To Uncle Sam
and
Auntie Evelyn

A momento of your visit.
To AUSTRALIA in 1975-76

with best love and wishes

Charles, Fay, Natalie and JACKIE
x x x

THIS IS
AUSTRALIA

OLAF RUHEN

PETER ELLERY

PATRICK TENNISON

MALCOLM MACKERRAS

Dr RUDOLPH BRASCH

PETER COWAN

MARTIN JOHNSTON

Dr PETER POCKLEY

Dr DAVID COHEN

IAN MOFFITT

JIM SHEPHERD

ROHAN RIVETT

REG MORRISON

Published by Paul Hamlyn Pty Limited
176 South Creek Road, Dee Why West, NSW 2099
First published 1975
© Copyright Paul Hamlyn Pty Limited 1975
Produced in Australia by the Publisher
Typeset in Australia by Terrey Hills Typesetters
Colour processing of Reg Morrison's photographs by
    Bond Colour Sydney Pty Ltd
Printed in Singapore by Toppan Printing Co. (Singapore)
    Private Limited

Publishing director: Phillip Mathews
Editor: Peter Hutton
Designer: Bruno Grasswill

National Library of Australia Cataloguing in Publication data

This is Australia/ [by] Rudolph Brasch . . . [et al];
    photographer: Reg Morrison. — Sydney: Hamlyn,
    1975.
    Index.
    ISBN 0 600 07358 0.

    1. Australia — Addresses, essays, lectures.
    I. Brasch, Rudolph, 1912-. II. Morrison, Reg,
    photographer.

    994

PAUL HAMLYN

SYDNEY

AUCKLAND

LONDON

NEW YORK

TORONTO

THIS IS AUSTRALIA

PUBLISHER'S NOTE

Australia settled comfortably into the good life in the quarter century following World War II. International political and ideological waves were, for the most part, mere ripples by the time they reached our shores; and the irony of the 'lucky country' tag was missed or ignored by a nation bent on pleasure.

But as the seventies began there were signs that Australia was stirring awake after its long and relatively undisturbed doze in the sun. A mood of challenge and change could be felt, and it seemed that the early years of the new decade were ushering in an exciting and significant period in the nation's history. The time was ripe for an honest, authoritative assessment of Australia—its heritage, its new values, its place in the world, its expectations.

That was the genesis of *This is Australia*. It is, we believe, a necessary book. We do not always share the views of our contributors, nor do we expect that all Australians will agree with every view expressed; however, we do share the general mood of optimism.

The publisher wishes to thank the following businesses for their assistance with this, the biggest book publishing project yet undertaken by The Hamlyn Group, Australia.

Acme Plastics Pty Ltd
Amalgamated Wireless (Australia) Ltd
Ampol Petroleum Ltd
Angus & Robertson Bookshops
Australia-West Pacific Line
Australian Record Company Ltd
Bell & Howell Australia Pty Ltd
Century Storage Battery Company Ltd
Civil & Civic Pty Ltd
John Clemenger (NSW) Pty Ltd
Commercial Union Assurance Co. of
  Australia
Corrigans Express (Australia) Pty Ltd
Cumberland Newspapers Limited
Festival Records Pty Limited
Gordon & Gotch (Australasia) Ltd
Ron Hodgson — Holden
Holyman Transport Pty Ltd
The International Correspondence Schools
  (A/asia) Pty Ltd

Johnson & Johnson Pty Ltd
K.G.C. Magnetic Tape Pty Ltd
Kodak (Australasia) Pty Ltd
Leyland Motor Corporation of Australia
Marrickville Holdings Ltd
Mitchell Cotts (Australia) Pty Ltd
National Mutual Life Asscn. of
  A/asia Ltd
Z. Nosek & Co. Pty Ltd
P & O Australia Ltd
Hon. Clyde Packer
Price Forbes Leslie Sedgwick (NSW)
  Pty Ltd
Radio Corporation Pty Ltd (Astor Records)
Simpla-Lux (Hunters Hill)
John Singleton
Sitmar Cruises
H. C. Sleigh Limited
Traveland International Pty Ltd
Waltons Stores Ltd

Acknowledgements
Extracts from 'The Kid' by C. J. Dennis (from his book *Songs of a Sentimental Bloke*), and from 'Australia' by A. D. Hope (from his book *Collected Poems*), are reprinted with the kind permission of Angus & Robertson Publishers.

Photographer Reg Morrison used Nikon and Mamiyaflex camera systems exclusively, with Kodak Ektachrome colour positive film.

CONTENTS

CONTRIBUTORS

Olaf Ruhen, a freelance writer, divides his interests between outback Australia and the South Pacific. Born in New Zealand in 1911, he started writing after early experience in outdoor occupations, particularly deep-sea fishing. After four years as an RNZAF pilot during World War II he moved to Australia, where he worked for eight years as a journalist with the Sydney *Daily Telegraph*, the Associated Newspapers organisation and the *Sydney Morning Herald* before turning to full-time freelancing and contributing to the *Saturday Evening Post*, the *Encyclopaedia Britannica* and publications of the National Geographic Society. His work, both fiction and non-fiction titles, has been published in the USA, the UK, Australia and New Zealand, and he reviews books for *The Australian* and the Melbourne *Age*.

Peter Ellery has watched Australia's post-war development as a juvenile participant and as an adult observer. As a cadet journalist with the *West Australian* he reported on agricultural matters during the period when Western Australians were turning bush into farmland at the rate of half a million hectares a year. He subsequently specialised in politics in Victoria and Canberra, returning to Western Australia to report on the mineral boom of the late 1960s. He has also worked for newspapers in Sydney and has been a contributor to the *Financial Times* and the *Economist*, specialising in natural resource development matters. He now works in public relations.

Patrick Tennison's journalism has appeared in every major Australian newspaper and magazine, from *The Australian* to *Walkabout*, the Melbourne *Sun* to *Forum*. He has also written for overseas newspapers, including Britain's *Daily Express* and *The Guardian*. He is a regular broadcaster of commentaries for the ABC, Radio Australia and the Voice of America, and broadcasting services in Britain, Ireland, Canada and New Zealand have commissioned his work. Since 1967 he has been lecturer in journalism for the Victorian Council of Adult Education. His first book, *Meet the Gallery*, was published in 1968, followed in 1972 by the very successful study of 'suburban neurosis' among housewives, *The Marriage Wilderness*; he has also contributed sections to books about Australian industry, crime and sport.

Malcolm Mackerras, born in 1939, is currently a lecturer in government at the Royal Military College, Duntroon, but is better known as Australia's leading analyst of election results. He is a regular election commentator on television and radio and in the newspapers, and is noted for the publication of his 'electoral pendulum' which shows seats according to their vulnerability. In addition to his many academic and journalistic articles he has published three books, including *Australian General Elections* which reached the best-selling list before the 1972 federal election.

Peter Cowan worked in various city and country jobs before taking an arts degree at the University of Western Australia. He became a teacher, and is at present senior tutor in the Department of English at the University of Western Australia. He has published four books of short stories: *Drift* (1944); *The Unploughed Land* (1959); *The Empty Street* (1965); *The Tins and other Stories* (1973). His two published novels are *Summer* (1964) and *Seed* (1966). He has also contributed to, and edited, a number of anthologies of short stories, and wrote a newspaper column on conservation. He has travelled abroad and in Australia, and is particularly interested in Asia. His favourite pastime is travelling by four-wheel-drive vehicles in national parks and other areas in Australia not much frequented by people.

Rabbi Brasch is chief minister of Sydney's Temple Emanuel, life vice-president of the Australian and New Zealand Union for Progressive Judaism, director of education of the Liberal Education Board of New South Wales, and a member of the governing body of the World Union for Progressive Judaism; he has pioneered Reform Judaism in four countries, has been president of the Australian Jewish Library Association and guest professor in Hebrew at St Andrew's College at Sydney University. The foremost Jewish lecturer, broadcaster, telecaster and scriptwriter in Australia, Rabbi Brasch has written many best-selling books including: *The Star of David*; *The Judaic Heritage*; *The Unknown Sanctuary*; *How Did It Begin?*; *How Did Sports Begin?*; *How Did Sex Begin?*. He writes a regular column on 'Religion and Life' for the Sydney *Sun-Herald*, and for four years has had a weekly television programme.

Reg Morrison's life with cameras began when he was 12 years old. He soon became 'a keen "bathroom" amateur', doing his own developing and printing, but it was not until he had been four years with West Australian Newspapers as a journalist that he moved into serious professional photography. That was in 1958. Since then he has worked with many different kinds of cameras covering many kinds of assignments; he has won Australian and international awards; and his photo-essay, *Australians Exposed* (1974), was widely acclaimed. In 1971 he joined The Hamlyn Group as pictorial editor and photographer, and in 1974 set off on a photographic odyssey which took him 35,000 kilometres around Australia by foot, Land Rover, rail, light aircraft and helicopter.

Contributing Photographers: Alan Birtles, Mervyn Bishop, John Carnemolla, Neville Coleman, Dr Paul Crowley, Neil Duncan, Wal Easton, Bob Edwards, Rennie Ellis, Val Foreman, Roderick Hulsbergen, Trevor Kolpin, Gary Lewis, David Moore, Michael Morcombe, Allan Power, Bill Russell, Rick Stevens, Ron Sullivan, Peter Wells, Richard Woldendorp.

Martin Johnston was brought up in Greece but now lives in Sydney, where he was born in 1948. He has published two books of verse, *Shadowmass* (1971) and *Ithaka* (1973), and has recently completed a third, *The Sea-cucumber*, and a novel, still untitled. He has written hundreds of book reviews, critical articles and radio scripts, and has also reviewed theatre, films and music. His first published article was on the arts in Australia. He has edited *Poetry Magazine*, been on the council of the Poetry Society of Australia, and has won a number of awards including the Combined Australian Universities' poetry prize in 1967 and the Book Design Award for book illustration in 1971. He has also judged several literary competitions.

Peter Pockley graduated from Melbourne University and gained his Ph.D at Oxford. His early efforts as a 'communicator of science' were in teaching, and in writing a standard text on physical chemistry for British schools. He returned to Australia in 1964 and became the first scientist employed full-time by the local media to communicate science to the general public. He was the ABC's Director of Science Programmes for nine years, and the first satellite TV shows for Australia and the Apollo space broadcasts were among his major credits. While with the ABC he was elected to the Science and Industry Forum of the Australian Academy of Science. In 1973, Pockley became the University of NSW's first Adviser, Public Affairs. He is a member of the Film, TV and Radio Board of the Australia Council, is actively involved in movements for the reform of broadcasting, and is Australian correspondent for the international journal *Nature*.

David Cohen is associate professor of education at Macquarie University in NSW, with key interests in the fields of curriculum development and educational media. After obtaining degrees in science and in education from the University of Melbourne and his Ph.D from Michigan State University, he taught for several years in Victorian schools and also lectured at the Toorak and the Technical Teachers Colleges. He has also worked as consultant to several parent groups in establishing primary schools, and his UNESCO activities have taken him to the USA, the UK, France and Poland. His publications include several books and numerous articles on education and science education. Dr Cohen received the G. S. Browne Prize for Educational Practice (1962) and the Australian Industries Development Association's Science Education Award (1966).

Ian Moffitt is the author of *The U-Jack Society: An Experience of Being Australian*, acclaimed as one of the finest books written about Australia. He has also contributed to many books on Australia, and writes fiction when he has the time. He has worked as a newspaper journalist for many years, including three years as New York editor for an Australian newspaper and is currently a feature writer on *The Australian* in Sydney.

Jim Shepherd has worked as a feature sporting journalist and columnist for two Australian newspaper chains. In a life almost entirely devoted to the observation and recording of sport he has written for more than 84 Australian and overseas newspapers and magazines, besides handling every imaginable commentary task as sporting director for the Sydney television channel, TEN-10 and for years before that for a Sydney radio station. He is now promotions executive for a large national company, specialising in the sponsorship of sporting projects, while retaining sports writing and commentating as a hobby.

Rohan Rivett graduated with first class honours in history and political science at Melbourne University in 1937, and began his working life as a reporter with the Melbourne *Argus*. After World War II he worked in Fleet Street and Europe until 1951, when he became editor-in-chief of the Adelaide *News*. During the 50s he represented Australian newspapers at four international conferences. His intelligent and urbane analyses of Australia's foreign relations, and his perceptive comments on international affairs, have been heard on the BBC as well as ABC radio and television; he has also written for many Australian newspapers. In 1974 he became president of the Melbourne Press Club. His publications include: *Behind Bamboo* (1946); *The Migrant in the Community* (1958); *Australian Citizen* (1965); *Writing about Australia* (1969).

THE LAND

Olaf Ruhen

**'By the time a second
generation grew . . .
they had come to
love the country . . .'**

Ernest Favenc the explorer discovered fine country in Queensland below the Gulf of Carpentaria and on over the Barkly Tableland to Darwin, but he must have carried disappointment like an ill-balanced pack, for what he really sought did not exist, never had, never could. His good mind must have told him so, over and over. Exploration fascinated him; his *History of Austral Exploration from 1788 to 1888* is authoritative, and in the motivations of other explorers he must have recognised desires akin to his own.

Yet he dreamed of finding a civilisation beyond the horizons, or the relics of one, created by people whose inheritance mirrored the likeness of his own. Eleven years after his explorations ceased he wrote a fanciful novel about Wouter Loos and Jan Pelgrom de Bye, the two Dutchmen marooned in 1629 for their part in the massacres connected with the *Batavia* shipwreck on the Abrolhos Islands off the Western Australian coast. In Favenc's reconstruction they travelled north and discovered a kingdom of civilised people whom he made responsible for the Wandjina art Sir George Grey had discovered in 1836.

This was the wildest fiction, but in an appendix Favenc discussed the possibility of the existence in north-west Australia at some previous time of a colony of semi-civilised people.

'The non-existence of ruins of any sort can easily be accounted for by the fact that they built their houses of mud which, after being abandoned to the mercy of successive tropical wet seasons, would soon disappear,' he wrote.

Favenc was not alone in his search for something, for anything with which, as a 19th century man, he could identify. Long before the discovery of the

Opposite: Early morning light on the mangrove-lined estuaries veining tidal flats on the north-west coast between Derby and Cockatoo Island, WA.

9

continent the dreamers of the northern hemisphere imagined a culture here that matched their own, just as today, when the first probes go out to other planets, scientists as well as fictioneers postulate the existence of other beings there and, more often than not, invest them with form and habits like our own.

From the time of Hesiod, about eight centuries before Christ, men's wishful guesses have invested the earth with such paradisical lands as the Hesperides, the Fortunate Islands, the Islands of the Blest. Perhaps more significantly, Plato introduced the legend of Atlantis, a concept so acceptable to the human mind that people have ever since believed it in whole or in part.

So, as the slow opening of the Australian continent disclosed only repetitions of what became a familiar pattern of unused kilometres, the land explorers must have felt the disappointment of anti-climax. The unfulfilled dream was a facet of the universal human experience, but the European mind, so long exposed to wonders, was the most susceptible to it.

The first explorations beyond the immediate environs of Sydney stemmed directly from the dream of Irish prisoners that a 'New World' existed south-west of Sydney. Under the leadership of John Wilson, a term-expired man, a hopeful party pressed ahead to the limits of its capacity. Its members discovered the lyre-bird and some other country oddities, but no New World. Perhaps Wilson had searched for it previously on his own account; he had left the settlement to live in the bush with Aborigines; not the first man to do so, nor the last, but the first to lend the bush-knowledge he gained this way to the ends of exploration and pushing back the boundaries.

Other such developments followed slowly. Little enthusiasm backed the desultory probes of the first 20 years until the promise of the wool trade indicated a need to develop land over and above the hectarage necessary for the colony's sustenance.

For a time the promise of the land lay all in grass, the prime essential for progress. Grass provided the power for land transport, through horses and oxen. Even the ships could not be built without the animals to haul the timbers and the fuel, to draw water and activate mills. In grass lay the promise of over-seas trade; in the empty kilometres the promise of grass supplied the enticement for the population the country needed.

While the first adventurous men went out, the stay-at-homes attempted to make the new land as much like the old as possible. Besides the introduced plants of economic value they planted their gardens with roses and lily of the valley, their stable-yards with oak and elm and poplar, their boundaries with hedges of hawthorn and sloe, their creek-banks with willows. And brought too, by accident or design, a host of introduced weeds. Goats and pigs ran free about their cottages, treasured rabbits crouched in backyard hutches, hens, ducks and geese made the air clamorous with familiar Old Country sounds.

Perhaps because of West Indian experience most officers had shared, the houses were built to designs more suited to the climate than the English cottage, but the householders made little use of Australian fruits or flowers or natural products. Few of these met the standards established in English, Irish or Scottish homes.

The introductions may have permitted the farmyards to approximate Old Country models, but the results of husbandry proved disappointing. When un-remitting work had cleared the mainly useless trees in the settled areas, the grey podzolic soils remaining were of low fertility. Flood plains provided a few sites where a rich tilth produced a better return, but on these Commissioner John Thomas Bigge, reporting on a colony more than 30 years old, made a scathing comment, surely not altogether without foundation:

'In these tracts I observed some decent habitations that had been established by the emancipated convicts; but there were also a great many that were within reach of the inundations of the river, the owners of which persisted in exposing themselves and their property to its ravages that they might indolently reap the benefits of the fertility that is left behind. The tracts on the shore of the river Hawkesbury have thus afforded support to many of the most worthless and **10**

The foundation of Australia's land mass is an immense raft of tough, ancient rock believed to be 2,500 million years old—more than half the currently accepted age of our planet. This raft was formed long before primitive life appeared on earth, and the rock is almost totally devoid of the fossils which tick off the ages of later, surrounding accretions. Australia was relatively unscathed by movements of the earth's crust that wrinkled and deformed most other land masses, and there were few volcanic intrusions. These boulders in Bunker Bay, WA, are fragments of such an intrusion, a protective chin jutting out from the south-west corner of the continent into the abrasive eastward drift of the great southern ocean. The 'mist' shrouding the boulders is the blurred wash of moonlit surf, recorded on film during a one-hour exposure.

indolent cultivators, and the produce has been diminished in quantity as well as quality, by the successive cultivation of the same grain, and by the admixture with it of rank weeds and wild vetches.'

The plain truth was that much more profit derived from trading, from shipping ventures, and from harvesting the rich produce of the virgin seas, sandalwood and sealskins for China and whale-oil for the lamps of the world. Development and establishment costs, in energy more than in cash, made pastoral enterprises much more rewarding than agricultural in spite of high prices for maize and vegetables of limited quality. But the increase in flocks and herds made the exploitation of new land essential, and sent the explorers out.

Within months of the conquering of the Blue Mountain barrier by Evans, following the lead of Blaxland, Lawson and Wentworth, Governor Macquarie ordered a road constructed, a task William Cox completed in another six months. Now the more promising interior lay open to development, and the explorers pressed home the advantage, discovering the westward-flowing rivers, the Lachlan and the Macquarie.

Oxley, having followed the Lachlan almost to its junction with the Murrumbidgee in 1818, went north the following year, pressing through to Port Macquarie and traversing promising country. John Howe made the first overland contact with Newcastle, assisting in the opening up of the Hunter, which had previously been approached only by sea.

John Kennedy, Hamilton Hume, Charles Throsby and others opened up the Southern Tablelands, seeking land for cattle, and once cattle were established on distant hectares, exploration became automatic and unceasing. From about 1817 the movement outward from the Port Jackson centre resembled the spreading of oil on cloth, filling up the valleys and flats as the liquid fills the veined hollows of the fabric. Rivers and creeks, hills and mountains and swamps, all were noted and mapped; and on the heels of the discoverers the herds followed close.

By 1826, the year before Cunningham climbed Mount Dumaresq and sighted the Darling Downs, it was decided to establish limits of location, boundaries beyond which land was neither sold nor let. Soon these enclosed 19 counties, comprising about 90,000 square kilometres of settlement. Commissioners appointed in 1825 apportioned the land into counties and parishes, but by 1830 their work devolved upon the Surveyor-General Major Mitchell. The boundary of the limits followed the Manning River in the north, then the Mount Royal and Liverpool ranges to Wellington, and linked Molong, Orange, Cowra and Yass, turning then eastward, approximately following the course of the Murrumbidgee and Moruya rivers.

But planning ever lagged behind necessity, and at this time something like a population explosion amongst domestic cattle and sheep forced an acceleration of the outward movement. Moreover, since publication of the Bigge report, free Englishmen were becoming more conscious of the possibilities latent in the colony, and a vast improvement in shipping enabled them to put their migration plans into action with greater ease. Not yet the ocean-going steamship, but the iron-hulled carrier with a more modern sail plan cheapened sea transport. In dozens and in scores people poured across the artificial frontiers.

In the Port Phillip district in the south, men like the Hentys, with ambitions as wide as the horizons they challenged, thrust inland from the coast. The better pastures of the south enticed Tasmanian adventurers, and still other explorers, eyes searching always for signs of good land (dominant tree types, matted grasses, a burgeoning wild life), joined the settlements with their overland tracks.

In 1830 Sturt discovered the Murray, doing some damage to the theory that the Darling, the upper waters of which he had already discovered, would turn out to be a great westward-flowing river that would offer easy access to the mysterious interior. But shortly after, a runaway convict, George Clarke, 'The Barber', who had thrown in his lot with a native tribe for the previous five years, told of the great river Kindur, which flowed to a northern sea that was visited sometimes by light-skinned savage natives sailing praus.

Mitchell too was a dreamer. Not only did he envisage a river, 'its course analogous to that of the Amazon's' and giving open entry to the interior, but he hoped to be the one to find it, and was impatient to put behind him the 500 kilometres to which settlement had now extended from Sydney:

'I felt the ardour of my early youth, when I first sought distinction in the crowded camp and battlefield, revive as I gave loose to my reflections . . . . It seemed that even war and victory, with all their glory, were far less alluring than the pursuit of researches such as these; the objects of which were to spread the light of civilisation over a portion of the globe yet unknown, though rich, perhaps, in the luxuriance of uncultivated nature, and where science might accomplish new and unthought-of discoveries; while intelligent man would find a region teeming with useful vegetation, abounding with rivers, hills and vallies, and waiting only for his enterprising spirit and improving hand.'

When his supplies failed to reach him, Mitchell had to abandon this probe which had opened up new country towards what is now the Queensland border. The extraordinary pressure of survey work postponed resumption of the explorations he loved for four years more. Then on the second of two expeditions to the south-west he discovered rich grasslands he called Australia Felix, and encountered the Henty family ensconced in a growing establishment on the coast, and ready to move inland.

Even while he was at the Henty homestead an Act of Council attempted to control the squatting boom by requiring annual licences at a cost of 10 pounds each. The system did not encourage any sound development of new holdings, for the licensees had no guarantee of tenure. They erected flimsy temporary buildings, usually no more than a framework clad with bark. Their fences were non-existent, and there were no surveys to determine their exact location had fencing been possible. But the boom in the wool industry ensured large profits.

Intrusions on native hunting grounds led inevitably to hostilities in which the natives had no chance at all. Their easy conquest by small parties of white intruders demonstrated that they would not cause a permanent or a difficult

Rodney Fox—a brush with death

World-wide reportage in film and print of his miraculous survival after his chest was crunched in the jaws of a Great White shark has made Rodney Fox the object of the curious interest of strangers, but it was his discovery of a rural life-style that led him to settle with his wife and three children on the outskirts of Port Lincoln in South Australia.

The glamour of underwater exploration had turned this one-time insurance man to the sea, an affinity which his near escape from death did not discourage, but rather the reverse. Today he combines abalone diving with motel-keeping and looks to the tourist trade for a future expansion.

'I've got a great liking and love for the sea,' he says. 'Port Lincoln has just been declared a city, and with ten thousand people it's just enough to keep me happy. For the children it's got everything—a choice of school, places to go and see. It's uncluttered.

'In Adelaide now it takes so long to go from one friend's place to another; in Port Lincoln they're all only five minutes away, even though they live the other side of town. And on the weekends you only have to go 25 or 30 kilometres to find a secluded place completely your own to set up a barbecue or go swimming.

'When I go away from Port Lincoln for a week or two at a time I can come back here, drive around the city, talk to three or four friends, find out exactly all that's been going on—all in a short hour. I'm keeping in touch with the place where I live and the business I'm associated with. I'm one of a community. For example, I know all that's going on in the fishing scene. So Port Lincoln is very acceptable.

'Then we have two local television stations, restaurants, picture theatres, good hotels and social clubs. And if that's not enough it's only 220 kilometres by air to Adelaide.

'Not only that, but I've made good friends on the farms. Farmers are generally very happy and friendly people and you don't seem to get the sort of person you get in cities where you have to be careful who you talk to. Where there's more people there's more trouble. In a small town they're more friendly.

'The town's based on wheat, fishing, transport and hasn't a great deal of industry. One of the largest natural harbours in Australia, a beautiful area, ideal for yachting. I keep in touch with the shark fishermen, the cray boats, the prawners. Then there's the tuna fleet and the scallop dredgers and in Coffin's Bay are oyster

leases. The sailing club's rather strong here, and I believe, for the amount of people, we've more boats than anywhere else in Australia.

'Most of the food comes directly from its source, the fish straight from the sea, and it's local lamb and beef. Local market gardens. And it's a very clean place, only one or two of the smoke-stacks that deter me from living in places like Port Pirie or Whyalla or Port Augusta, all fast-growing industrial towns. Port Lincoln's growing slowly, and I can keep in touch with it.

'It's a pretty place, with Boston Island out in front. A lot of history round here, great potential in the tourist industry. Just out there is a whole area called Whalers' Way with terrific marine scenery—rough conditions, a contrast to the harbour.

'And the big game people are interested in coming across, having a crack at the Great White shark, the largest dangerous shark in the world.

'I don't know how I regard the plans for making Port Lincoln a superport for the hundred-thousand tonners. I don't want to see masses of machinery and a concrete jungle. But in a superport for superships arrivals and departures will be fewer. Supermachinery will clear the port faster.'

Libanangu settlement, Wattie Creek, NT, was established in 1965 by Gurindji pastoral workers who walked off nearby Wave Hill station in protest against personal exploitation and the uncompensated loss of tribal lands. They began their own pastoral and mining company, and in 1975 finally won the right to lease the land on which they squatted—the first victory of its kind for Aborigines.

problem; authorities thereafter displayed no interest in securing any rights to the tribal occupiers. But the small annoyances and complaints arising from the spearing of sheep did lead to the establishment of a Border Patrol of the Police Force, and in 1839 the levy of a tax on cattle pastured beyond the boundaries. While settlement on Crown lands could be discouraged or controlled, there was no way, in those unfenced wilds, in which the government could stop the pasturing of stock.

In Tasmania a highway, which in 1818 linked the northern and southern settlements, encouraged the spread of settlement. Land grants and the provision of cheap convict labour for settlers gave additional impetus, and once the wool export began in the same year, 1818, a rural prosperity emerged. Wheat for New South Wales and cattle for Mauritius swelled the exports and by 1825 when the colony of Van Diemen's Land was separated from New South Wales, prosperous farmers were building substantial homes in the English style.

The excitement of establishing a splinter settlement at Port Phillip in 1836 created another boom; during the previous years most of the best land south of Bass Strait had been settled. Indeed, when Governor Arthur in 1831 abolished free grants in favour of an auction system the land remaining was not of that potential liable to create excitement. Yet not much of the alienated land had been cultivated. Most of the best tracts, in the broad valley which lay between Hobart and Launceston, were held by a few individuals who saw their best returns in the breeding and marketing of stock.

On the mainland so far the explorers had been barely ahead of the settlers, and sometimes behind them. From Goulburn in 1839 Angus McMillan struck south to find new pastures in what is now Victoria. From a station on the Tambo River, which the Omeo Highway largely follows today, he established a route to Corner Inlet, after repeated attempts on the heavily timbered country. This gave a Victorian outlet to the pasture production of the Monaro. He named many Gippsland features, including the Mitchell River which runs into the Tambo.

In both Western Australia and South Australia a confusion over land tenure arose for a variety of reasons, one being that land contracted for or bought in Great Britain was not surveyed. When bankruptcy of the State ended the period of systematic colonisation in South Australia in the early 40s it was put on the same footing as the other Australian colonies. Western Australia made such little progress, from an apparent lack of labour, that in the mid-century settlers successfully petitioned the British Government to make it a convict settlement.

In 1842, under the pressure of migrations from the south, a ban on free settlers in the Moreton Bay district was removed. In the opposite direction the movement flowed down the wooded hills and the Paul Strzelecki routes through Gippsland to Port Phillip.

Life for pioneers was harsh but not unduly so. Typically masters of improvisation, they lived in huts wrested from the materials at hand. A sturdy framework of poles, pegged and morticed, carried a cladding of bark or slab walls; the large bark sheets stripped readily from river gums and a few other eucalypt varieties represented almost the only labour-saving innovation Australia had to offer. A more permanent building had walls of timber, split and slabbed rather than pitsawn; the stubborn hardwoods were most easily handled thus. The workmanship which raised the buildings was excellent; at least it proved so in those that are still preserved today, and they are not truly rare, with only the roofs several times renewed.

These were primarily of bark, fastened down with small logs slung over the ridge, or thatched with rushes when these were available, or sometimes with the more unsatisfactory mountain grasses. Floors were the natural earth, fireplaces of stone or timber plastered with clay. In warmer districts fireplaces were set outside. Where settlers feared native attacks, holes in the wall that served as windows could be closed with heavy shutters. Fear was more prevalent than was justified, yet the earliest of the pioneers, those farthest out, were an intrepid lot.

Peter Cunningham in 1827 listed the normal ration for convict farm workers, and one cannot imagine that the free-ranging settler fared much better: 'Their usual allowance: a peck of wheat (two gallons, or about fifteen pounds) ; seven pounds of beef or four and a half of pork; two ounces of tea; two ounces of tobacco; and a pound of sugar—weekly, the majority of settlers permitting them to raise vegetables in little gardens allotted to their use, or supplying them occasionally from their own gardens'. There were not many natural products of the land to supplement such fare and orchards and vegetable gardens took time to establish.

Rachel Henning, writing from the Rockhampton district of Queensland in 1864, described the weekly rations as eight pounds of flour, two pounds of sugar, a quarter pound of tea, and a nominal 16 pounds of beef, though actually this latter was unlimited. People could also pay for pickles, vinegar, currants, sardines and jam, items brought by wagon and ship from Sydney. The store also carried tapioca, rice and sago. Beef not used immediately after killing was salted down or smoked.

The Hennings, proprietors of a well-financed enterprise, established themselves there in 'a long low building, built of dark-coloured slabs of wood with a verandah in front, and the doors and windows opening into it. It contains five rooms: the first is our bedroom, the next the store and the next the parlour. At the back of ours is Biddulph's and Mr Hedgeland's room and at the back of the parlour is another bedroom wherein reside any other members of the "staff" who happen to be at home—more than half are always at the outstations. The kitchen is next door to the house and behind are the men's huts, sheds and gunyahs, etc.

'The house stands on a low hill at the foot of which runs the creek which supplies us with water, and a very pretty creek it is, with deep banks covered with trees and shrubs. We have a piece of ground fenced and dug for a garden at the foot of the hill, but at present it only contains some pines and pumpkins and some petunia cuttings . . .'

She described the verandah chairs: two straight poles held together by cross-bars and leant against the wall. A strip of strong canvas of the sort used for wool-bagging nailed to the bars formed the seat and back. 'The most comfortable kind of easy chair I know,' endorsed Miss Henning.

Australians do not share the passion of Americans for saving samples of pioneer furnishings. Seldom did the weather keep them housebound to work at their crafts. Such items as they contrived were frequently thought too rough for future generations to treasure; the white ant and the timber borer usually assisted in the decision to discard. In the gunyahs the furniture was often stabilised by being tamped into holes in the dirt floor.

HARSH LIFE FACED OUTBACK SETTLERS

Opposite: A scrap of vegetation sucks life from the small mound of dust marking the death of a steer near the southern edge of Lake Eyre. And so life cycles evolve with the grim simplicity characteristic of much of this arid continent.

For the men on outstations amenities generally were fewer. Normally they waited until relief; the weekly rations carried out to them on horseback. They were remote from any company save that of the stock they guarded and the birds and animals of the wild. Natives constituted their chief enemy in some areas at least, but even without these their lives were constantly at hazard. A broken leg, sustained some days before the rations were due, could mean death. Even a toothache could be afforded no relief.

Small wonder that, on the first day of temporary freedom, most of them turned to the bush shanty and its colonial rum. When company was available conversation and group singing provided the chief amusements; books were rare, though the illiterates numbered less by comparison than in English communities.

The lonely life unhinged the minds of many shepherds so that people called them 'hatters', and for nearly a century the class was recognisable. Edward S. Sorenson, in his *Life in the Australian Backwoods*, described one Jack the Rager:

'Only the flies by day and the mosquitoes by night disturb the peace, only the cries of the birds and the rustling of leaves break the quietude. To the

16

Continued on page 33

In contrast to the barren heartland of Australia the eastern seaboard is relatively rugged and fertile. This towering finger of rock is one of the Glasshouse Mountains, a group of residual volcanic plugs bared by the erosion of the coastal plain north of Brisbane. They were named by Captain Cook on his passage northward after the Botany Bay landfall in 1770.

Following page, left: Early morning along the serried ridges of the New England Ranges in northern New South Wales.

Following page, right: A waterbird breaks the symmetry of sandbars in the tidal shallows of Norfolk Bay on the Tasman Peninsula, Tasmania.

RICHARD WOLDENDORP

A climate of harsh extremes demands evolutionary specialisation. These Baobab or bottle trees, native to the drought-prone northern areas of Australia, are so named for their ability to store water in their trunks.

This skeletal forest in western Tasmania recalls the huge bush fires that ravaged vast areas of the island in 1967. Even the unique fire resistance characteristic of much Australian vegetation cannot withstand the appalling heat of such fires.

23

MICHAEL MORCOMBE

MICHAEL MORCOMBE

Geographically isolated and relatively inhospitable, Australia provided a refuge for many primitive species of flora and fauna.

Opposite page: A bearded dragon lizard and its prey recall the struggles that took place between their monstrous ancestors millions of years ago.

Above: Pockets of Antarctic Beech, *Nothofagus moorei*, like these in the New England Ranges, NSW, also survive in southern New Zealand and at Cape Horn. They support the theory of continental drift away from Antarctica.

Bottom left: A group of Black Gins, *Kingia australis*, a member of the primitive grass tree family.

Bottom right: The spiny anteater or Echidna, *Tachyglossus aculeatus*, is one of the world's only two surviving egg-laying mammals or monotremes.

Many species of wildflowers and birds bring jewel-like colour to an often drab landscape.

Top left: A carpet of 'everlasting' daisies, *Cephalipterum drummondii*, sprung from the red soil of north-west Western Australia's mulga country after late-year rains.

Top right: Everlastings near Lake Moore, Western Australia.

Right: *Coreopsis lanceolata*, a naturalised exotic, butters railway and road verges in western New South Wales at spring time.

Opposite page: A Rainbow Bird, *Merops ornatus*, comes home with a dragonfly dinner.

Following pages: Calcium leached from the upper layers of a sand dune and deposited in seepage channels deeper inside the dune formed these calcium-cemented pillars, later uncovered by wind erosion of the surrounding sand. This array stands in Nambung National Park, Western Australia.

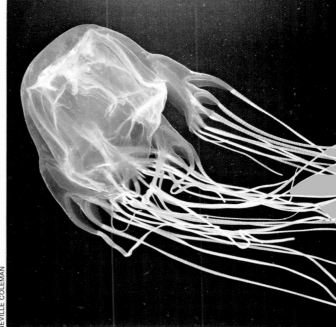

Australia's northern waters offer contrasting extremes of beauty and danger.

Opposite: A Baler shell (*Melo amphora*), twilight and the incoming tide on the vast stretch of Eighty Mile Beach in north-west Western Australia.

Top: A brush with the deceptively delicate tentacles of the beautiful *Chironex fleckeri* or sea wasp will bring the most agonising death in a matter of three or four minutes. It is probably the world's most efficient killer, and also the main reason for Australia's northern beaches being deserted during the summer months when the risk from *Chironex fleckeri* is greatest.

hatter by temperament this is an ideal state of existence, and a man who loves to talk, but likes to do all the talking himself is suited by a dog listener as well as any . . .

'It was election time and Jack was putting up for No Man's Land. Standing beside a gidgee-stump on which stood a quart-pot of water and a pannikin, he orated with great *empressement*, punctuating with hand-clapping and ''hear hears'', interjecting and making sarcastic remarks and wheeling this way and that to reply thereto. Now and again he would point his thumb at the wilga-bush on his left and tell the mulga-tree on his right that a gentleman wanted to know what he was going to do about his deceased wife's sister . . . . He had closed a successful meeting when he was suddenly semi-paralysed by hearing a real clap and a real ''hear hear'' in the darkness beyond. It was the boss.

'Sometimes, as cranks of the bush often do, he amused himself for hours at a time, trying to match the spiral columns on the lids and bottoms of (cylindrical) wax-match boxes, by playing peg-knife and other silly games. If you came quietly on his camp at night it was not unusual to hear a heated discussion going on between him and the fat-lamp. As he tersely put it when surprised, ''Just a little argyment between me and Slushy''. Sometimes they had a row and an imaginary fight, and Slushy was kicked out of the tent. At other times he sulked as a result of the pigheadedness of the other fellow and wouldn't speak to the fat-lamp for a week. He would even ''see him further'' before he would light him.'

Hope, more than anything else, led the colonists into the wilderness where there seemed a very good prospect indeed for even the penniless to establish a family fortune. Hope faded in the early 40s when trade languished in the Mother Country, still so called, and the expanding production of Australian pastures met with little buyer interest.

Then Henry O'Brien of Yass recommended the export of beef tallow and this proved a resounding success. Almost immediately the wool market improved. In April 1845 the *Sydney Morning Herald* proclaimed that 'sheep-farming, which two years ago was pronounced on all hands a losing concern, is now the most profitable investment in the country. What with the high character of our tallow and the remunerative prices of our fleece, our pastoral interest—the ruling interest in Australia—was never in a more auspicious position than at the present moment'.

In his *Sydney in 1848* Joseph Fowles reported 'our denizens of the pasture-plains boiling down into tallow sufficient meat, per annum, to feed nearly half a million of persons because we have not mouths to eat it; and our denizens of the city luxuriating in all the delicacies which the well-appointed hotels and restaurants of Sydney provide on the most princely scale'.

Pasture lands could still be had at reasonable rates, either bought or rented from private owners or occupied under licence from the Crown. A flow of recruits to the pastoral industries became a flood under the influence of the gold discoveries of the 50s. Australia became a frontier offering adventure as not the least of her attractions. The great distances from Europe meant that most new citizens were young, a great many in their early 20s or younger. Assisted migration encouraged couples with young families, and the children could more than earn their way on remote holdings.

Goldfields communities created new markets. Also the more sober among the successful miners looked to put their easy earnings into investment; the failures had to offer their abilities wherever they could be used. As the easy alluvial gold worked out and the big companies moved in to work the deep reefs, an abundant supply of labour was released to encourage development of farms and stations. The country's transport system developed almost overnight, both as to the roads and the vehicles using them, and the beginnings of a railroad system emerged.

Gold also introduced a strong reinforcement to the American influence established in Australia with the whaling fleets. Americans landing in substantial

THE NEW FRONTIER ATTRACTED THE YOUNG AND VIGOROUS FROM EUROPE

Opposite: Wave erosion of the cliffs near Port Campbell, western Victoria, has carved this set of island fragments known as The Twelve Apostles.

numbers brought with them New World economies in land clearance and stock handling. These were important, but supplemented innovations already in existence. Men who numbered their animals in thousands and counted their employees on the fingers of one hand could not be expected to attend the birth of each lamb in a hurdled pen, or to remove a fleece by the ancient methods of the United Kingdom.

A political factor that encouraged the outward movement of the pioneer was the advent of responsible government in a grouping of competitive States. Poor in natural trade channels, the eastern States yet possessed the Murray, Murrumbidgee and Darling rivers. As a river trade developed, both Victoria and New South Wales moved with alacrity to forestall the channeling of the rich products of the major valleys through to South Australia at the Murray mouth.

Such moves encouraged the sound development of country towns with their secondary industries. No longer were men issued with wheat to grind for their bread, sometimes in small hand-querns they contrived themselves. Milled flour was everywhere available and there were roads of a sort on which to carry it.

The richer land-owners, amply financed from the start, had developed their more settled stations until some of them resembled small villages. The great barns of colder climates were never necessary here; only the most aristrocratic of stud beasts were stall fed, and year-round grazing over most of Australia was interrupted only by accident of flood or drought.

But the shearing-shed was a necessity for woolgrowers, and accommodation for not only the permanently employed hands but also the great host of transients the shearing seasons required. As affluence encouraged the grazier families to move to even grander houses, those they vacated became available to the key men. A stable, a shelter for the less rugged vehicles and machines, lofts for grain, a cow-byre and piggeries and poultry-yards—the buildings proliferated.

By the time a second generation grew in the big house the settlers were no longer intent on introducing plants from the Old World; they had come to love the country with its native products for itself. Typically, they still did not understand it. The first of their predecessors had mined its productivity rather than nourishing its source; when drought brought a scarcity of grass they slashed the scrub so that the animals might browse. To keep life in their breeding-stock they brought the plants to the point of hazard. And after the boundaries were fixed and the fences built, their overstocking impoverished a soil that, as a rule, had no great stability.

Such effects were not always immediately apparent. The first big paddocks might contain 250 square kilometres or more, and in this territory waterholes formed gathering points for stock. Whenever rain provided surface water they fed out into the less-used growth at a distance, allowing scrub and grass near the water to regenerate. When fences subdivided the area a heavier stocking ate each section bare. Hot sun converted the soil to dust, blustering winds took it over the horizons. Smaller holdings produced a comparable effect; efficiency was seldom tempered with the wisdom of restraint.

More characteristic were the battlers, the people hoping to wrest a fortune from the soil but settling for a living. Typically they lived in a remoter district, and lived harder, their personal expenses and their family's cut to a minimum, their operating costs higher because of the distance from the transport streams and their dependence on primitive facilities and make-shifts. Ruthless in their dealings with the land they fired the bush to clear it, and fired the grasses each year for the sake of the succulent new shoots on which their animals thrived. And typically, after years of progress when good seasons favoured them until their confidence was high, concurrent seasons of drought destroyed their equity.

When the ploughs went in to the low rainfall areas nearer the continent's centre, the topsoil blew away in dustclouds that harassed their family's existence, and reddened sunsets across the Tasman in New Zealand.

The search for new land, good land, developed a new kind of person. The early pioneers, with short stages in front of them, moved with heavily laden wagons as, even at that time, the narrow-bodied Conestogas moved across the

American prairies. The later adventurers stripped down to essentials. In Australia they needed little or no protection; no wild beasts menaced either the people or their herds; the natives in most districts were harmless and indeed could be enlisted as helpers. The men moved out with what they could carry on horseback; half a dozen men with half a hundred horses could move swiftly and lightly over the country.

Cattle running free in the enormous, unfenced holdings were controlled because of the scarcity of surface water over much of the country. On the huge quondam sea-beds the sparse rainfall drained swiftly away through the limestone that had once been caved coral, and many kilometres separated the watercourses. Cattle usually grazed no more than eight kilometres or so from the waters and therefore a few men could control six or seven thousand square kilometres. The pastoralists right from the start learned to make use of the trained ability of Aborigines to read signs. For the black man's survival ability this skill was essential; the white man learned to turn it to economic advantage. If cattle had not drunk at a waterhole they were not, in normal seasons, in the hills beyond. Simple deductive ability enabled the mustering teams to scour in a few days holdings larger than many an English county.

A droving team of six men could and often did convoy in safety herds that would have required the attention of more than 30 American trail-herd hands, and take them over rougher country, the packhorses maintaining mobility in country that would stall American chuck-wagons, light and adaptable as they were. Over the whole of the Australian continent a man could travel in safety, his only hazard the snake, his only necessary gear a blanket and groundsheet, though in seasons of rain the mobile team might stretch a tent-fly over a sapling.

A man who travelled with cattle rejected even such elemental furniture as a sleeping-bag—the constriction it afforded could be a fatal handicap in the event of cattle rushing. He made most of his gear himself, usually from rawhide,

RESOURCEFUL DROVERS MADE OVERLAND TREKS OF MONUMENTAL DISTANCE AND HARDSHIP

Eric Hampson—rector in the tropics

The Venerable C. E. Hampson is a bearded, confident, almost flamboyant figure in the Queensland north, very assured in the beauty of the religious atmosphere of which he is warden. In Mount Isa, a tropical mining city which has grown in population from 3,000 in 1947 to more than 28,000 in 1973, Eric Hampson is Rector of St James the Great. Centre of its shire, the city is a base for the Royal Flying Doctor Service and School of the Air.

Tertiary education in South Africa, where he grew up, followed war service, and after religious experience there and in England he became a Bush Brother of St Barnabas, serving in North Queensland. A research scholarship at the Queen's College in Birmingham enabled him to study the spiritual background and presupposition of the Brotherhood movement.

'After 20 years, academic work in a theological college was most stimulating, though I suppose it also pre-conditioned me to react favourably when the Bishop of North Queensland asked me to return,' he said recently. 'The distances, isolations and related human heartbreaks were familiar to me. However, from being involved in rural society to service in a mining city was another prospect, and I suppose some sense of adventuring is necessary to grapple with a new task, so I came to Mount Isa, and as much supervision of the 1,000 kilometre long "bush area" as is possible for the Bishop's Archdeacon.

'I enjoyed enormously the advantages of the heady mini-metropolitan flavour that is Mount Isa. First I enjoyed a house, after years of camping in the back of a hot little "god box"; after years of being welcomed in the homes of graziers it was a delight to be able to return the compliment. The Rectory soon became a centre of social activity and hospitality. If anyone was blessed with the rumbustious passing parade I was.

'Some came for healing. The days of the old style confessional seem to have gone but the same needs for compassionate understanding and the assurance of forgiveness are still there. I have never quite got used to the confidence people have in their priest; but to be patient and tender and firm and sometimes "surgical" is very exhausting. A man is deserted by his wife and small children. You feed him every night for five months and hear snatches of agonised phone calls. You hope there will be some reconciliation. But he commits suicide.

'Then there is the large range of unexpected guests, usually about 1.30 am. Typical: two concerned truckies wondering what to do with a young couple and an infant they had picked up in the Northern Territory. The truckies are on their way early next morning but the couple stay a week to get work, get clean and get the baby healthy.

'The church here is a delight. Simply to have a building that "prays of itself" as Sir Ninian Comper used to say. A sanctuary where all one's work begins and ends, a ladder, as Jacob dreamt, set up from earth to Heaven. It is swept and garnished once a week by careful hands, decorated with fresh flowers, lit by many candles, charmed with music, warmed by prayer, eased with fellowship and watched by angels. No wonder the architect designed a building to mirror the great Mount Isa Mines workshop across the railway line.

'The community is young and not godless, so many attend to the rites of league, tennis, squash, stock cars, golf, etc. The devotion is fanatical. And as the moralists say, there are worse things to do.

'The great cure climactic stage-managed by the three Rotary Clubs comes at the end of the winter season—the annual rodeo, an amalgam of heat, dust, horses, beef, swaggering men, booze and guitars. But like all the best orgies it is cathartic.'

Eric Hampson leaves you with the impression that his role, in isolation or in the crowd, will always be a significant and rewarding one.

sometimes from tanned hides he bought. A man with pride might plait his own stockwhips, or plait a bridle from the superior, glossy kangaroo hide. Handiwork of this nature filled otherwise unused evening hours: every good stockman could pad his own saddles, riding or pack, sew his own packbags and saddle and belt pouches, shoe his own horses and make their hobbles, or lay up a rawhide rope. For hobbles the ubiquitous rawhide was unsuitable—horses with the cunning of Satan would soak their legs in surface water until the rawhide loosened and they could work the hobbles off.

Nat Buchanan, who came to Australia as a six year old, joined the gold-rush to California in his early 20s and returned unsuccessful to find that mismanagement had lost him the station he owned with his brothers in the New England district. He became an overlander, moving stock and sleeping by his saddle, and then worked a station near Longreach in Queensland. Poor prices broke him, and at the end of 1877 in search of new country he explored the Barkly Tableland between Rankine River, near the Queensland border, and the Overland Telegraph line, more or less on the route of the main road north to Darwin today.

He thus opened up some of the very rich country of the North. He pioneered the Murranji track, with its seasonal dry stage of 180 kilometres which invariably took a toll of cattle lives and endangered men. The jeopardy in this 180 kilometres between waterholes is best measured against the 13 or 16 kilometres which grazing herds, unpressed, took a day to cover. Buchanan won stockman renown when he took Australia's largest travelling herd, reputed to be 20,000 cattle, from the south-west corner of Queensland to Glencoe and Daly River in the Northern Territory.

In 1883 the Durack family, having held outback stations at Thylungra on Cooper Creek, took 8,000 cattle in four mobs right across the top of Australia to found a Western Australian dynasty. They lived two and a half years in the wilds.

The Jardine brothers, when their father was appointed Superintendent at Somerset, farthest north on the Australian mainland, went on the road with 42 horses and 250 cattle from Rockhampton. In his magistracy, Jardine senior was expected to keep a supervisory eye on the troublesome sea traffic from a completely lawless New Guinea. Ten months on the track, the sons lost 30 horses and 50 cattle from plant poisoning, and a number of the survivors weaved in crazed and agonised pain from eating the macrozamia cycad, which today is still a hazard on that route.

Such losses were not high compared with some in the waterless centre. In 1901 a good drover, Jack Clarke, took 500 bullocks out of Queensland along the Birdsville track for millionaire owner Kidman, and reached Marree in South Australia with 72 survivors.

Independence of action, among the worst sort, fostered some crime. Probably the most famous episode was Harry Redford's theft of a thousand cattle from Bowen Downs in Queensland in 1870. He pioneered the stock route along the Thomson, Barcoo and Strzelecki rivers by which he took them to South Australia. Unknown cattle duffers 10 years later lifted a smaller mob from Queensland for sale in Adelaide. The owner, from Bullee Downs, tracked them and reached Adelaide just in time to claim the proceeds of their sale at auction but the cattle had changed hands at least once, and the duffers had disappeared.

The foundations of not a few fortunes were laid in stolen cattle. The lifting of branded mobs had its dangers, but many a herd was augmented with musterings of cleanskins. And I knew one station owner in the Northern Territory whose proud boast it was that though he owned 6,000 cattle he had never bought a beast.

Tough and amoral, callous of the rights of others, some of these men abused the Aborigines in remoter districts to a scarcely believable degree.

Opposite: Gelding improves the tractability of stock-horse teams, and is a common practice. At Hidden Valley station, NT, this young stallion has just been castrated in the traditional manner—with a penknife—and is terrified at the sight of 12-year-old Duncan Elliott, a visitor from Birrimba station.

Following page: With the rest of the herd yarded for the night, this lone runaway provides a few moments' sport for dogs and stockmen at Anna Creek station near Lake Eyre.

In March 1919 the Reverend James Watson, ex-chairman of the Methodist Aborigines Mission in the Northern Territory, was reported by the Melbourne *Argus* as saying: 'If there be such a thing as conscience then there are white men in Australia whose consciences must have the lash of scorpions. I have stood in a compound where the blacks have been driven and men, women and children shot down. We speak of the atrocities of the Hun with horror but there are men with the same instincts in northern Australia. Scattered and raided with musketry by these white devils, whole communities are wiped out.'

The smaller holdings of the dairy farmers, the cane farmers, the orchardists, the vintners, the growers of garden produce, hugged the towns and cities, their markets. The prospects of stock raising seemed unlimited until the great droughts of the last years of the century. After one slashing bad year in 1888 the weather ameliorated, but in the cities the boom was breaking and markets dropped more because of manipulative excesses than any inherent weakness in the country. From 1895 the dry years began again, and in 1902 all the southern States experienced their worst year on record.

Overstocking, from holding stock against the poor markets of the early part of the decade, undoubtedly contributed. Thirst and weakness slashed the numbers of Australian sheep by half. A compensation was the subsequent more careful husbandry, which brought about a greater weight of fleece and meat for the average marketed animal thereafter.

But neither in the far Outback nor in the closer settlements did Australia have time to develop in significant proportions a yeomanry, an establishment over several generations of people wedded to familiar land. The short history of the rural development was itself unsettling. Not only did the establishment

Tom Hare—outback administrator

Tom Hare, Executive Officer of the Reserves Board of the Northern Territory, first saw the parched dusty little township that was Alice Springs as one of 29 RAAF signallers sent to man stations in Darwin and Ambon in December 1941, and in process of transfer from four days in a baking, overcrowded train to four more in hotter, dustier and more overcrowded road trucks.

After the Japanese bombing in the north they endured some arduous conditions, but at the point at which he had lost quarter of his trim body weight, Tom had the luck to be posted to a teleprinter station in Alice Springs for six months. In 1949, after three years in the New South Wales public service he returned to make his life there.

'I'm really no city person,' he says, 'though I lived in Sydney from 1936 to the beginning of the war, except for a short spell in Cootamundra. The Public Service seemed dull. I couldn't see anything but routine advancement, and I never had the feeling of doing anything really important.

'I'd served under Colonel Lionel Rose when he'd been District Veterinary Officer in Cootamundra, so when he came to me in Sydney and told me he was going to start an Animal Industry Branch in the NT, that it was the first organisation of its kind, and that he wanted me to take the senior administrative job with him, I thought the prospects exciting. I'd be able to do something for the pastoral industry.

'In 14 very happy and useful years these prospects were realised. Colonel Rose was almost a double of Field Marshal Montgomery in appearance, quick-witted, short-tempered and never suffered fools gladly; unnecessarily rude at times, but an excellent administrator and a veteran of two wars. He worked hard and played hard. He built up a great organisation.

'The difficulties of the pastoral industry when he came included the lines of communication; cattle were walked out, often over 50 to 60 kilometre dry stages. He set about with a great deal of vigour to reduce the distance between watering points to 24 kilometres and doubled stock route bores from 70 to 140 or 150; then when truck transport came in, built trucking yards. In the early 60s I accepted this position with the Reserves Board.

'Alice Springs has changed tremendously from a population of 1,500 when I came here to something over 13,000 today. Now it's a very modern town and has lost a lot of its atmosphere. Once we knew everyone and parties were on at the drop of a hat.

'The outstanding developments have been in the transport and tourist trades, and these are interlinked. It's where the rail traffic to Darwin is transferred to the road and this promotes all the transport service trades. Then tourist requirements have given the building industry a big boost. Alice Springs used to be a cattle town with a bit of mining. Mining has fallen to nothing and the cattle industry has just about reached its height. There's a limit to the herds you can run under open range conditions.

'The growth of tourism—which with transport will bring the population to 50,000 by the end of the century—affects the Reserves Board vitally. People are there before we are ready for them. Ayers Rock is a classic example of more people than you can handle with the facilities available. It also has problems associated with Aboriginal mythology, it's one of the places best known to overseas tourists, and tourist organisations have promoted it vigorously. Our draft master plan will mean the development of a new tourist village and airfield outside the boundaries of the national park and people will only be permitted to visit, in daylight hours, only certain spots. These drastic measures are the only ones that will prevent more environmental damage.

'Let's look at development. Of course things like the gas field west of Alice Springs could have an effect, if the gas is retained in Australia as it should be. And if by some chance it is kept in the Northern Territory for the industries associated with mining in the north, then this could have an effect on Alice Springs. But I'm not sure of the elements needed to develop a natural gas industry.

'There's a 64-dollar question about Aborigines—and with so many experts in this field I hesitate to make any comment at all. But the policies adopted in the past aren't going to solve the problem—a problem of people who haven't any purpose in life, and who I doubt could revert to traditional life even if they wanted to. What people tend to overlook of ever larger herds on larger holdings tend to move the young country worker to new locations, but the large areas worked by skeleton staffs encouraged the constitution of a large nomadic grouping of seasonal workers with no tradition of stability. Then three-quarters of a century of significant gold strikes, not only in Australia but also in California, New Zealand, and several Pacific islands but especially New Guinea, tended to promote a general restlessness. Not only gold, but other more or less temporary excitements supported this influence. The Australian, unlike the European, regarded the cutting of domiciliary ties as a normal precursor to a life in the country.

This became almost a tradition when, beginning with the Boer War, a series of overseas conflicts exerted powerful recruiting influences over young Australian men. The response was particularly strong in the Outback, and Australians, used to living on horseback, relaxed for days in the saddle, established a reputation for cavalry dash and a kind of rebellious efficiency. In the Boer War, and later in World War I, their horsemanship ensured them a place in the spectacular front of major engagements.

Home again, their experience in and out of hostilities increased a rural dissatisfaction with the lack of amenities in the Outback. But in a parallel development they brought a modernisation programme to the farms and stations. From World War I many learned the use of machinery and on their return introduced it to their work and adapted it. Even aircraft: in 1922 P. J. McGinness and W. Hudson Fysh inaugurated the first civilian service in eastern Australia with the first flight of Qantas. The feat aroused imagination with its spectacular solution to some of the isolationary problems of the Outback. The growth of such services and also the introduction of other machinery brought new skills

is the birthrate: years ago primitive people couldn't support large families, but now the Pitjantjarra people west of Ayers Rock and on the Docker River have families of six or eight, and they're typical. So the problem is escalating. The employment opportunities are not here even if they wanted to work. I'm not being critical. It seems to me they might have the right idea. They live and lived for today, and we seem to be living for tomorrow all the time.

'But there's a lot more of them. They're not working and so there's a constant problem. But the same problem of displaced people must have been faced elsewhere and probably even solved. What has been promised the Aborigines since the advent of the Labor Government has achieved nothing except a lot of aggressiveness, and I do believe there will be physical violence in the end.

'This brings me to the question, am I going to live in Alice Springs when I retire? I've always said I didn't understand people living in a place all their lives and taking off when their work is finished, because they'd have to make new friends and adopt another way of life. But I've been thinking it over. I've a wife and young family to consider and this Aboriginal problem might in fact be the one that's going to drive me off. I doubt if I'd want my girls being brought up in this atmosphere.

'Because of the large uninhabited areas in the Territory people tend to think we don't have much need for conservation even in this fragile country where the desert areas are very sensitive to the impact of people. This is exemplified by pastoral leases being granted in very marginal country which stretches out into the Simpson Desert. Eventually, all that this will achieve is the encroachment of the desert areas closer and closer to Alice Springs. I know one property of which the owners were on drought relief the second or third year it was occupied. This indicates a lack of appreciation for conservation not only by people here, but by higher authority.

'In the Top End which is better able to withstand the onslaught of people you have the same lack of appreciation. The classic example is the Kakadu National Park we've been asking for since 1955. While we were doing so, it was alienated for pastoral purposes. Then when we almost got to the stage of getting the inferior country that was left, uranium was discovered and it will get preference. There's only lip service paid to conservation.

'We don't miss any of the so-called blessings of city life. People have said, "You must regret that you can't go to good entertainment, to symphony concerts, to art shows, things which enrich your cultural outlook". When I ask how often they've been in the past year they'll say, "Oh, I haven't been at all, but I just like to know I can go if I want to". So probably people from remote areas see more of these events than people who live among them, because when they go on leave they are hungry for them and seek them out.

'I'm more interested in natural culture. In the city any section of the community can hold others to ransom and this offends my sense of independence. The rights and wrongs of a situation don't come into it at all. You're subjected to blackmail day by day. I have my birds and if I went to a city the conditions would not be good for them. I keep these beautiful Gouldian finches, among many others—and I want to be able to see them in large numbers in conditions as natural as I can contrive for them—for example with living trees in the aviaries where they can nest, and where they spend their lives.

'People in the Outback do look to the fleshpots more than they used to. You can't really call the Alice the Outback. We enjoy the things people enjoy in cities and towns that are nearer cities. But when you go a little bit away from this town you're on your own, and if you don't carry what you need to sustain you, you could be in trouble. People seem frightened of this, but when they are involved with it they enjoy it. I know that when people are bogged here two or three days on a bus tour something really unusual happens. This becomes the highlight of the tour for them, rather than what they paid for when they left home. Those who live here take it as something that can happen any time. It's a challenge.'

to country centres, diversifying the population. At the same time, the openings they provided in the urban world seduced many country youngsters to city opportunities—far more than in previous generations.

Amongst the effects of the struggle for amelioration of country conditions came the birth of the Country Party. The fiscal protection which smoothed the way for urban workers was to some extent paid for by farmers: their product sold on world markets at open prices; their needs had to be procured at the high Australian price brought about by imposts on imports to protect the local manufacturers and their employed workers. The Labor Party introduced a federal land tax, designed to break up the big estates, and that seemed another urban raid on the farmer. Accustomed to the paternalism that supplied most material wants and only minimum wages, some farm workers also supported farmers in their opposition to less than moderately successful Labor attempts to increase farm wages.

So farmers' associations generally recognised the desirability of separate political representation. The first move had come in Western Australia in 1914 when a newly formed Country Party secured direct representation in the State Parliament and gave some effective voice to wheat-grower interests. At war's end other groups were established in Queensland, Victoria and New South Wales, and a federal organisation was formed which adopted a programme in 1919. Today its strength still lies in an independent trading ability whereby it gains concessions in payment for support, and it has not indulged in dreams of dominating government.

Some of these concessions may have seemed to threaten rural ideals of private ownership and control of land, which remain dominant. But the promise of better financial returns has wedded these to the establishment of a variety of government marketing boards and co-operatives, and government-strengthened rural credit.

Between the wars a severe recession in the early 20s and the world's worst depression in the 30s smudged the economic picture, a process assisted materially over most of the continent by the hungry drought years of 1919 and 1927.

World War II, more than any other single event in history, instituted changes in the rhythm and tempo of country life. Perhaps the most spectacular was in the field of aviation. During the war the Empire Air Training Scheme trained 38,000 aircrew, 10,000 of them overseas. Some at least adapted the new techniques to their peacetime existence. Need for capitalisation slowed the introduction, but dozens, then hundreds of aircraft were employed in top-dressing, seeding, crop-spraying and vermin destruction. In 1956-7, the first year for which figures are available, the areas so treated totalled nearly half a million hectares. In the next decade this area increased more than tenfold. On hundreds of outback stations pastoralists could inspect the condition of stock and pastures from small aircraft and direct and supply mustering teams. Today the helicopter too plays a significant part.

Where the aircraft was thus introduced it also performed a social function, carrying the pastoralist to country race meetings and other leisure functions, cutting down the time spent on travel.

The war introduced thousands more Australians to modern techniques of roadmaking and to heavy machinery in the construction of roads and airfields sometimes in country as difficult as that in New Guinea. Farm machinery increased in power. The ringbark mentality that cleared a tree at a time gave way to overnight clearing of huge areas. This was exemplified by the clearance from Central Queensland of square kilometres of the acacia known as brigalow.

The introduced disease of myxomatosis reduced the rabbit population and brought back huge plague-barren tracts into production, or permitted their development. In nearly all instances where introduced animals have thrived at all they have thrived too well and even those useful beasts of burden, the horse, the donkey and the camel, have become pests in country they have adopted when becoming feral.

Opposite, top: Byron Nathan is a man of two worlds—the old Australia and the new. He was born about 1885, in western Queensland, to a young lubra and an English adventurer. The arts of black-tracking and desert survival came naturally to him, and he taught himself to read and write after his father was speared to death. Well known for his fine horsemanship, he spent most of his life working cattle until, at the age of 68 when most men would be retiring, he became his own boss with a small pastoral lease near Boulia, some 350 km north of Birdsville. He successfully ran his station, Jimbrella, for the next 20 years.

Opposite, bottom: The homestead generator has broken down, and hurricane lamps light the dinner table for Irene Lewis at Hidden Valley station, NT. The property was carved out of a virgin lease taken up in 1946 by her son-in-law Dick Scobie. Although paralysed by a car accident in 1968, Scobie and his wife Thelma continue to run the station with the help of one permanent stockman and occasional assistance from friends and relatives at nearby holdings.

43

Joe Talbot, one time proprietor of the hotel in Hammond, SA, takes his evening stroll through the crumbling hamlet. Situated in what used to be a thriving pastoral area at the southern end of the Flinders Ranges, Hammond finally died in 1972 when the old hotel was refused a renewal licence after 95 years of trading. Joe Talbot's only remaining companion is Maurice Case, a former mayor of the town; they pass their evenings on the hotel verandah, laying plans for Hammond's revival.

Machinery has replaced them all. The motor-cycle has replaced the stock-horse in sheep country farthest out, and with the trapyard strategically placed at the waterhole, the long arduous weeks of muster are reduced. The beach buggy has replaced the camel and, used without restraint, seems likely to do irreparable harm to the fragile ecology of the sandy deserts.

With the use of machinery, farms are being shaped into highly productive units. More and more, with the employment of contractors, one person manages a larger unit. Sometimes the power under the control of a single individual is used unwisely. Up on Cape York Peninsula the wholesale clearance of the rain forests does not seem to promise any permanent profit from the thin coating of soil; the native animals and plants have disappeared with the trees, and the first year's exuberance of abundant crops has given way in subsequent seasons to a proliferation of weeds. Science with its chemicals can control the weeds, but each application seems to affect the ecology and some native life suffers.

Chemicals seem inefficient against the locust plagues even though the aircraft pour ever-increasing quantities upon the swarms. The locusts seem to have been increasing and perhaps the farmer, who for generations has eaten the locust-eating bustard, a gastronomic prize, is much at fault. Other operations of farmers discourage other birds and animals that keep plagues in check; the foxes, cats and pigs that they introduced have created a rarity of ground-nesting birds.

Plagues of imported mice do untold damage, appearing in unbelievable numbers. In the 1917 plague 550 tonnes of mice were destroyed near one South Australian town. Seven tonnes of mice were poisoned alongside a single fence at Sheep Hills, in the Victorian mallee country.

With awareness the battle against the trials of the land is conducted ever more energetically. Aerial bushfire patrols augment older precautions in seasons of danger; pesticides save most threatened crops; dams are an obvious weapon against droughts and in their cycle against floods; hormone sprays control the introduced plant plagues of lantana and blackberry; and scientists keep searching for weapons against such potential and actual dangers as the giant toad, introduced to control the cane beetle in Queensland. Possibly most effective in the long run will be the educative programs instituted to meet the continually changing challenges of nature.

Education, direct or indirect, has made the biggest change in country life. Part of this came with the return of Australians from overseas war service looking for standards of life they had encountered or at least seen on their leaves, even though they may have had little opportunity to enjoy them. Other aspects of information arrived with the influx of workers brought by an accelerated migration scheme.

When contracting companies for the Snowy Mountains hydro-electric and irrigation schemes brought thousands of migrant workers to Cooma, the small mountain village they invaded underwent a metamorphosis. An outlet to the Monaro, Cooma had a brief regular winter influx of snow skiers at that time, but their numbers were not great. Temporary or permanent residents who sought relief from the mundane routines of country life had a choice between the single hotel and a 'greasy spoon' cafe. Fund-raising dances and picture shows closed the list of entertainment facilities.

Within months of the arrival of overseas workers three cafes opened, presenting menus equivalent to anything in Sydney and probably superior, at that time, to Canberra. Entertainment with meals became a commonplace. The construction workers, on high wages and danger money, began by example to instruct the locals in sophisticated leisure usage.

Developments not quite so dramatic influenced other country towns. Probably the most effective excitation came from the intrusion of the arts into the smaller centres. Typically these had been represented by the School of Arts Library, usually furnished with a large collection of classics with well-worn spines. Amateur talent, invoked at annual celebrations, monopolised any available stages.

Broken Hill Flying Doctor Jeffrey Harrild launches a supply-filled aerial torpedo, part of a relief air drop to the flood-isolated inhabitants of White Cliffs, an opal mining town in western NSW.

Right: Tibooburra, in the northwest of the State, was also flood bound. During ward rounds at Tibooburra Hospital, Dr Harrild examines a premature baby he delivered two weeks earlier.

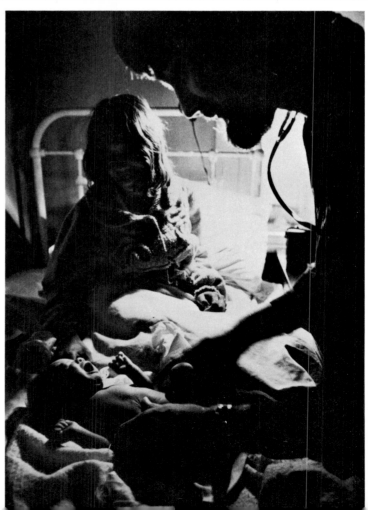

But travelling theatrical companies began to invade the smaller towns and some of them, subsidised by government, presented plays of high quality, singing and dancing of metropolitan standard. Travelling exhibitions induced a familiarity with more static visual arts. New systems of recording brought higher standards of music to the Outback.

Two Australian innovations, largely copied overseas, reduced the handicaps of the lonely stations remote from their neighbours. The Flying Doctor Service, linked with a huge amateur radio network, ensured that medical advice was available on the instant, that medical practitioners could be called to most emergencies.

The associated School of the Air, utilising the same network, brought erudition to the homestead children. In the afternoon the isolated wives, donning good clothes, chatted once or twice a week in air-linked meetings, describing their apparel as they introduced themselves to unseeing friends. Communication with the outside world eliminated many fears and apprehensions.

Post-war availability of efficient machinery improved the arterial roads out of sight. As late as the mid 50s, the main highway along the Queensland coast, Australia's Number One Highway, was in places no more than twin ruts stretching shakily across grass wallows where any day vehicles became bogged. Towns like Bowen were cut off on their land approaches for weeks at a time in each wet season. By the 60s a vast improvement was apparent—and the general principle of 'Long Service Leave' crowded the roads with Australians, some of whom were able for the first time in their lives to realise a dream of seeing their own country.

The principle of Long Service Leave was set out in a decision of the Commonwealth Conciliation and Arbitration Commission in September 1959. Prior to this, on a road like that linking Alice Springs with South Australia, the traveller might meet three cars in a lucky day. Immediately after the grant was made I passed 130 cars on an ordinary day on that same road, and found cars and caravans on minor roads in remote territories. Among them were tourist buses, equipped sometimes with camping gear.

The influx of people interested in their habitat promoted historical societies in country centres, often subsidised by town and county councils and guided by the older societies; promoted, too, such good restaurants as established themselves. Catering for tourists they found themselves with a small town and regional clientele as well.

An unbelievable number of small towns found excuses for holding festivals connected with the vegetation of the district. Grafton promoted its jacarandas, townships in the Adelaide Hills their autumn leaves, Bowral its tulips, the Barossa Valley its vintage, Innisfail its sugar, Ballarat its begonias. Centres like Port Macquarie, which had spent a century concealing or destroying the evidence of its convict history, began instead to display it. Port Lincoln embarked upon a Tuna Festival, extolling the main source of its sea wealth. Everywhere the centres began to see logic in attracting outsiders.

And some displayed new potential. Tamworth, a country town with the State's largest egg production, supported by wool, fat lambs, flour and other grain products, a freezing works, a timber industry and a number of manufactories, became known also as a centre for country music.

Still other towns benefitted from the establishment of centres of tertiary education. In Bathurst, the Mitchell College of Advanced Education brought numbers of students, and summer schools held in its precincts during term or semester breaks interested still others. The numbers of these people are perhaps not so important as the influence they carry, and the practical demonstration for talented country youngsters from families unable to afford them the opportunity for study elsewhere that they can compete with the best.

Moreover when, for example, mining ventures required the establishment of new towns, or such government pursuits as weapons testing at Woomera, administrators found that some deference to the arts valuably aided the establishment of a more contented work force.

Practically all such developments followed the century's halfway mark. Their net result was to reduce the difference between country living and the city. Where the population warranted it, the establishment of television and radio stations brought to most rural people an approximation of the evening entertainment of suburbia.

Some centres that made no overt moves in any of these directions died on the vine, or leaned on more thrusting neighbours. But the pattern was always one of a closer liaison between the farmsteads and their nearest centre.

On the farms, machinery had already reduced the number of hours worked. A horse teamster, working his team for seven hours 'tight-chains' in the day, that is to say, effectively moving farm implements for that time, could expect to start at 4 am by bringing his team in to feed and groom them, and typically would finish 17 hours later. At weekends his horses and their harness demanded still some hours of work.

The tractor driver, finished when he stops his motor, works short hours for more money and is paid overtime for extra effort. Awards dictate the time he shall spend working, and in general his employer stays within a similar allotment of working hours.

More and more country people have become specialists, offering specialist services. And more and more the conditions of employment have approached those offered in the city. The dust, the flies and the distances remain. Against this the open-air life and the absence of weary commuting hours make compensation. The television programme they watch, the radio they hear, offers the same entertainment as their city cousins enjoy; their late model car transports them to any other entertainment they fancy.

No longer valid are the chief enjoyments of the pioneer—the fierce joy of self-sufficiency proved; the prime satisfaction of wresting a living directly from the soil; of demonstrating, from the well-tried resources of the inner person, an ability to cope with the land and the seasons; of establishing a homestead and holding where the generations unborn can grow and develop; of celebrating inwardly the small quiet triumphs of improvisation. Independence is no longer possible, and the person on the land is no more than the firing chamber in a machine largely beyond his control. The tightening constriction of communities striving to adapt their form to the necessities of the global village is unwelcome always, but it still allows freedom to sample the great delights of life beyond the haze of city smoke.

The person in the Outback has an inheritance from generations for whom the realisation of dreams lay always over the lip of the horizon; for this Australia's ancestors left their native lands only to find, as the modern individual will find, that like the foot of the rainbow the dream will move ahead, forever in sight and just out of reach.

Opposite: A stockman waits for stragglers to cross a salt pan during a cattle drive near Lake Eyre, SA.

Water is scarce and livestock feed sparse in the vast arid tracts of central and northern Australia. Land holdings have to be big to run cattle successfully. The biggest, and one of the most successful, is Anna Creek station near Lake Eyre. Owned by a pioneer family, the Kidmans, the property is a group of stations covering 31,000 square kilometres, an area about the size of The Netherlands.

Above: After resting at a water hole, stockmen drive the mob towards nearby holding yards at Stuart Creek station, one of the Anna Creek properties.

Above right: Butchering a steer to replenish the camp larder.

Right: Twilight comes suddenly in the clear dry air, but there is little evening leisure. Work begins again at dawn.

Following page: Yarding the mob at sundown.

Camels were introduced from India's North West Frontier in the 1860s, and for more than half a century proved invaluable in the development of the dry interior. Displaced by motor transport, most of the few survivors run wild.

Right: One of the last three working camel teams—all three teams are at Anna Creek.

Below: Flanking the main herd, the camp wagon and a mob of spare stock horses wind through barren salt country near Lake Eyre.

Above: Bushfires, often started by lightning, are a constant threat in the Outback. Containing them can become a nightmare when whirlwinds or willy willys (like the one beyond these termite mounds) suck up the burning embers and scatter them far from the fire's main front.

Right: Dairy pasture in northern NSW. The ring-barked trees, a common sight in most Australian dairy country, reflect the short-sighted attitude of early settlers.

Opposite: A scene symbolising the most crushing fear of pastoral Australia—drought!

Rural development in this century has been handicapped by the one-way stream of young country people headed for 'the big smoke'. Recently, however, small groups of city dwellers have been moving in the opposite direction to escape the social pressures and commercialism of urban life. Many of these small groups are attracted by the relatively healthy, simple and tranquil qualities of the bush life. They establish communes in which to practise their chosen life style. These vary greatly but are usually based on an inter-dependent family social structure—a structure cherished by the Aborigines for longer than human memory.

Left: A commune meeting at Nimbin, northern NSW.

Below left: Tjilgiyiri, or 'Tiger Lily' as he is known around Ayers Rock, poses in an old US Cavalry uniform and army cap with members of his family.

Below: For all his 93 years Tom Pether has lived in central Queensland. He spent most of his life prospecting, mainly for opals. Now retired, he lives in a small iron shack at Winton.

Top and opposite: Independent and matriarchal, Mrs Annie Wharton lives in a tent in the bush near historic Wilcannia, western NSW. According to her family's calculations she is between 100 and 120 years old, and has lived in the area all her life. She remembers Wilcannia being built, and recalls working bullock teams with her father, de-snagging the Darling River. Annie Wharton was a good horsewoman, and worked as a horsebreaker, cattle musterer and drover. She also raised a family of 14 children.

Right: George Kulka has worked for 20 years in the cane fields around Mossman, on the north coast of Queensland.

Following page: The Family Hotel at Tibooburra, a remote and desolate corner of north-western New South Wales, is a unique kind of pub; it boasts work by two of Australia's most famous painters. Patrons, like station manager Jack Williams, may take their choice of this mural by Clifton Pugh in the front bar, or a delicate felt-pen sketch by Sir Russell Drysdale on the other side of the wall in the lounge.

Although long regarded as a nation of beer drinkers, Australia has in the last decade or so become a major producer and consumer of wine. But local wine-growing is not new. Some of the family wineries that pioneered the industry a century ago are still thriving.

More valuable than wine, especially as an export, is Queensland's sugar. Machine harvesting has all but replaced cane-cutting by hand, and seasonal work, well-paying but back-breaking, has declined.

Left: Roly Birks has been making wine at Wendouree Cellars since 1917. The vineyard, in the Clare district north of Adelaide, SA, was started in 1892 by his father.

Below: Mechanisation has reduced the large seasonal workforce once employed by the wine industry, but picking is still done almost wholly by hand. Here, a picker and her son take a lunch break at Seppeltsfield, SA.

Opposite: Morning tea for a cane field labourer near Innisfail.

As Australia's people have adapted themselves to the country's varied landscapes and conditions, so too have the various breeds and cross-breeds of sheep. There are ten times more sheep than people in the continent.

Below: Mick Hayes of Caltowie, SA, was for 60 years a drover in the northern reaches of the State.

Following page: Not all of the pastoral land is reckoned in hectares per beast. This valley near Tilba Tilba on the south coast of NSW is typical of much of the lush, productive pasture found along the east, south-east and south-west coastal fringes of the continent.

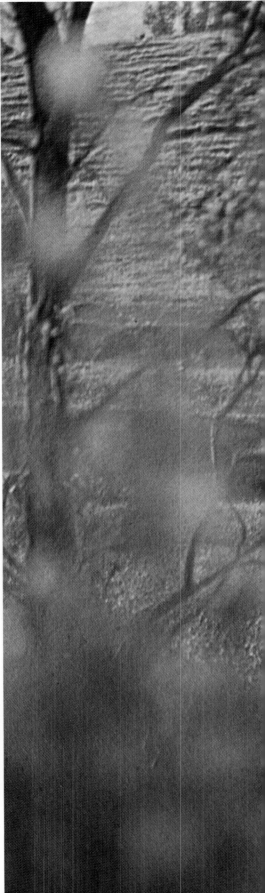

Top left: The Great Western Tiers are the backdrop to rich paddocks near Devonport, north-western Tasmania.

Bottom left: Evening idyll near Bermagui on the south coast of NSW.

Below: A poetic landscape near Wagga Wagga, on the Western Slopes region of NSW along the Murrumbidgee River.

Heavy (and controversial) expenditure by the Federal Government converted a sparsely populated area of north-western Australia into a rich pocket of intensive agriculture. Known as the Ord River Project, with irrigation water supplied by a dam on the Ord River, it is a major source of cotton and rice, supplementing the harvest from eastern Australia.

Right: Aerial spraying is the only effective, economical method of combatting constant attacks by disease and pests.

Left: Haematite, valuable as iron ore, stains these tidal flats in north-western WA.

Top: A glimpse of sunlit cliffs through the limbs of a dead fig tree in the north-west.

Above: Rain produces gentle, short-lived colour among the twisted stems of desert shrubs.

On the desert floors and the sands of the coastal fringe, wind and water create their ever shifting patterns.

Opposite: Coastal lagoon in Western Australia.

Above: Extreme tidal fluctuations along the north-west coast leave their tortuous mark on the mud-flats of bays and estuaries.

Left: An insect's trail competes with sand ripples on a dune near the Birdsville track.

77

For every kilometre of coastland populated (in season) by surfers and holidaymakers, there are many more where not even a lone fisherman is likely to move through the emptiness.

79

THE ECONOMY

Peter Ellery

'Seven decades of uninterrupted protectionism . . .'

In the 1970s Australia still conveys to the world the image of a nation of lean, laconic, sun-bronzed individuals wresting a living from the sheep's back, the wheat paddock or the mine shaft.

True, time has modified this. Pharmaceutical efficiencies on the sheep run, large-scale operations on the biggest wheat paddocks in the world and massive mining machines which move hundreds of thousands of tonnes of ore a day where a man once hauled dozens of buckets have allowed the trim figure to relax and spread slightly with prosperity. And the bronzed prototype has become confidently articulate in the eyes of the world.

If there is a less honourable variation on the image which accompanied us into nationhood more than 70 years ago, it may be of the smooth promoter, still lean, but with his sun tan paled by luxury living and with a mining property to sell or a real estate deal to put together.

But images are outward reflections which do not necessarily reveal character. Increasingly in the 20th century Australians have become a nation of factory workers.

One Australian in every four in a workforce of six million is employed in manufacturing industry and the proportion is growing. The world's most urbanised nation has also become one of the world's most industrialised nations on a per capita basis. Though the products of the rural and mining industries continue to dominate overseas trade, the factories account for more than 25 per cent of the gross domestic product. The value of factory production has increased more than fivefold in the past two decades, and now approaches $9,000 million a year.

A drive through or flight over the approaches to the great cities of the south-eastern seaboard, or Perth, the western capital, is evidence of this industrial strength which had its beginnings before the turn of the century in the need to turn out special machinery for the peculiarities of Australian agriculture, and which gained a broader base in two world wars.

Opposite: Until recently sales like this one, in Western Australia, were the yardstick of the nation's economic health. Today, minerals have a slight edge over wool as the major export in financial terms, though the rural sector still contributes mightily.

81

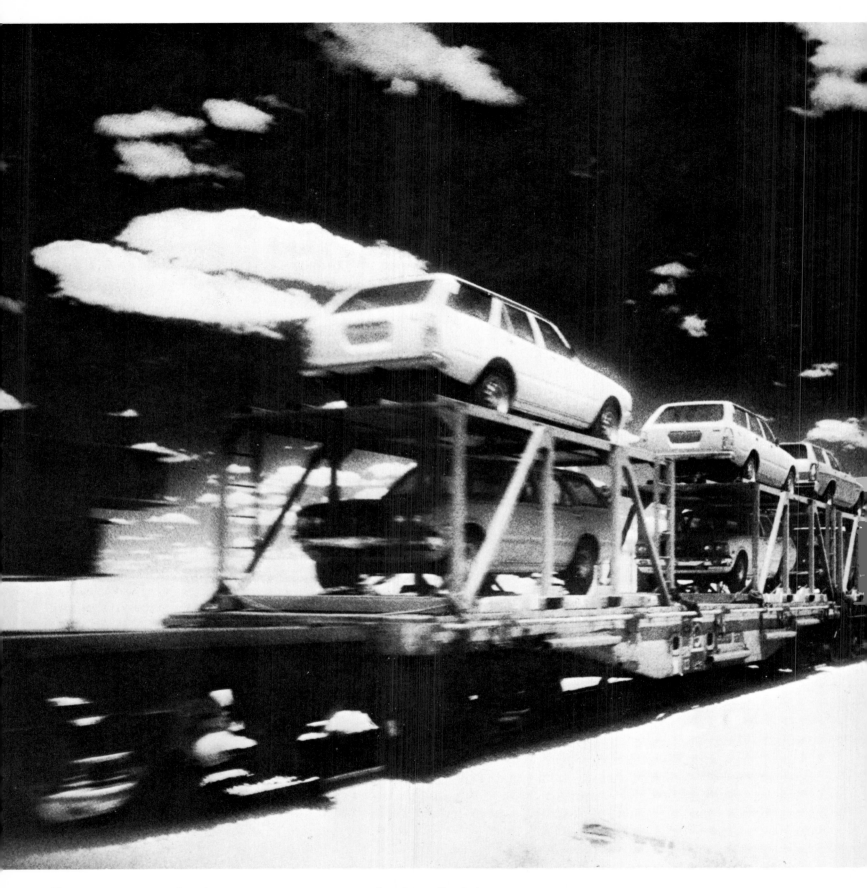

For many years camel trains were Alice Springs' only supply link with the south. The widely respected Afghan camel drivers have disappeared, but today's 'Ghan', a fast, airconditioned diesel train (successor to older coal burners, now museum pieces) recalls their name and the vital role they played in opening up the arid interior. Rail competes with road and air transport for the valuable tourist trade, but cars for the Alice arrive on 'The Ghan'.

Thousands of hectares are devoted to factory buildings—dun coloured structures with serrated roofs generally set in a splash of green lawn amidst an olive-dun Australian landscape of gum trees, security fences and bitumen paving.

Though the waterways of the factory areas are often polluted, modern industrial Australia has largely escaped the gloomy, polluted environments of the industrial nations of the northern hemisphere—except for the older (pre-1940) industrial suburbs of Sydney and Melbourne.

To the predominantly young population—the great majority of which has grown up with the era of industrialisation—it may seem that factories have always been part of the Australian scene. But manufacturing has not come easily and does not fit naturally into the economic life of a nation which owes its prosperity and ascendancy in trade to vast primary resources which respond, sometimes with lavish rewards, to the application of relatively little labour and a great concentration of capital and technology.

Before the Federation of the Australian States in 1901, the relatively few factories operating principally produced goods for local consumption—stump-jump ploughs, crop strippers, shearing appliances, pickles, ham, furniture, bricks, and clothing made from imported fabrics. Facilities existed for the repair of imported machines rather than their manufacture, and considerable energy was devoted to the preliminary processing, such as wool scouring and saw milling, of staple primary products.

Federation removed interstate trade barriers and introduced a uniform protective tariff, creating an umbrella of artificial protection under which manufacturing industries flourished. This growth quickened with World War I which curtailed the availability of manufactured goods from abroad and boosted local demands.

Australia's industrial giant, the Broken Hill Proprietary Co. Ltd, took the momentous step from mining and smelting lead ores to making steel during the war, and the orders flooded in, commencing an extraordinary saga of company growth which has always paralleled and sometimes outstripped the greater national move to industrialisation. The burgeoning new steel-maker generated the establishment of a host of related and subsidiary industries. Extensive manufacture of machinery was also begun and a wide range of products such as textiles, metal and electrical goods were added to Australia's previously modest output of manufactures.

The end of the war saw the creation, in 1921, of the Tariff Board which further assisted new manufacturing industries by means of protective tariffs against overseas competition.

Expansion of manufacturing continued unchecked until the Depression of 1929-33 which caused many factories to close their doors and put one Australian worker in every three on the dole.

A slow return to prosperity from 1933 onwards, together with tougher import restrictions and a depreciation of the Australian currency, brought renewed activity and when World War II broke out in September, 1939, Australia had a well-established industrial base from which to supply the Allied cause in the South Pacific and east of the Suez Canal. Once again, fired by the furnaces of war, Australian factories went to work to supply the Australian people and their allies with goods which had previously been imported from Britain and Europe. And once again, the wartime expansion brought on-going benefits.

With peace came a steady flow of migrants to Australia from the war-torn old world—almost two million in 20 years—bringing new skills to the factory floor and rapidly expanding the home markets for Australian produced goods.

The inflow of new settlers, coinciding with a period of unprecedented prosperity and growth for the basic rural and mining industries, created the climate for rapid industrial expansion in terms of both volume of production and diversity of products.

The Australian motor vehicle industry was born in the early post-war period and has grown to become one of the biggest employers of factory workers. Today it produces some half a million new vehicles a year, of which nearly a fifth are exported to more than 70 different countries.

The domestic appliance industry mushroomed to supply the demands of the newly prosperous Australian housewife. The demands of ebullient consumerism in turn created new opportunities for the heavy industries.

Overseas capital flowed in a steady stream during the 50s and 60s to increase petroleum refinery capacity, establish new fertiliser plants and chemical complexes and turn out an increasing range of pharmaceutical products, machine tools and electronic equipment. Breweries, strongly Australian owned and always healthily productive and profitable in the thirst-forming climate, flourished as never before.

Australian mechanical ingenuity, originally born of a need to improvise in the Outback, produced a range of products for local markets which became competitive abroad. Though only an eighth of all factory output is exported, it makes up 25 per cent of total exports. Australian-made cranes were used to build the world's tallest building in New York, Australian telecommunications equipment is exported to 50 or 60 different countries, Australian agricultural machinery commands a market in all comparable agricultural situations throughout the world.

As a generalisation, the State capitals are the centres of labour-intensive light and medium manufacturing. Heavy industries such as steel making, metal refining and shipbuilding are concentrated in Newcastle and Wollongong, which together with Sydney form the great urban concentration of central New South Wales, at Geelong in Victoria, Whyalla in South Australia and Kwinana in Western Australia.

Coal from the vast alluvial beds beneath and around the city fires the blast furnaces and hot strip mills of Newcastle, oldest and smokiest of the Australian industrial centres. But its surf beaches, and the Hunter River which links it to the vineyards upstream, distinguish it as a typically Australian city.

Wollongong, sprawling untidily beneath the Illawarra escarpment, populated by one of the heaviest concentrations of migrants in Australia, was the fastest growing urban centre during the expansion of its steelworks in the 50s and early 60s.

Geelong, on the western side of Victoria's Port Phillip Bay, is the centre for a major alumina smelter and petrochemical plants superimposed on the solid structure of an old pastoral port and service centre.

Whyalla, set on the dry western shore of the Eyre Peninsula, near the head of Spencer Gulf and in sight of Iron Knob, the great mountain of iron that is the reason for the city's existence, is also heavily peopled by migrant factory workers from the old world. Australia's third steel making city, it has also become the centre of the government-subsidised shipbuilding industry.

Kwinana, 40 kilometres from Perth on the flat sandy coast of Cockburn Sound, is the best planned of the heavy industrial centres. Hundreds of unoccupied hectares of sparse scrubland separate its giant metal refineries and the oil refinery which is its source of energy. Ships discharging cargoes of crude oil and fertiliser feedstock, or loading metals for overseas destination, anchor out from sandy beaches, many kilometres of which remain accessible to the public.

Beyond the heavily populated south-east coastal crescent stretching from Brisbane to Whyalla, and the concentration of people around Perth in Western Australia, there is little manufacturing industry of consequence.

The decentralists dream of—and plan for—great industrial complexes based on the richness of Western Australia's Pilbara iron ore deposits, and the vast coal reserves of Queensland's Bowen Basin.

Less ambitious and more easily realised plans to establish light and medium industry at Albury-Wodonga on the New South Wales-Victorian border, at Bathurst-Orange in New South Wales and in other large provincial towns are already being implemented. Queensland, with its resources evenly spread along its coastal strip, has shown a natural tendency towards decentralisation of industry to a greater degree than the southern States.

But by and large, in the most spacious land on earth, the dream of decentralised industry has many philosophical adherents and few practical activists. Government ministries for decentralisation have been set up, but withered away from time to time with little to show for their efforts.

Urban Australians may curse the spread of their manufacturing complexes which are swelling the growth of and breeding future pollution problems for their traffic-choked cities, but few are willing to establish new factories and new industry in the Outback.

But if decentralisation of manufacturing poses a socio-economic challenge for Australia in the last quarter of the 20th century, it is nothing compared to the challenge of tariff reform.

Seven decades of uninterrupted protectionism in Australia have spawned and nurtured a major industrial civilisation beneath the clear southern hemisphere sky. In many ways it is more admirable than the industrial civilisations of Europe, America and Japan. Australian factories are newer and cleaner, working conditions are better and aggressive trade unionism, combined with fortuitous economic circumstances, ensures that Australian factory workers are as well paid as any in the world. Industrial development has fulfilled a national aspiration which pre-dates the formation of the Australian nation from a group of pastoral colonies—the desire for economic independence and a wider range of job opportunities than could be provided by a rural based economy.

But the voices of many economists, amongst others, contend that a surfeit of protectionism has also nurtured many industries which are inefficient and an unnecessary drain on the national economy.

The Tariff Board has been replaced by the Industries Assistance Commission which has the monumental task of instituting significant tariff reforms. The challenge is to remove undesirable forms of protection without disrupting the economy, and in particular the level of employment. Judging by initial performances, and considering the broad spectrum of the vested interests opposed to tariff reform—from employers to employees—it will not be easily achieved.

If the blue-overalled factory hand driving to his work in an outer suburb in a small late-model car is the prototype of the modern Australian, the grey-suited office worker is the archetype. By occupation, seven out of every 100 Australians are administrative, executive or managerial workers—the serious denizens of the sombre concrete and glass towers of downtown capital Australia.

These are the business decision makers, the cautious, conservative, wheeling-dealing, money-spinning doers, who in two decades have transformed Australia from a sylvan backwater, albeit an urbanised one, to a voice to be heeded in the world's trading circles.

Decisions made in the executive offices and boardrooms atop the tallest buildings, combined with a lot of luck and the blessing of bounteous natural resources, have enabled Australian governments in the 70s to be sought out and fawned upon by nations in a world undergoing a major shift in its trading relationships. Supported by an army of clerks—out of every 100 Australians employed 16 are clerical workers—the Australian archetype runs the manufacturing companies, the mining houses, the uniquely Australian stock firms, which dispose the products and supply the requirements of the rural community, the retail establishments and the capital raising financial institutions, which occupy the central city areas.

As the nation has grown fat on the successes of the capitalist system, Australians have tended to take for granted or find fault with the vital role played by the private sector financial institutions in their daily lives. The banks, stock exchanges, building societies, merchant banks and finance companies have gone about their daily business unheralded and largely ignored except when some weakness or aberration in the system has thrust them unfavourably into the headlines and public notice.

Yet they have played and continue to play a major part in the formation and mobilisation of massive amounts of new capital that has been essential to

HIGHEST RATE OF HOME OWNERSHIP IN THE WORLD

the post-war leap from promise to prosperity. During the period of high growth in the 1950s and 1960s some 90 per cent of all new capital invested was drawn from domestic savings. This has been largely overlooked because of the publicity devoted to a chauvinistic concern about the role of foreign capital. Investment from overseas has accounted for a mere 10 per cent of total new capital. But it has attracted a disproportionate share of unfavourable attention because it has been channelled into areas of high risk and high profit return. Sometimes such investments have affected resources of potential strategic significance but more often objections are vaguely articulated nationalistic misgivings.

Much new capital has been channelled into the economy by the life assurance groups, traditionally the main vehicle for private savings, which, in the words of one writer, straddle the country like a medieval colossus. From behind the discreet facades of their functional steel, glass and concrete head office blocks, they dominate the Australian property market and the markets in ordinary and fixed interest securities and government bonds. In terms of assets they tower over all but a handful of the more visible industrial and mining companies, and in the late 60s and early 70s their rate of growth exceeded the rate of growth in national income. Sums assured in force at December 31, 1973, totalled $45,800 million, an increase from $39,400 million in 1972. Annual premiums were close to a $1,000 million in 1973, and have since passed that point.

Most of the assurance companies are mutual societies, owned by the policy holders. Some are of foreign parentage, particularly British, but their associations with Australia generally began in the old colonial days. Until recently they enjoyed a privileged existence in comparison to other financial institutions, pampered by government tax concessions, but obliged by law to invest at least 30 per cent of their life office funds in government and other securities. Before the 1960s they generally confined their non-government investments to the safe and secure property market, loans on mortgages and to a lesser extent the share market.

Criticism of this conservative approach, and the opportunities offered by the 1960s are encouraging a move into more adventurous areas including huge mining and pastoral developments. A mobilisation of the life assurance contributions of thousands of ordinary Australian families through the giant Australian Mutual Provident Society, biggest by far of the life houses, has increased Australian equity in projects such as the Mt Newman iron ore mine in Western Australia, and the Gove bauxite-aluminium undertaking in the Northern Territory. Capital requirements for these projects were too great for other Australian institutions to contemplate.

As the principle vehicle for personal savings in Australia, and with a billion dollars in premiums to invest each year, the assurance companies are likely to remain a major source of capital for growth for years to come. If they continue to follow their new investment policies, they also offer a practical alternative to the use of overseas capital in the high risk, high reward areas of natural resource development. Moves to divert savings from the private sector to the public sector in recent years may have some impact on their role, but they are too well established and too much part of the Australian scene to be much affected by anything short of drastic new policies which totally restructure the economy.

Unlike the assurance companies which conduct their monolithic business under close government control but relatively free of public debate, the less-controlled securities industry has been exposed to intense public debate in recent years.

The share market became a conversational set piece for every social gathering during the spectacular boom and crash of 1969-71 as Australians talked of those they knew who had made fortunes overnight, and later of those who lost them. The aftermath of the boom has seen a continuation and intensification of the debate on the role of the market in the economy, and the need for more self-imposed and government controls. It has also seen a sharp decline in the value of new share issues from a peak of $1,000 million in 1969-70 when the tiny speculative mining company Poseidon NL rocketed to overnight fame, and later infamy, on the hopes generated by its discovery of a rich nickel deposit at remote Mt Windarra in Western Australia's parched eastern goldfields.

Poseidon had the goods alright, and the Mt Windarra mine which began production five years after the discovery is now making its contribution to the nation's wealth in an efficient and unspectacular way.

But the events which sent its shares rocketing from less than a dollar to a peak of $280 in the space of weeks, and which generated such euphoria that honourable men forsook their principles in a scramble for instant wealth, has left a deep scar on the Australian securities industry at home and abroad which may take generations to erase. Much of the money raised by the speculative mining companies in the Poseidon boom was wastefully dissipated by amateur management, or found its way into questionable investments for which it was never intended.

But the market for manufacturing and commercial securities was also pushed to record high levels in the boom and the well-established companies which took advantage of the inflated share prices to raise new capital at that time are today reaping the benefits.

The share broking fraternity, though severely chastened by the experiences of the boom and its aftermath, and by the public inquiries which followed, has moved only slowly to implement the reforms which are so glaringly necessary.

Given the market's proven capacity to raise a billion dollars in a year towards the fulfilment of Australia's economic aspirations, there is a clear incentive to ensure that it is seen beyond all doubt to be reliable, effective and efficient as a mobiliser of capital. But given the Australian's penchant for the long chance—they have turned increasingly to the super lotteries of prizes ranging from $100,000 to $500,000 since the share market lost its promise of instant wealth—the final form of regulation adopted must leave some room for chance if it is to attract the breadth of public support it requires.

'Black Jack' McEwen—an unlikely protectionist

The manufacturing industries have flourished and grown fat in post-war Australia, sheltering under an umbrella of tariff duties held aloft by the most unlikely of protectionists, Sir John McEwen.

A grim-faced farmer from Victoria's Goulburn Valley, Sir John was a towering and controversial figure in Australian politics almost from the day he entered Parliament in 1934 until he retired as Deputy Prime Minister in 1971. For the most influential part of his political career he was responsible for trade and manufacturing matters, and a powerful protagonist for the protection lobby in the Federal Cabinet. Even as he prepared to retire amidst the plaudits of his colleagues and the public at the end of a long and distinguished career he was fighting a spectacular last stand for protection, in this case by attempting to emasculate the Tariff Board which was becoming increasingly disenchanted with his policies.

No individual can claim to be singly responsible for the growth of modern industrial Australia, and yet it is probably his monument more than that of any other man. His political strength and determination in the 1950s and 1960s created a favourable climate for the investment of thousands of millions of dollars in new manufacturing plant, creating hundreds of thousands of new blue collar jobs.

If John McEwen, orphaned son of an Ulster-born Presbyterian minister, farmer and leader of the farmers' Country Party, ever saw any irony in this he has apparently never acknowledged it.

Born in 1900, McEwen grew up in Ned Kelly country, the farming settlements of central northern Victoria which were the haunt of the notorious bushranger of the late 19th century. He served in the Australian Imperial Force during the 1914-1918 war, and on his return to civilian life took up a 35 hectares irrigation farm under a Soldier Settlement scheme at Stanhope in the Goulburn Valley.

A tall, Lincolnesque figure, he was forced by necessity to participate in the politics of the struggling soldier settlers movements of those difficult days. He was elected to Federal Parliament in 1934 as a representative of the Victorian Country Progressive Party, later joined the Country Party and almost immediately found himself involved in a series of leadership feuds in which he is credited with bringing down two party leaders, Sir Earle Page and Mr A. G. (later Sir Archie) Cameron. His feuding did not stand him in good stead when he opposed Page for the leadership in 1940. After two ballots and two deadlocks the party installed Sir Arthur Fadden as its leader and the tougher, more ruthless McEwen was relegated to a lesser position for 17 years.

But he played a leading role in the formation of the Liberal-Country Party coalition which was elected to government with Sir Robert Menzies as leader in 1949 and remained in power for 23 years. In the government McEwen was successively Minister for Commerce and Agriculture, and Minister for Trade and Industry which he combined with his role as Deputy Prime Minister when he was finally elected Leader of the Country Party in 1958. There was undoubtedly a degree of opportunism which persuaded the representative of rural interests to see the advantages for himself and his party of a close association with the financially powerful manufacturers lobby, but the results of that association produced dynamic economic and social changes for Australia.

Apart from encouraging manufacturing industry, his most notable contribution to contemporary Australia was the negotiation in 1957 of a Trade Agreement with Japan which paved the way for the massive mining industry expansion of the 1960s, primarily to supply raw materials to Japanese industry.

In 1971 Sir John retired from politics to divide his time between his farm Chilgala at Stanhope, now grown to more than 1000 hectares running 1,800 beef cattle, and a town house in the plush Melbourne suburb of Toorak. With his retirement the anti-protection lobby has gained strength and marked up some notable progress. But 'Black Jack' McEwen has achieved too much for his policies to be easily unscrambled.

To regulate wisely without being too heavy handed is a challenge for the securities market, and the Australian Government. But to ignore the need for regulation, or to procrastinate indefinitely, will threaten the continued useful existence of the securities industry.

If there are doubts about the manner in which the securities industry is discharging its role in the Australian economy there are none of any substance about the banks. Like the life assurance companies, they are revered national institutions, bastions of security and discretion tightly regulated by government and their own collective desire to avoid unseemly competition, creators of credit and vital to the stability of the national economy.

This has not always been so. Australian banks closed their doors during the great financial crash of the 1890s and some were severely shaken again during the Depression of 1929-1933. Today, by virtue of the government's long established central banking policies which proscribe a statutory reserve deposit and closely regulate every facet of traditional banking activity, they appear impervious to all but the most calamitous of economic shocks.

Structurally the banking system is organised into the Reserve Bank, the Australian Government's central bank which administers banking policy and regulates reserves, the Commonwealth Banking Corporation with its trading and savings banks, 14 trading banks including the six privately owned major banks, and government and privately owned savings banks. In addition the Commonwealth Banking Corporation administers a Development Bank with special functions to assist primary and secondary industry development, and the major trading banks have established the Australian Resources Development Bank with the main object of assisting Australian enterprises to participate more fully in the development of the nation's natural resources.

The banking scene has been remarkable in the past decade or so for the rapid development of merchant banks and finance companies which are challenging the deposit banks in some areas of their traditional business. But an examination of this development reveals that all the major trading banks have extensive interests in these quasi-banking organisations. Their existence is to a large extent an indication of the growing sophistication of the Australian financial system, and of the economy which is creating demands for new services and specialisations within that system.

Even more spectacular than the development of the quasi-bank institutions has been the growth of the permanent building societies. The societies have always existed in Australia but they have been achieving high levels of growth only since the middle 60s. To a large degree this mirrors the increasing prosperity of the lower income Australians, arriving at a situation where for the first time in their lives they can consider putting their savings into something more rewarding than an old sock or local post office branch of the savings bank. It is also testimony to the techniques used by the societies to capture the small investor's dollar, techniques which have raised some disapproving eyebrows in the competing savings banks.

But whatever the savings banks may think there are many hundreds of thousands of Australian home-owners who would not be home-owners if it were not for the hard-sell, investment-winning ways of the building societies. Loans advanced by the permanent building societies rose spectacularly from $375 million in 1969-70 to $1,000 million in 1972-73. Deposits in the same period rose from $950 million to $3,250 million—far exceeding the money harvesting prowess of the great grey insurance companies.

Since then deposits in the societies (and their rate of lending) have declined and there has been some unease about their stability. Though they have performed well, their image over many years has been tarnished by the history of the building society collapses which occurred during the crash of the 1890s. They depend for their borrowings on the prosperity of the small investor which in the middle 1970s was being increasingly eroded by endemic inflation. Drawing on the least sophisticated end of the lending market, they are far more susceptible than the other financial institutions to volatile movements in their deposits.

Although the increased lending capacity of the building societies has filled an urgent need, it has failed to sustain the high rate of home ownership which has been a source of Australian pride since 1901. Of the four million private houses and flats in Australia, some 70 per cent are owned, or are in the process of being purchased, by their occupiers. This is the highest rate of home ownership in the world, but represents a reduction of a few per cent over a decade. That it is occurring is a source of some concern—but the reasons are almost certainly related more to the increasing congestion of the big cities and the pressures toward higher density living than to economic circumstances alone.

With few exceptions, every young Australian couple desiring to own a home can do so today, though it may require the sacrifice of the young wife working for a few years. The homes are being built bigger and better than ever before, and with the munificence of the building societies there are mortgages to match for those who can afford the interest. If proof of this is needed, it is in the statistics. The proportion of homes built in the high class materials of brick, brick veneer, concrete and stone has increased by 250 per cent since 1950 while the proportion built from humble timber has fallen by 90 per cent. Built-in amenities and appliances have become a standard feature of the Australian home of the 1970s, a contrast with the spartan square three-bedroomed cottage without trimmings of any sort which was the norm in pre-war times.

Like the troubled securities industry, the home building industry is a super-sensitive barometer to the national economy. Though it has been prosperous more often than not in the post-war years, it has had its share of downs as well as ups. Since 1960, shifts in government fiscal and monetary policies have severely reduced the rate of home building on several occasions, sometimes by accident and more often than not by design.

Though home ownership is within the reach of every Australian who cares to strive for it, the striving is becoming more arduous as land costs increase along with the cost of materials and labour. Provision of low-cost housing for the lower income groups, traditionally an area for government concern, lags well behind requirements for the same reasons.

Despite its many problems, the home building industry has kept up a staggering pace, more than doubling the number of homes in existence since the end of the war in 1945. In doing so it has covered the broad hectares surrounding the old pre-war cities with vast landscapes of three-bedroom brick and tile cottages within each of which resides a small segment of the Australian dream.

If the home builders have managed a cracking pace, the builders of commercial and high rise big city buildings have in their own way been devastating. A survey in 1972 showed a total of 41 new skyscraper office blocks worth a total of $185 million under construction in Sydney, with another 57 worth $328 million approved but not yet started and a further 52 projects awaiting consideration by the City Council.

Sydney was not a special case. Australians, aided often by overseas investors, began to reshape the centres of their big cities in a big way in the 1960s. For more than a decade the skylines of all the State capitals have been distinguished by a fretwork of partly built office towers and lean, busy cranes. The downtown areas have been brutishly gutted of their medium-rise pre-war buildings, subjected to the incessant din and dust of demolition and construction and remodelled in standardised concrete and glass to resemble every other big city in the western world.

There is evidence that the office building boom peaked before the mid 70s when it was realised that it was creating a king-sized and long-lasting glut in office space. Now the rush to redevelopment is more sedate, the inner city noise levels more tolerable, but still the work goes on.

Increasingly though, the developers have been turning their attention to the opportunities for value-increased land utilisation and construction offering beyond the central city. Tourism and recreation have provided lucrative openings. So too has a revolution in retailing which has seen the development of

American-style enclosed shopping centres which fit like a glove into Australian suburbia with its sprawling residential areas and emphasis on the car. The first such centres were built in Sydney and Melbourne in the early 1960s. Since then they have spread and prospered until they cluster around the middle and outer suburban circumferences of the cities like satellites around a celestial body—each occupied by its own department store branch, variety store, food supermarket, attendant smaller retailers and a host of local solicitors, dentists, doctors, travel agents and real estate agents and other services of the inner city.

Australian retailers employ more than 10 per cent of the workforce or some 600,000 people. Annual sales have increased steadily and occasionally spectacularly during the prosperous years and in 1972 topped $10,000 million for the first time. It is a highly competitive and almost wholly Australian business. Ultra-fine profit margins and the forceful personalities of many of the home grown and occasionally self-appointed merchant princes are likely to keep it so.

Anomalously, while retailing remains highly competitive it is also increasingly concentrated into the hands of fewer and fewer big companies which are increasing their power over manufacturers because of their buying strength.

Because of competition, retail price maintenance among food lines disappeared in the 1960s, and in all other areas in the early 1970s. The appearance of the discount house in strength during the early 1970s has provided further opportunities for the Australian housewife to obtain genuine retail bargains.

In the Australian suburbs the housewife shops for her bargains. In the cities, their sprawling industrial fringes and the large provincial towns, 11 million Australians go about their daily business very much in the way of the urbanised people throughout the western world. There is little direct contact for average urbanites with the wider land, rich in resources and opportunity, which begins where the suburbs stop. They see it fleetingly on annual leave, a strip of land at most a few kilometres wide on either side of the bitumen which carries them to a coastal or mountain resort. They may visit or fossick around the ruins of a ghost mining town or rubberneck at Ayers Rock and Alice Springs in the dead heart. The archetypal executive frequently sees it from 9,000 metres as he jets between the capitals sipping a scotch and soda and referring importantly to the notes he carries in his ubiquitous briefcase.

TAPPING THE VAST OUTBACK RESOURCES

But every day the Outback and the continental shelf impinge indirectly on the life of the suburban Australian, like the hot westerlies which blow over Sydney in the summer, or the cool southerly busters which bring change, thunder and rain.

Only two million people live outside the State capitals and the big provincial centres. They live on the scattered farms and pastoral station homesteads, in the rural townships, the forestry camps and fishermen's shanties and in the transplanted air-conditioned plastic push-button suburbs which have been built to make life liveable for the workers at the isolated new mining enterprises of the outback.

Australia has a population density of slightly more than four persons to 2.5 square kilometres over the whole continent, which makes it as sparsely settled as any land on earth. But if the densely populated coastal regions and their populations are extracted, the figure is something less than 1.5 persons for the same area. It is those two million people, and those 6.5 million square kilometres, which distinguish Australia economically and socially from the rest of the world and which give it more reason for confidence than most other nations in the crisis which looms for the western economies in the last quarter of the 20th century.

Some 4.7 million square kilometres of Australia's total land surface of 7.5 million square kilometres are taken up by agricultural and pastoral holdings. Much of this is semi-desert, capable of carrying only a few animals to the square kilometre. Though rural production—agricultural, pastoral, dairy, horticultural and viticultural—makes up only six per cent of the gross domestic product, it accounts for around 50 per cent of the nation's exports. Roll the contributions of the other primary producers, the miners, fisheries and foresters, into the export account, and they amount to more than 75 per cent of the annual exports which are now worth more than $7,000 million. Without this contribution the thin blue line of the balance of payments surplus would quickly become the thick red line of a deficit, and the standard of living which Australians have become accustomed to would be impossible to sustain without mortgaging the the future against massive borrowings from abroad.

The rural industries have played a key role in the development of Australia since the first settlers erected their tents on the shores of Sydney Cove in 1788. Attempts to produce grain to supplement the rations brought with the First Fleet began almost immediately, but without conspicuous success. Two and a half hectares were planted to wheat and failed. Of the small flock of sheep which landed with the First Fleet, only one animal survived its introduction to the cheerless colony.

From this discouraging start, by a slow process of trial and error, success and disappointment, in a harsh environment totally alien to the plough and the shepherd, have evolved a wide variety of rural industries, rich in production and frequently profitable to their farmer practitioners, though they are sometimes reluctant to admit that their life is not always struggle and adversity. Over the years, and because of the strong and continuing influence of the politically well-organised farming community, governments at both State and federal level have introduced a complicated structure of guaranteed prices, subsidies and controlled marketing to sustain the farmers against adversity, either natural or economic.

Though only one sheep from the First Fleet survived, John Macarthur, an enterprising officer with the soldiers sent to protect and maintain order among the first settlers, soon imported more. The British market for wool was booming and he decided to breed specifically for wool. The first clip he exported from New South Wales in 1807 attracted a good price and much interest because of its quality. By 1827 the struggling colony, perched precariously on the edge of the unexplored continent, was competing more than successfully with the woolgrowers of Saxony who had dominated the trade for centuries. Within 40 years of Macarthur's first commercial clip New South Wales was producing more and better wool than any country in the world and settlers were pushing out through the grasslands of the colony's unknown interior to take up more land and to let their flocks multiply.

Multiply they did. Throughout the 19th century and far into the 20th, Australia's economy rode proudly, and sometimes it seemed almost exclusively, on the sheep's back. Not any old sheep mind you, but the Australian Merino offspring of the first Spanish Merinos imported by John Macarthur in 1797, the dumb, diligent producers of the finest quality wool in the world.

Macarthur's Merinos proved to be superbly adapted for life in much of the Australian interior save the most arid of the deserts. Even there they flourish in the occasional wet years. The Merino led the first settlers into what was to become Victoria, and wool quickly became the staple product of the six main Australian colonies.

Sheep numbers increased from 20 million in 1861 to 180 million in 1970 when the clip peaked at 923 million kilograms. Australia is by a long way the world's biggest producer of sheep and wool. There has been a decline in sheep numbers and the size of the clip since, partly because of drought which from the earliest days has periodically decimated the flocks, but mainly because of a prolonged downturn in wool prices during the 1960s which reached a trough in 1970-71 causing many wool men to diversify into beef and other more profitable avenues of production.

The downturn in prices appears to have been the inevitable result of competition from synthetic fibres which may finally have broken wool's pre-eminence in the Australian economy. But it may be premature to write wool off. For 170 years the industry has roller-coasted from boom to recession, subject to all the **91** marketing uncertainties of a staple natural commodity which produces according to the laws of nature and sells according to the whims of man.

In 1970, concerned by the industry's problems, the Australian Government established a statutory body, the Australian Wool Commission, to support prices at auction, and exercise some pressure on the whims of man—more specifically to wool buyers of Japan, Britain and elsewhere. The Commission, since renamed the Australian Wool Marketing Authority, ended its first year owning a million bales of wool. A strong revival in the market saw it making a profit from the stockpile. The recovery was not sustained, however, and wool continues to face serious economic problems. Close to half a million Australians are dependent on the industry for a living and their investment exceeds $8,000 million. An unhealthy proportion of the 100,000 or so sheep farmers are in serious debt.

Whether it has entered a permanent decline or a temporary eclipse, wool will remain important to the Australian economy for the forseeable future. Its supremacy as the premier item of export is being challenged by wheat, coal, and iron ore but there is too much invested in wool growing in Australia and in the manufacture of woollens elsewhere for it to slip quickly into oblivion as a vital industry. And as the promoters of wool are quick to say, its natural fibres have qualities which the synthetics cannot emulate.

In the meantime, it has carried Australia into maturity and the spin-off from its economic impetus over almost two centuries has contributed enormously to the development of other rural industries. It has also stamped itself indelibly on the Australian character. The lean, laconic, sun-bronzed Australian of the popular image is a sheepman first of all. He may also be a wheatgrower.

Whatever else they may have learned when they lost their first two and a half hectare crop of wheat at Sydney Cove in 1788, the early settlers learned that if they wanted to grow wheat they had to work at it. For many years they laboured with dismal results, spurred on only by the knowledge of the vast distances which separated the tiny colony from a more reliable source of grain.

While the economic successes of first wool, and later gold mining, attracted romantic attention to the bountiful new Australian colonies, a handful of small landholders battled to grow a few miserable hectares of wheat against seemingly insuperable odds. Gradually some breakthroughs were achieved. It was recognised that the varieties of wheat imported from the old world were largely unsuitable for the Australian climate and experimentation with the breeding of new varieties began. More than 1,000 new varieties of wheat have since been bred to suit Australian conditions, increase yields and also increase resistance to disease.

The soils seemed particularly inhospitable to cereals until it was discovered that there was an almost universal deficiency of phosphates in Australia's ancient, weather leached soils. The introduction of superphosphate fertiliser boosted yields substantially. The advent of the tractor and the development of large sophisticated seeding and harvesting machines and bulk handling equipment overcame another problem—the chronic shortage of labour which had prevented farmers from cropping the broad hectares required to produce reasonable sized crops from the comparatively low yields that were attainable.

On the marketing side wheat demand and price fluctuated with disturbing unpredictability, leaving the farmer with large surpluses and low prices when growing conditions were best, and high prices and shortages of grain in times of strong demand. Most of the wheat crop is exported, and is thus dependent on overseas markets which are subject to sudden variations depending on world-wide crop and economic conditions.

The establishment of a wheat stabilisation plan guaranteeing a firm price for all production and the surge in world population and grain demand since the end of World War II encouraged a major increase in wheat growing capacity during the 1950s and 1960s. In Western Australia, the discovery that trace mineral elements would substantially boost crop yields increased agricultural potential enormously. Some eight million hectares of new land were brought into production for wheat and sheep raising in the 20 years from 1949. Not even the Canadian prairies or the Russian steppes have witnessed agricultural land development on such a grand scale.

In 1968-69 wheat farmers delivered some 14 million tonnes of grain to the Australian Wheat Board—a crop record which has not been surpassed. The enormous volume strained handling and storage facilities and over-supplied the market to such an extent that a quota was thereafter imposed on production in each State. Since then the market has improved while the farmers, restrained by the quota system, have diversified into other cereal grain production. But the demands of a hungry world and the long struggle by Australian farmers culminating in their ability to produce satisfactory grain yields in low rainfall areas from land that is naturally infertile will ensure the continuing strength and vitality of the industry. Australia now ranks third in the world after the United States and Canada as an exporter of wheat. The vast spread of the wheat-growing lands, in all States except Tasmania, gives a fair guarantee against catastrophic crop losses caused by drought.

Wool and wheat are the staples of the Australian agricultural and pastoral industries but they are by no means the only primary products of significance. The variety of production is expanding rapidly as farmers are pushed by economic necessity and increasing confidence in their own mastery of the environment to experiment and diversify.

The coarse grains, barley and oats, have always been grown, but production has risen significantly since limitations were imposed on the wheat crop. Sorghum, maize, rice and oilseeds have become important crops in the past two decades.

Some 20 million tonnes of sugar cane are produced each year on about 200,000 hectares of fertile soils in the tropical north of New South Wales and in Queensland. The yield of refined sugar is well above two million tonnes a year of which about three quarters is exported, making Australia one of the major suppliers of the world's sugar markets.

Meat, long a traditional product of the agricultural and pastoral areas, has acquired new significance with the world population explosion and the hunger for proteins. Australia's cattle herds have had their own population explosion in the past decade, rising to a total exceeding 30 million animals, mainly destined to become beef. Australia has now replaced Argentina as the biggest meat exporter in the world. The herds are widely distributed through the agricultural and pastoral regions. Cattle graze intensively in the cool pastures of the southern States and with rather less enthusiasm or effect on the harsher native pastures of the northern Australian cattle stations, one of which may comprise up to 400,000 hectares of land and run a beast to every 2.5 square kilometres in a good season.

Intensive pasture improvements in the southern areas have boosted stock carrying capacity for both cattle and sheep. In the north irrigation feed lotting is being experimented with to boost cattle carrying capacity.

How many Australians now in their late 30s and early 40s recall the popular teaching in the schools of their childhood—that the Australian continent, then supporting six or seven million people, could at best support 20 or 30 million, that its agricultural lands could not support many more, and that some of its vital mineral resources were already in danger of exhaustion if not carefully conserved for future generations?

The population has almost doubled in the 30 years since those pessimistic times but the application of science, technology, faith and elbow grease to the often parched and poverty striken countryside of the post-Depression days has wrought miracles. With wool, wheat, meat and virtually every other rural product the challenge is no longer 'Can enough be produced?' but 'Are the markets big enough?'

The multitude of marketing authorities and statutory bodies which have been established to supervise this delicate end of rural business have been aggressive and successful. Until the 1960s Australia relied on Britain and to a **93** lesser extent western Europe to take most of its surplus primary produce. When Britain contemplated entering the European Economic Community Australian farmers slept less soundly. But Japan and the United States have become major customers as Britain and Europe have declined in importance. In recent years vigorous selling has established flourishing new markets for Australian primary produce in Japan, eastern Europe, the Arabian Gulf and Africa.

The Australian rural industries were imposed on an alien and inhospitable continent by the human need to survive, and having survived, to prosper. By virtue of their export strength and long-established institutions they dominate the economy and politics of the country to a greater degree than the newer, larger manufacturing industries and mining.

FROM GOLD RUSH TO MODERN MINERAL BOOMS

Though the mining industry has been established in Australia for 130 years it does not have the same record of continuous growth as the rural industries. From time to time in the brief history of the nation it has burst spectacularly into the economic limelight, played a short, dazzling role, then disappeared amidst applause to wait in the wings. Now there are indications that mining may have achieved stardom.

The first Australian mineral boom came with the discovery of gold in New South Wales and later Victoria during the 1850s, and gave substance to the tiny colonies. The great gold rush boosted the population of Australia from 350,000 in 1851 to 2,500,000 in 1881. A smaller gold rush to Western Australia increased the population of that colony more than fivefold in the 20 years to 1911. In 1885 the boundary rider Charles Rasp discovered the fabulous silver, lead and zinc lode at Broken Hill, in western New South Wales, giving rise to a share boom which made the great Poseidon boom of 1969-71 look like a church-hall bingo game, and setting in train a chain of events which was to establish Australia's iron and steel industry and much later its near self-sufficiency in crude oil.

Gold boomed again in the West in the 1930s, creating an island of prosperity in the midst of the Great Depression and providing a stage for one of the most colourful of Australian entrepreneurs, Claude de Benarles.

There were other rushes: for base metals on the west coast of Tasmania, for gold in Queensland and New Guinea. Profits from the Mt Morgan Mine in Queensland financed an oil exploration programme in the Persian Gulf which led to the establishment of what is now British Petroleum—one of the seven great oil companies in the world.

But by the early 1950s the Australian mining industry was going nowhere. Broken Hill continued to flourish and, together with Kalgoorlie, the gold city in the Western Australian desert, had established a tradition as the custodians of Australia's mining skills. The great Mt Isa base metals mine in central Queensland was emerging successfully from a long struggle to survive. Black coal mining flourished in New South Wales and extraction of brown coal from the world's biggest deposits in Victoria's La Trobe Valley was becoming a vital industry. Tasmania's base metals miners were still hard at work. But in Western Australia and elsewhere the gold mines, which had been the main source of inspiration to new prospecting and discovery, were beginning to close down.

As has so often happened in the Australian primary industries in the past, the prospectors and exploration geologists began to look for other metals as a means of surviving. The early prospectors, traversing outback Australia in search of gold, had found plenty of evidence of other minerals such as iron ore and nickel, but there was no market for high bulk, low value metals in remote areas in those days, and more often than not the discoveries were not even recorded.

In 1889 the geologist H. P. Woodward, on an expedition through north Western Australia, noted the abundance of iron ore and wrote prophetically that there was enough to supply the whole world. Some 60 years later a company geologist, cruising by boat beneath the red cliffs of Weipa on Cape York Peninsula, recognised that the redness was due to enormous deposits of bauxite and recalls that he kept thinking that if it was all bauxite there must be something wrong with it since no-one had recorded it before. Black coal had been mined intensively in New South Wales for many years, and to a lesser extent Queensland, but initially for local use only. Though there were indications that the deposits might be vast, there was no incentive to explore their extent beyond the foreseeable demands of local use. There was virtually no market for uranium until the advent of nuclear energy in the post-war period—so no-one looked for it.

Today coking coal, iron ore and bauxite, the mineral of aluminium, are among Australia's biggest export commodities, with the value of coking coal exports totalling $1,000 million a year and displacing wool from the premier position it has held for 170 years as the nation's principal export commodity. Australia is the world's largest exporter of bauxite, which was being imported into the country until 1960, and has 40 to 50 per cent of the western world's uranium deposits. Nickel was discovered in commercial quantities in 1967 spurring an exploration and share market boom which has incidentally increased the inventories of other mineral reserves, notably mineral sands and possibly base metals.

Mineral exports have risen dramatically in value and now exceed $2,000 million a year. As a percentage of total exports they have gone up from around five per cent to more than 25 per cent in a decade. Mining accounts for about three or four per cent of gross domestic product, but the huge volume of the major minerals produced is well in excess of the demands of Australia's 13 million people, and exports continue to grow in value and volume.

It is largely because of the country's vast mineral resources that Australian ministers in the 1970s can strut the world stage speaking importantly of resource diplomacy and seeking special trading favours for the benefit of the Australian people in return for assurances of continued supplies of mineral commodities.

In a world where the Arab oil producers have abruptly overturned traditional trading patterns and disrupted the western industrial economies which rely heavily on imported oil, Australia is seen as a restraining influence on the

Hancock of Hamersley—peerless prospector

The vast mining industry expansion which has thrust Australia into the economic limelight in the resource conscious world of the 1970s owes at least as much to the ingenuity of man as it does to bountiful nature.

The mineral deposits which are now making the nation rich were laid down aeons before the advent of man. In many cases they were known to the early Australian settlers. They assumed economic value only to satisfy the seemingly insatiable needs of industrial man in the second half of the 20th century, and because of the initiatives of a handful of men like Lang Hancock.

A thickset man with his oiled hair parted in the middle, and eyes of steel, Langley George Hancock is generally said to be Australia's biggest taxpayer and most right wing politician. Above all else though, he has been the most successful and enterprising Australian prospector.

He was born in 1910, scion of a pioneering pastoral family from the dust red Pilbara region in north Western Australia. In those days the scion of a pioneering family from the most arid pastoral region in the poorest Australian State did not have a lot in terms of security.

The family property was lost through drought and Hancock's father became the manager of Mulga Downs station. Young Hancock completed secondary school in Perth and returned home to help. Clever, inquisitive and ambitious with a mechanical mind and visions of a great future for his harshly beautiful, heat-seared Pilbara, he rode around the station looking after the sheep, mending windmills and fences and scheming for great things.

In the 1930s with an old school friend, Peter Wright, he set up a plant to treat blue asbestos which was being mined in one of the great gorges in the flat-topped Hamersley Range near the station homestead. A major mine developed and was sold to the Colonial Sugar Refining Company.

Hancock had discovered that flying was the only way to move quickly over the long distances of the virtually roadless region, and acquired a light aircraft, which he used in prospecting expeditions. After quitting his blue asbestos interests he continued an active mining career, and began a political odyssey to obtain special taxation treatment for the forgotten north.

In 1952, flying low over the headwaters of the Turner River to avoid a thunderstorm, he recognised massive iron ore deposits in the cliffs above the river. Iron ore was a prohibited export in those days. He worked to change that and to interest major overseas companies in his deposits. Finally the Rio Tinto Zinc Company, later amalgamated to form Conzinc Rio Tinto of Australia Ltd, signed a prospecting and royalty deal which was to make Hancock and his partner Wright enormously rich. In 1960 the Commonwealth Government lifted its embargo on the export of iron ore to encourage prospecting and within six years, Hamersley Iron, formed by the CRA group, had begun exporting on a massive scale, generating royalties amounting to millions of dollars a year for the men who had shown the potential of the Pilbara.

Most men in Hancock's position would have retired to the south of France. He has continued prospecting however, and has now acquired title to the major proportion of the vast iron ore deposits which have been discovered in the Hamersley Range. He has also established a newspaper and founded a political party with the object of persuading Western Australians to secede from the Commonwealth.

The secessionist movement is hardly likely to succeed, but if it does the rest of Australia would be poorer without the iron ore discovered by Hancock.

wilder aspirations of the resource rich nations because she ranks so highly among them, now and in future considerations.

Australian coal exports will play a vital role in assisting Japan and other lesser nations to reduce their dependence on oil as an energy source, and for the future, Australian uranium is seen as a major crutch to reduce world dependence on oil for energy.

Of the major mineral commodities Australia is deficient only in crude oil—the most vital of them all. A major discovery in the Bass Strait, south of Victoria, in the 1960s supplies almost 70 per cent of the nation's crude, and there is minor production from Barrow Island off Western Australia and Moonie in Queensland. Large reserves of natural gas in the Bass Strait and central Australia are being produced to supply the needs of south-eastern Australia and huge discoveries in deep water on the north-west continental shelf await development. However, prospecting for petroleum has been the most disappointing feature of the nation's mineral search. Further large deposits may await discovery in the very deep water of the continental slope but unless this hope is realised there will be increasing oil imports to offset decreasing local production and to cater for increasing consumption. It may be that Australian ingenuity in the utilisation of super abundant but less convenient energy forms such as coal and uranium will be necessary to offset the oil deficit. While these short term solutions are being considered, scientists are already studying the ultimate solution—harnessing energy from the sun which on an average day bathes Australia with more hours of light at a greater intensity than it does any other continent.

The spectacular growth of Australia's mineral industry in the past decade was made possible first by the enterprise and ability of Australian prospectors and exploration geologists, combined with the entrepreneurial flair of individuals such as the iron ore prospector Lang Hancock and companies such as Western Mining Corporation which pioneered firsts in iron ore, bauxite and nickel. But initially it was left for foreign mining companies, particularly from the United States, to risk the huge capital sums necessary to establish large scale mines, often with their own railway systems and ports, in remote and forbidding areas.

Australian companies are now following the example of the foreigners. Indeed Australian enterprise on the vast scale that is required for the new mining projects has been made possible to a large extent by direct association or indirect benefits generated by the foreign companies.

But an increasingly prosperous Australia has also become increasingly nationalistic in outlook. There is widespread concern at the large extent of foreign ownership of our mineral industries—estimated at between 38 and 65 per cent depending on the point of view being argued. There is little doubt that public sentiment and government policy will not allow foreign ownership to grow beyond this level.

Australians are also concerned at the prospect of being regarded simply as a convenient quarry for Japan, which is the biggest customer for mineral commodities, and the other industrialised nations. There are strong pressures to ensure maximum processing of minerals in Australia in the future. The spin-offs from this, for the economy generally and the manufacturing industries in particular, should be enormous.

By a process of struggle and good fortune Australia has arrived, three quarters of a century after achieving nationhood, at full economic maturity. Her ability to produce abundant surplus foods and fibres and the vast mineral and energy resources being discovered often in her most unprepossessing regions, have cast her in the role of a food bowl and quarry to much of the world—a nation of 13 million people ranking among the top trading nations.

The long term future, despite any temporary setbacks, appears to be boundless as long as the mythical lean, laconic sun-bronzed individual of earlier days does not allow himself to run too much to fat.

Opposite: Huge ingot moulds throw up a shimmer of sparks from newly poured steel at BHP's Whyalla steelworks, one of four major steelmaking centres recently developed in response to the vast iron ore finds in the north-west.

RON SULLIVAN

Above: Tailings left by opal gougers at White Cliffs in western NSW show no sign of the technological revolution that has taken place in other forms of mining in recent years.

Above right: At Cockatoo Island, the oldest major iron ore mine in Western Australia, giant ore-carrying trucks ply the switchback roads of the open-cut workings.

Bottom right: Underground mining has also been transformed. At Mount Isa, in western Queensland, machinery makes cavernous drives in place of the mole-like burrows of older methods.

In the appropriately named Oph-
thalmia ('inflammation of the
eye') Range is the giant of the
north-west iron ore ventures, the
Mount Newman Project, with ore
reserves estimated at 1,000 million
tonnes. Mount Whaleback, part
of the range, is being cut away by
mobile cranes with cabs three
storeys high, and huge ore trucks
carry 150-tonne loads down the
mountain to the crushing plant.

The crushed ore is moved in
trains, more than 1,500 metres
long, to Port Hedland, 420 kilometres away at the end of the
biggest privately owned railway
in the world. Pelletised ore is
shipped from Port Hedland to
Japan or to Australian iron and
steel works.

Bottom right: An ingot ready for
the rolling mill at Whyalla, SA.

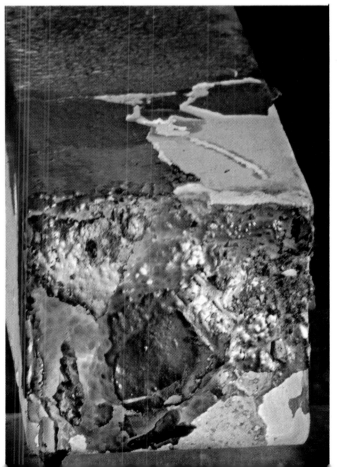

Below: Now a thriving crayfishing base, the Abrolhos Islands off the central coast of Western Australia were the scene of one of the bloodiest episodes in the history of European man's contact with Australia. A Dutch trading vessel, the *Batavia*, laden with passengers and treasure, was wrecked here in 1629. The captain, Francois Pelsaert, set out in an open boat for Batavia (today's Jakarta), 3,200 kilometres away. In his absence a vicious mutiny broke out among the survivors, and 70 men and women were massacred before the mutineers' ringleader Jeronimus Cornelisz was caught in a trap only hours before Pelsaert's return. Retribution was grisly. Two of the 40 mutineers were set free on the mainland, but disappeared without a trace.

Opposite: Far more valuable than sunken treasureships or the $50 million a year crustacean industry is the offshore oil discovered in Bass Strait by the Esso-BHP consortium. Five production platforms are now sited over four fields, and two more are under construction. Crude oil and natural gas are piped to Longford near Sale, Victoria, for processing and stabilisation: 'sales' gas, mostly methane, is then piped direct to the Melbourne market; stabilised crude oil goes to storage tanks (*right*) at Long Island Point, Westernport; ethane, propane and butane also go to Long Island Point for fractionation.

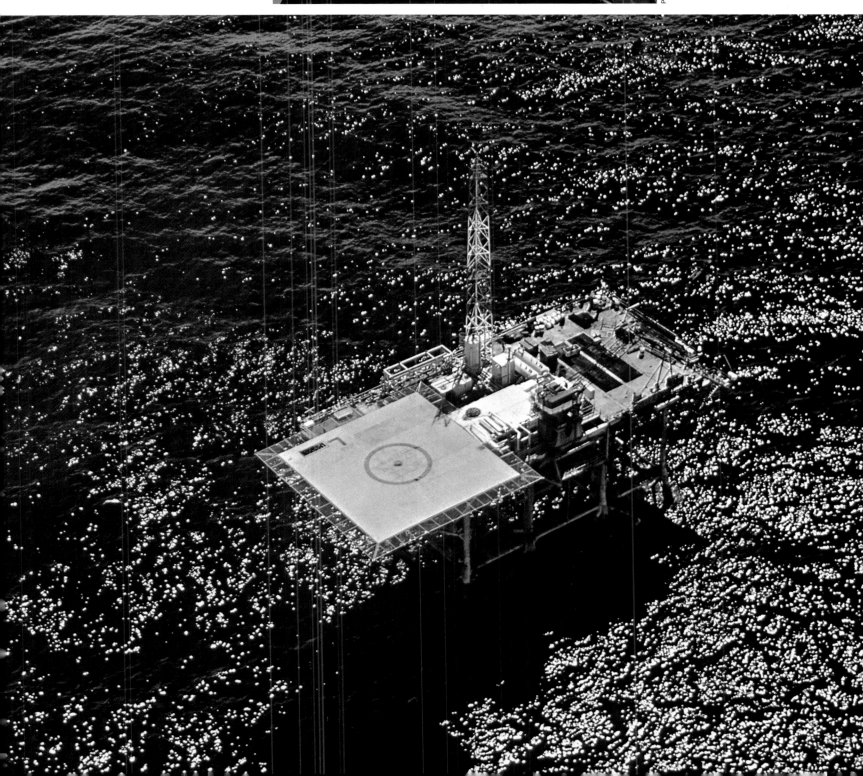

The vehicle manufacturing industry is one of the biggest employers of factory labour in Australia. It produces about half a million vehicles a year, and nearly a fifth of these are exported to more than 70 countries. Even more labour-intensive are the big domestic appliance and electronics industries which thrived under tariff protection during the 60s and early 70s. An easing of tariffs caused rationalisation and consolidation, particularly in the electronics industry which is now successfully entering the South-east Asian market against European and Japanese competition.

Opposite: Rising fuel prices, increasing traffic congestion and the growing awareness of air pollution contributed to the small-car boom of the 70s. These Minis were among the first to roll off the production line at the expanded Leyland plant in Sydney.

Top left: A large part of the annual output of four-wheel-drive Land Rovers is exported to South-east Asian countries.

Centre left: A metal finisher touches up a rough spot on a newly welded Mini body.

Left: Hundreds of new colour television sets stand 'soaking' (a running-in and test procedure) at the AWA-Thorn plant in Sydney.

Australia's first grain crop—2½ hectares of wheat planted in 1788 —failed; of the small flock of sheep brought by the First Fleet only one beast was alive at the end of the first year. It was an inauspicious beginning for a country that has prospered for almost 200 years on a rural-based economy.

Opposite: A cereal crop on the fertile downs near Toowoomba, southern Queensland. Australia is one of the world's top grain producers and exporters.

Above: Superphosphates and small doses of mineral trace elements put new life into the ancient, weather-leached soils of Western Australia's otherwise marginal lands. Fertilisers, and the use of a new wheat strain (one of a thousand developed to suit Australian conditions), produced this harvest near Merredin, WA.

Left: The cultivation of secondary cereals such as oats, rye and barley has increased since wheat production was limited by a quota system. New crops flourish in this rich, cool country north of Adelaide.

107

Opposite: Leaf from Australia's only commercial tea estate, near Innisfail, Queensland, began to reach the nation's teapots in the early 70s after years of experimental growth and trial harvests. Lacking the cheap leaf-picking labour of Sri Lanka, India and Assam, Australian growers have developed bushes that grow in dense uniform hedges suitable for plucking by specially designed mechanical harvesters.

Top: The table wines of tomorrow ferment in a clinical array of steel tanks at Tolley, Scott and Tolley's modern winery in the Barossa Valley, SA.

Left: Shovelling white wine lees from a fermentation vat at Hamilton's Ewell winery, Adelaide.

109

The fertile 1,700-kilometre coastal strip from the NSW border to Mossman, north Queensland, has become a major source of the world's sugar in recent years. The annual production of refined sugar is two million tonnes, of which about three quarters is exported.

Top: A husband and wife team plant cane on a small family farm north of Mossman.

Right: Young cane on the rich coastal flats south of Cairns.

Opposite: A permanent smoke haze hangs over the cane belt during harvest months, and the night sky is reddened by big cane 'burns'.

THE CITIES

Patrick Tennison

**'A determinedly
urban society . . .'**

Australia's 'outback' myth that seems to get most international attention is exactly that—a myth. Sure, mate, it is a sunburnt country. Or most of it, anyway. And it has certainly got sweeping plains. But who lives on them? Any sunburn felt by Australians is more likely to be of the week-end ration—and a larger dose on annual holidays.

From the earliest times of white settlement Australia has been a determinedly urban society. Today, 82 per cent of the 13 million population live in cities. And that, despite Henry Lawson, 'Banjo' Paterson and all the other bush pushers, is a world record. Almost a quarter of the population, a group edging close to three million, lives in just one city, Sydney.

Big, bustling and brusque, Sydney is the birthplace of the Australian nation. A scrambling scrimmage of a city, erupting with life. Like Venice, Rio or Capri, it is a city where water is a vital complement to the land it is built on. Blue tongues of water from Sydney's harbour spread into dozens of craggy bays and coves and inlets.

SYDNEY

Also, within 32 kilometres of the city centre there are stretches of more than 30 ocean beaches. Here surf and sun abound in a relaxing climate that gives Sydney an air of physical freedom no other Australian city enjoys quite as much. Nature seems a close neighbour of the air-conditioned purpose that fuels the city's business boilers.

Here, in a calm little bay on the harbour shoreline, on January 26, 1788, landed an unlikely band of people destined to found a new nation. That First Fleet, as history now calls it, comprised 11 small sailing ships; two warships, three storeships, and six convict transports. In all, less than 4,000 tonnes of wooden vessels. They had sailed from England, by way of South America, on a voyage of almost 23,000 kilometres that took eight months. In command was Captain Arthur Phillip, appointed by King George III as the first Governor of New South Wales. He named the inlet where they landed Sydney Cove, in honour of Britain's Home Secretary, Viscount Sydney.

Opposite: Every State capital saw a building boom in the 60s. The mineral boom prompted massive injections of foreign capital that set the business pulse of the country racing.

Australia has the dubious distinction of being the most urbanised
nation in the world, but the
growth of the cities continues.
This workman stands at the top
of Sydney's newest and tallest
office tower overlooking Circular
Quay and the western arms of the
harbour.

The settlement that grew from that motley bunch of none too willing pioneers took its name from the place where they first came ashore. They numbered just 1,030 'souls', as recorders of those times liked to call people. There were 736 convicts—188 of them women—17 convicts' children shipped with them, 211 marines with 27 wives and 19 children, Arthur Phillip and his personal staff of nine, and another group of 10 comprising other officials, their wives and two servants. Another 13 men were drafted from the crews of the ships to serve in the new settlement.

During the long voyage from England, 36 men and four women had died. On the same journey, seven children had been born, some of them to the convict women. In the storeships came a variety of grain seeds, plants, horses and cattle. The list included even vine cuttings, to ensure that the new colony could be self-supporting in wine. From their accommodation aboard, the first settlers moved to tents ashore. Then, a few weeks later, they launched Australia's first industry: brick making. And the building programme begun then continues today. Phillip wanted Sydney to be a well-planned city. Streets, he ordered, should be 200 feet wide. But then, as now, Sydney displayed a wayward attitude to anyone wanting to lay down firm rules. The streets were built where people walked, and the first buildings beside those streets. Today Sydney does have a few avenues '200 feet' wide. But they came long after Arthur Phillip.

Now, almost two centuries later, Sydney has matured into a worldly-wise city of wealth, poise and agreeable disposition. Nature ensured its basic handsomeness. Sydney's profile is a dramatic skyline of tall modern buildings that give it lines that seem, at times, more rigid than graceful. To compensate, the city has acquired a number of architectural gems. Sydney's latest is the $100 million Opera House, its white billowing roofs stretching out over the harbour waters. Close by too, spans the bridge of grey steel, arching high into the sky, an earlier symbol of the city's adventurousness.

In the bitumen and concrete canyons of the commercial heart thrums the beat of people, cash registers and computers. Hilton and David Jones, AMP and IBM, consulates and protest groups. At night the streets become neon glitterways. Below ground, high above ground, people gather, work, travel, dine. Like an ant's nest, a giant circling cave has been dug out beneath the city to cope with transport pressures. Into it, day and night, the red and blue electric trains burrow through the eternal subterranean darkness with their human cargoes.

Sydney presents always a frenzy of movement, colour and shapes. Its big buildings are usually grey, white or black, though one, rising tall on the north side of the harbour, is a glowing pink. Fed by the vitamins of ambition, enriched by the protein of success, each year they grow taller. Ingenuity is stretched to find for them new, different shapes: square, round, curved, triangular. In Park Street towers the highest residential building in the Southern Hemisphere: the Park Regis. In its basement, six metres below street level, diners sip their drinks as they watch the steaks sizzling on the iron grill. High above their heads, separated by 44 floors of steel and concrete, swimmers play in the rooftop swimming pool.

Fanning out from the city, spreading north and south beside the beaches, and creeping westward to the mountain range rising 45 kilometres from the sea, Sydney's suburbia sprawls determinedly. Again, variety. Discreet Wahroonga on the upper class North Shore ignores the challenge of trendy Woollahra, just east of the city. Redfern looks old and tired from struggle. Mt Druitt, way to the west, appears younger and better equipped. Balmain, old but in the process of rejuvenation, clings to its own little corner of the harbour. Paddington, its terrace houses rediscovered after a century of disinterest, demonstrates the arts of the investor, the decorator and the promoter of that 'something new and different' that always excites Sydney.

But close to the hub jostles the ever-lively Kings Cross. Here the street spruikers and wayside amplifiers chorus the siren song of Sydney's permissiveness. Here strippers strip, gamblers gamble, dawdlers dawdle in a brassy orchestration with counterpointing flesh and fantasy. Yet here too, as every-where, change intrudes. Now it's new tunnels and rock channels for rail and road extensions. Bitter conflict flares between developers whose money is on high rise and the antis who want no change in the status quo. Struggles like this are embedded into Sydney's history.

Approaching its 200th year, Sydney is enjoying the peak of good health and survival despite an often chaotic past. Today the city handles the chaos of modern change and the burden of people and traffic congestion as it has handled past political, industrial and economic disturbances.

In 1788, when it was all just beginning, Arthur Phillip wrote enthusiastic-ally of his selected site as having 'the finest harbour in the world, in which a thousand ships of the line may ride in the most perfect security'. To the shores of that harbour have gathered more people than Phillip ever imagined, to live in life styles far different from those of his time. This is the curious plot of the drama of Sydney, that two centuries later it is fulfilling the original plan Phillip had in mind for it. He sought to make a settlement that was viable, secure and eventually prosperous. Sydney today stands proud and high in the list of the world's big cities that are agreeable to live in.

MELBOURNE

Between Sydney and Melbourne there is a bitumen ribbon 900 kilometres long called the Hume Highway, a railway system converted to a standard gauge only in 1961—and a certain rivalry. But it is a rivalry discussed more in Sydney than in Melbourne. 'Surely,' Melbourne is inclined to say, 'everyone can see for themselves . . .'

Melbourne is 57 years younger, born in 1835. And less populous with 2.5 million people. But Melbourne considers itself somewhat better mannered. And it is wealthier, having inherited much of the lush legacy of the gold discoveries in its provinces last century. Most of the gold, naturally, flowed through Mel-bourne and a lot somehow stayed. It sparked a boom in population, develop-ment and business energy. Except for brief Depression lulls in the last century and during the world-wide 1930s slump, that boom has continued unrelentingly.

Melbourne always wanted to be big, but without the hectic bustle. Mel-bourne yearned to be great, but also gracious, and the remaining older architec-ture still murmurs that attitude. This is proclaimed by the stately State Parlia-ment building in Spring Street; by the older churches in Collins and Bourke; by the domed vastness of the Exhibition Building, erected with equal measures of haste and care for an international show-off in 1880. Even the city's older banks remain, appropriately, the most ornate in the country. Melbourne has always been circumspect, never grabbing too quickly at new-fangled fads that might later go out of acceptable fashion.

Melbourne had Australia's first steam railway, which opened for business between the city and Port Melbourne on September 12, 1854. But it was more than 100 years later that, unlike most of the other capitals, it sanctioned a State lottery. It also approved more permissive (by Australian standards) liquor laws. Bless Melbourne's conservative heart, the city has even retained its tramways . . . and come to be glad of it. Today and for many years ahead Melbourne's citizens will be riding these great green juggernauts. Long before anti-pollution became a cause, Melbourne decided trams were preferable to buses. Like the city itself, these ancient but steady conveyances follow their pre-set route. Both, too, seem to have acquired the steady knack of keeping to timetables.

Melbourne's most jealously protected endowment is the vast spreads of park-land, both in and right around the central city area. For every 1,000 citizens it has been estimated that the city has 2.5 hectares of parkland. At South Yarra, the Royal Botanic Gardens retain, in an era of motor freeways and soaring concrete offices, the rare delights of large sweeping lawns, leafy trees, multi-coloured gardens and a lakes complex populated with swans, ducklings and myriad species of visiting wildlife.

You could say that civilisation was so keen to extend itself to Melbourne that not one but two founders rushed in and vied with each other for the honour of launching the project. First, but not quite legally, came the noble-minded John Batman. On June 8, 1835, with an adventurous little band of settlers from Tasmania, he rowed up the Yarra River and stepped ashore to proclaim his immortal line: 'This will be the place for a village'. Batman spearheaded an imaginative immigration approach on behalf of a conservative and rigorously right-minded group that called itself the Port Phillip Association. They had studied various earlier explorations, including a brief landing by Matthew Flinders, of the Port Phillip Bay area which Melbourne now straddles. They reasoned that land beside the river feeding into the bay would make an ideal settlement site. Their aim was 'free' settlement, as distinct from the earlier convict-based inaugurations of Sydney and Hobart.

It was arranged that Batman would 'buy' the site from its traditional Aboriginal holders. And so was drawn up a formal Deed of Sale for 600,000 acres. The Aborigines were paid in goods reckoned as more useful to them than the whites' paper currency: tomahawks, flour, blankets. It was all as formal as it was later deemed illegal. The British Crown had already proclaimed itself title holder to the land and a transaction like that could have no official recognition.

Hardly had the ink dried on Batman's quaint document when along came a second founding party, this one led by the more prosaic John Pascoe Fawkner. He arrived on August 29, 1835, with a squad of craftsmen eager to get down to the job of establishment without any of the frills of negotiations. The two founders brought with them different notions of settlement. Fawkner brought journeymen ready to begin at once the hard work of construction, a different approach from Batman, who represented the softer-handed investors interested in financial speculation. A steely confrontation between the two parties existed until the Law sorted out the legalities. But for the building of Melbourne to proceed, speculative finance and trade skills were both needed.

Throughout its history, the development of Melbourne reflects the positive union of both skills. By May 1836, 13 homes had been built. But the place still had no definite name. Among several suggestions was one, Batmania, which citizens since are grateful was never adopted. Instead, in 1837, the settlement beside the Yarra River was officially named Melbourne, in honour of England's Prime Minister, Lord Melbourne. That same year, on June 1, Melbourne planned its first legally authorised land sale, but first the Assistant Surveyor-General of Sydney, Robert Hoddle, arrived to lay out a street plan for the city. From the street muddle already evident in Sydney, the authorities had accepted the lesson that only advance planning would ensure a more orderly growth in Melbourne. Hoddle is scarcely remembered today, but the generously wide streets and open space areas he drew on his first maps remain a silent monument to his farsightedness.

At that first land sale in 1837, small central city properties fetched prices as high as 150 pounds. Only two years later some were changing hands for 10,000 pounds. Melbourne had started early on its course of becoming the wealth capital of the nation. Gold, discovered a few years later, accelerated the inrush of money and people. It became a favourite site for the headquarters of mushrooming new companies. Being the most centrally situated settlement in Australia was another factor. That was important, too, in the choice of Melbourne as the first national capital from 1901 until a fledgling Canberra opened for the business of politics in 1927.

Melbourne has somehow always managed to accept the inevitable historical changes with serenity. Like the River Yarra which flows unhurriedly right through the city and suburbs, Melbourne prefers the stable and the functional to the hasty and spectacular. The tourist showplace, the National Gallery in St Kilda Road, was completed on schedule for its opening on August 20, 1968. It cost $13 million, exactly what it had been budgeted to cost. Australia's finest art gallery, it faces the country's finest avenue sweeping straight and curved in a wide, tree-lined swathe from the city almost to the sea at St Kilda. On this route 100 years before the builders began erecting the gallery, bushrangers bailed up travellers making the journey by night. On a hot evening 50 years later Dame

Nellie Melba, a name she took in salute to the city of her birth, took rides in an open carriage in the cool evening air while her patient Town Hall audience would wait for her to return and continue her concert.

Melbourne has also given Australia more political leaders than any other city: men as diverse in their views as Bruce and Scullin, Menzies and Calwell, Deakin and Holt. Here a lad named Peter Thomson, later to become Australia's most famous golfer, first played golf on the Royal Park course. Here, at Fisherman's Bend, was born a car they called the Holden. Any listing of national figures produced by Melbourne would be almost as diverse as it would necessarily be long: tennis player Frank Sedgman; satirist Barry Humphries . . . Gough Whitlam, Labor Prime Minister, was born in suburban Kew. On October 9, 1964, a 16 year old Aboriginal boy won a bout at Melbourne Stadium that was the first rung of a climb in boxing that would see him ascend nearly four years later to a world title. His name . . . Lionel Rose. Three years before Rose's fight there, another 16 year old who had migrated to Australia from France had his first professional fight. He was Johnny Famechon, who also went on to be a world title holder after making his boxing debut in Melbourne Stadium.

Since the late 1940s, Melbourne's atmosphere has undergone a dramatic change as a result of a major influx of migrants. It has become home to more migrants than any other Australian city. After Athens and Salonika, a Greek ethnic population of 115,000 makes Melbourne the world's third largest Greek-speaking city. Prahran High School's enrolement of 1,100 comprises 90 per cent of students with a migrant background. A Housing Commission high rise block of flats in Fitzroy houses 3,600 people who speak a total of 24 different languages.

With traditional understatement in its operations, Melbourne continues to fulfil the City Council's motto 'We Gather Strength As We Grow'. Here, in

'Dick' Hamer—polished and thoughtful

Rupert James Hamer is one of Australia's most unlikely politicians. But one of its most successful.

He became Liberal Premier of Victoria in August, 1972, a touchy time for a new Liberal leader with the whole country about to swing to Labor under its new band leader Gough Whitlam. In December 1972 and again in May 1974, Victoria swung with the rest to the Whitlam victory beat. But in between, in May 1973, at the Victorian State election it stepped out of that solid beat to declare itself firmly pro-Liberal. Or, more accurately, pro-Hamer.

Not as tall and handsome as Whitlam. Not as young and dapper as Dunstan. Not as flamboyant as Askin, nor as inflexibly fierce as Bjelke-Petersen. Hamer's style is as quietly low key and coolly determined as the slogan his party used for his 1973 success: Hamer Makes It Happen.

More important than the 'nots' in his make-up, Dick Hamer is a thinker. A genuine humanitarian. A hard-working assessor of what the community thinks, believes and aspires to. He can translate Greek verse as nimbly as, his Scottish blood aglow, he will give a private demonstration of Scottish dancing. He can be mild mannered when conciliation requires it, urgently forceful when delivering his policies from the hustings. A political opponent, whose child attended the same primary school as Hamer's young son, arrived late one day to collect his offspring. He found the youngster on Hamer's knee

chatting to the Liberal leader until his Labor Party father came to collect him.

'It's hard to think of a man as a political adversary when he's as warm-hearted as Dick Hamer,' the Labor man commented later.

Born in the Melbourne establishment suburb of Kew in 1916, he was nicknamed Dick after an uncle killed at Gallipoli. Hamer went to Geelong Grammar School, then to Melbourne University to study law and was admitted to the Bar in 1940. In World War II the graduate who had been the State's top law student, with honours in all subjects, joined the AIF Intelligence Corps.

Five years' war service took him to Tobruk, El Alamein, New Guinea and Normandy, where he took part in the 1944 Allied landing. Came the peace and he slipped unobtrusively into the Melbourne legal scene until, just as unobtrusively, he entered the State Parliament in 1958.

Four years later he was given the first of a string of ministries that led him to the Deputy Premiership and finally the Premiership of the State. He was the choice of and successor to the long-reigning Sir Henry Bolte. Hamer's smooth, cultured, calm contrasts sharply with gravelly country-cured Bolte. But as Bolte seemed right for the less tame 50s and 60s, the Hamer urbanity arrived on the Melbourne scene as the more sophisticated electorate was wanting something more polished and thoughtful.

Hamer's 1973 success, against many pre-poll predictions, reinforced that view.

'I am not ambitious,' he has confessed. And he has quietly turned down all Liberal offers of a safe federal seat. 'I believe my style includes reason, persuasion and looking ahead.'

He has been described as conservative, but not negative. As Chief Secretary, he allowed the musical *Hair* to be shown, nude scenes and all, in Melbourne. Any transcript of his personal conversations could be published without the need for expletives to be deleted. Close colleagues can recall only one angry moment when he bitterly described a group of opponents as 'those bastards'. They say he seemed more shocked than his listeners when he said it.

Rare among politicians, he has an intense enthusiasm for art, music and the theatre, and enjoys also playing tennis, boating and an afternoon at the races or football. He once said he would rather attend an afternoon at a Melbourne Grand Final than at 10 Downing Street or the White House.

Part of the reason for his success is that he has made very few if any enemies. At a personal level, a high measure of respect exists between himself and Prime Minister Whitlam. Like Whitlam, Hamer represents something very timely in the power corridors of our major cities: the politics of education, efficiency, and closely studied reason. Any study of Dick Hamer demonstrates the difference between a politician and a statesman.

1956, the world looked to the first Olympic Games ever staged in Australia. Here are the headquarters of most of Australia's biggest companies: BHP, CRA, ICI, Myer. Here, to span the Yarra near its mouth, is being built the Westgate Bridge, a structure higher and longer than any other bridge in Australia. Soberly adventurous in its own circumspect way, Melbourne is also the only city that declares a public holiday every year for a horse race, the Melbourne Cup.

But it sees nothing unusual in that.

In Brisbane the mixing of parts old and new is, well, different. It is, first, the nation's most tropical State capital, basking the year through in an average of nearly eight hours of daily sunshine. So it goes about its various businesses in a more casual way than most cities its size.

Brisbane, at many points, has installed its new buildings and features right beside the old. Today and Yesterday are often neighbours in a sometimes surprising mixture of different generations. This can startle at first. But then, like a newly-discovered cocktail, the recipe can be most stimulating. On Wickham Terrace, beside the original Observatory built by convicts in 1829, stand modern office blocks, motels and smart restaurants. In suburban Bardon, set amid today's homes, schools and nearby shopping centres, the historic 1865 mansion Fernberg sits, where State governors have resided since 1910.

Australia's great post-war building boom reached Brisbane later than it swept through most other capital cities. Until the mid 60s the city had changed little from the preceding 20 years. Then very swiftly, as usually happens, in just one decade, the Brisbane skyline changed utterly and dramatically. Now the city took on the true late 20th century look. As new buildings soared, freeways snaked out from the city on major traffic routes. As part of the new look, the city also got more open space. A stack of dreary old buildings in front of the imposing City Hall were ripped down to make the enlarged King George Square one of the outstanding city squares in Australia. Beneath the square is tucked a car park, a modern solution to the internationally modern parking problem. In this same recent period, some of Brisbane's older theatres were renovated. New ones sprang to life. A wide range of new restaurants suddenly appeared, to give appropriately flattering treatment to the local sea food and fresh fruit that still rank as expensive delicacies in other cities. Brisbane began attracting tourists who were not merely transients on their way to the nearby beach resorts of the Gold Coast or to more tropical parts farther north.

Credit for many of the city's advances deservedly goes to the only Australian Lord Mayor who ranks as a national figure, Brisbane's Alderman Clem Jones. A surveyor who retired with a comfortable fortune made by the time he was 35, Clem Jones was first elected Lord Mayor of Brisbane in 1960. 'Clemism'—it means 'getting things done'—is the term specially coined for his method of action. In 1972 he took office yet again for a record fifth three year term as head of the nation's biggest municipal complex. A duchy of almost 1,000 square kilometres, this State within a State employs a staff of 10,000 to supervise the city's transport, electricity system, road construction, water supply and all development. Given this vast amount of locally centralised power under Lord Mayor Jones, Brisbane has embarked on its greatest period of expansion.

One advantage that Brisbane inherited was a city centre rail system, conveniently underground. Brisbane was Australia's first capital to tunnel rail routes underneath the city, more than 50 years ago. With a population approaching 750,000, Brisbane spreads easily over a complex of low hills that offer an endless variety of elevations and views. Through it all lumbers majestically the broad Brisbane River. Five traffic bridges cross the river. All are modern in design. All are different. Each has its own special strength and beauty to complement the impressive power of the forever twisting and turning river. One of these vital arteries, the William Jolly Bridge near the city centre, is built in a 'through arch' design unique in the southern hemisphere. Brisbane's multi-columned City Hall, site of municipal power, commands attention and affection as the city's outstanding major building. Its clock tower looms proudly

100 metres above the street. An observation platform near the pinnacle offers visitors a 360 degree panorama view of the city. Inside the building, the city's main concert hall commands attention too for its unusual circular design.

Befitting its welcoming sub-tropical setting, Brisbane has set aside 50 square kilometres of its land for parks, gardens, recreation areas and forest reserves. Outstanding among these is Mt Coot-tha, rising more than 300 metres in its own reserve just eight kilometres from the city centre. Especially at night, its summit offers breath-taking views of the city spread below. Closer to the city and on the river bank, New Farm Park displays 12,000 rose trees, as well as avenues of jacaranda and poinciana trees which bloom each spring making a profusion of colour. Typical of the mixing of different eras, the State Parliament House, a fine example of French Renaissance architecture built in 1868, is sited in its own garden of tall trees facing the splendid Botanic Gardens set on the curving river bank. Behind the Parliament building, the new Riverside Expressway links with the Captain Cook Bridge to speed cars between the river's north and south banks.

It was close to where that expressway now begins, at North Quay, that the New South Wales Surveyor-General, John Oxley, stepped from a rowing boat on September 28, 1824, and decided to establish a settlement. A convict settlement had already been set up that year on the coast 45 kilometres away at a place called Humpybong, now, thankfully, named Redcliffe. But conditions there were less than ideal and so, on December 24, 1824, the grim little colony within a colony moved to Oxley's new site.

At first it was named Edinglassie, before it was given a new name in honour of the Governor of New South Wales, Sir Thomas Brisbane. Among the first stone buildings erected was the Colonial Stores. It was later enlarged, but the original ground floor walls still remain near the river bank. In unrelenting heat the convicts sometimes suffered barbarous treatment. Free settlers were forbidden by law to come closer than 80 kilometres to this area where strict military rule operated unchallenged. In the circular mill, now the Observatory, men were forced to walk a treadmill as many as 14 hours a day as the mill ground hominy, a kind of maize used to make porridge that was an important part of an inadequate diet. A century later, in 1929, Australia's first experimental television signals were beamed from this same building.

In 1839 the Sydney authorities decided to abandon the penal settlement and by 1842 free settlers, who had been moving into nearby districts in growing numbers, began establishing homes in Brisbane. But the city's early growth was very slow. At the first land sale on August 9, 1843, centrally sited allotments could be bought at up to 250 pounds an acre. By 1846 Brisbane's population was still only 829. But other areas in what is now the State of Queensland were developing more quickly. And on December 10, 1859, the State was proclaimed a colony separate from New South Wales. At the time of that proclamation, the population of Brisbane was 5,000, in Queensland it was only 25,320, and the State Treasury held exactly two pence.

But Brisbane grew as population and industries expanded throughout the State. Thanks to its wide, deep river Brisbane held its position as the major port as beef and dairy herds flourished on inland pastures. Coal was discovered in abundant quantities 40 kilometres to the west at Ipswich. The vast wheat lands of the Darling Downs, farther west, opened up. And then the sugar industry to the north. Later came the gold discoveries at Gympie, 150 kilometres north, and later in the State's far north.

As the capital of an essentially agricultural State, Brisbane remains a commercial metropolis with a vital agricultural background. Texans boast of the size of their State; Brisbane is the capital of a State more than twice as big. Where once bare-bodied convicts sweated to carve a colony from the wilderness, today air-conditioned offices stand amid smartly displayed shops.

With its historical links with yesterday, and a kindly balmy climate, Brisbane stands uniquely among Australia's capitals as a cross-section of all the major factors that are themselves uniquely Australian.

Adelaide ranks as Australia's most remote capital—in terms of temperament, not kilometres. It has been neat, trim, almost obsessively proper and quite passionately work-oriented from the day of its birth. That is the way Adelaide appears to most visitors. Neighbouring Melbourne gets into an escapist mood every autumn for the fun get-together called Moomba. That curious word just happens to translate from the Aboriginal as 'backside'. More demure Adelaide in the same season stages a higher browed Festival of the Arts. But only once every two years. As surely as South Australia's Don Dunstan is the nation's most carefully dressed and spoken Premier, Adelaide would never, but never, consider staging anything as prankish or abandoned as a Moomba. Well, not as an official occasion.

And the 700,000 residents who live close by the gentle River Torrens like Adelaide for that. And for its cultural achievements and its innovative social legislation which today is often well ahead of other State's statutes.

This is the city where, as a child, Judith Anderson roamed the hills of its eastern border picking wild blackberries and stuffing them in her newly laundered bloomers. She later went on from there to become an internationally acclaimed actress, collecting stage and screen honours and being made a Dame on the way. As she was doing all that a young man was stunning the cricketing world with his batsmanship, becoming Sir Donald Bradman before turning to the more sober career of stockbroker. Two of Australia's most prestigious scientists were launched here: Sir Howard Florey and Sir Marcus Oliphant.

Millions of Australians have lived in homes or bought properties probably not knowing a debt they owe to Sir Robert Torrens. It was he, as South Australia's Premier in 1857, who introduced a Bill in the State Parliament to simplify the laws of land transfer. Torrens Title has since been nationally adopted as a system to simplify and safeguard land sale transactions. Like its talented sons and daughters—and the list of sons should properly include also the great vaudeville comedian Roy Rene—Adelaide's own story is one of diverse talent used with unswerving dedication to score deserved success.

World authorities rank Adelaide with Washington and Edinburgh for the successful thoroughness of its planning. King William Street, 40 metres from side to side, is the widest main street in any Australian capital. Four broad terraces, named for the points of the compass, provide a perimeter for the city proper. They in turn are girdled by a Green Belt, with industrial and residential areas beyond. Whether the facility is old or new, a town plan or a cultural festival, Adelaide has always striven for excellence. St Peter's Anglican Cathedral in Pennington Terrace summons worshippers with a peal of its eight bells that are classed as the finest in Australia. Over at West Beach, sea lions and seals, dolphins and sharks, as well as other varieties of sea creatures, are on view or perform daily at Marineland, which is the largest completely enclosed aquatic complex of this type in the Southern Hemisphere.

One of Australia's early explorers, Captain Charles Sturt, first conceived the idea of settling this particular region. In 1828 he accepted a commission from Governor Darling in Sydney to lead an expedition to trace the courses of the Murrumbidgee and Darling Rivers. This journey of more than 6,500 kilometres led him inevitably to the Murray River, which he followed to its mouth. He later published a detailed account of his expedition. It contained some thoughtful suggestions for a new colony somewhere near the Murray's mouth. As early as 1801 the ubiquitous Matthew Flinders had surveyed that part of the coast. Thirty years later Captain Collet Barker and a party trekked inland from the sea and decided this area between the hills and the coast would be ideal for settling. Sturt's writings clinched the whole concept.

In 1835 a committee was set up in London to foster a migration scheme to the new area. One of its patrons was the Duke of Wellington, no less. And the name chosen for the new settlement was Adelaide, in honour of the wife of the ruling King William IV. As first governor, the King appointed the distinguished naval officer and veteran of Nelson's battles of the Nile and Trafalgar, Sir John Hindmarsh. It was to be a free settlement—no convicts—and one where the most welcome would be hard-working, God-fearing people, prepared to invest their physical energies as well as any money they had into the venture.

Adelaide's first settlers were the nearest Australia had to the Puritans who had sailed to America in the Mayflower 216 years earlier, except that they were not fleeing from religious persecution. In July 1836 the ambitious band landed at what is now the Adelaide beach suburb of Glenelg. Despite all the careful organisation, a bitter dispute soon erupted among them. Hindmarsh and the settlement's planning surveyor Colonel William Light, both very determined men, fought vigorously over the issue of exactly where the new settlement would be sited. Light won. A grid plan he set out was finally adopted and put into practise. Hindmarsh was recalled to England. Following the ideal of keeping rigorously to systems, a municipal body was inaugurated in 1840 to provide local government in the area, becoming the first civic body of this type in Australia.

With the settlement well established, the colonists turned to the education of its future leaders. In 1847 the Collegiate School of St Peter opened with that purpose largely in mind. It continues the same task today. Among the nation's capitals, Adelaide has always enjoyed some status as being slightly different, even insular. The reputation as 'the city of churches', a commodity with which Adelaide has always been well endowed, has perhaps enlarged this image. But what is often overlooked is that the creation of Adelaide presented some special difficulties that made stern demands on early inhabitants. In many ways the climate is less kind than other capitals enjoy. Summers are long, hot and dry. The annual rainfall is the least of all capitals.

From the beginning, too, home-builders were unable to obtain adequate local supplies of quality timber to build their homes, and Adelaide today has a higher proportion of brick and stone homes than other major cities. But it does have the luxury of more than 30 kilometres of wide and sandy beaches less than half an hour's travelling time from the city centre. From Outer Harbour in the north to Seacliff in the south, these are a prominent suburban feature. Also, to the east, are the famed Adelaide Hills; a splendid Natureland and vast green oasis beside the busy metropolis.

Since 1968 particularly, new building developments have brought some major transformations to the city's skyline. In that year alone, a record 44,500 square metres of new office space were added to Adelaide's commercial life. This sort of expansion has continued every year since. In 1973 the extra office space added was more than 20,000 square metres. Originally a building height limit of 40 metres restricted high rise development. That was increased to 61 metres, but that limit too is passing.

Post-war years brought an inrush of industrial development to balance the State's essentially primary production of the pre-war era. Expansions in the motor car industry have proved especially valuable, making Adelaide today one of the nation's strategic car manufacturing centres. Natural gas discoveries in the State are expected to give further impetus to this type of development.

With the calmly idle River Torrens and its complex of lakes forming a picturesque centre-piece, Adelaide's well planned beauty comes from a neat mixing of its buildings old and new. Outstanding among the new is the $6.5 million Festival Theatre, opened in 1973. Behind an eye-catching modern exterior, it contains a 2,000 seat auditorium that has won high critical acclaim as a concert hall, opera house or for whatever other purpose it has been put.

But the old buildings are cared for too. That list includes the Holy Trinity Church of England built in 1838 and the oldest church in the State. In its tower, still working, is the original clock made by the clockmaker to King William IV. Still preserved, too, is Grange, the home of Charles Sturt built in 1840. In it still are some of the furnishings Sturt's family brought from their original home in Cheltenham, England. On North Terrace the National Trust now cares for Ayers House, helping it earn its keep as a restaurant and reception centre. The land this house stands on was bought in 1837 for 12 shillings. In 1846 a chemist, William Paxton, built on it a two storey stone cottage. Nine years later it was bought by a prominent politician-businessman, Henry Ayers, who commissioned architect George Kingston to plan a series of extensions. Among additions made over the next six years was a ballroom ranked in its time as the best in the State and still preserved today.

Whether in a sparkling new theatre or a 19th century mansion, Adelaide demonstrates special qualities of purpose, stability and durability. They remain a continuing reflection of the people of dedication who dreamed of a city here and insisted it must be a good one. People like Sturt, Barker and Colonel Light, whose original plan remains a remarkable national, as well as local, achievement.

In the family of Australian capital cities, Perth displays an open freshness, a sense of freedom and youth that none of the others can quite match. Perth is, to many, what San Francisco is to Americans. Visitors invariably proclaim Perth the friendliest and most welcoming of the major Australian cities. The city is unsophisticated, nurtured in a gentle climate, living a life that is less hurried, less worried. Some of Perth's most famous sons demonstrate its special qualities in their public performances: the direct but often humoured frankness of ACTU President Bob Hawke . . . the fierce determination of Sir Charles Court . . . the irreverence and flair of publisher Max Newton.

Since 1961, when Perth citizens burned their lights all night to guide American astronaut Colonel John Glenn on one of his high and perilous earth orbits, Perth has been known as the City of Light . . . but it equally deserves titles like City of Air, City of Sun, or City of Grace. Graceful in name and reality is the Swan River which curves through the metropolis. Graceful are the major streets such as wide, tree-lined St George's Terrace, one of the country's outstanding boulevards. Graceful are the green-lawned and uncluttered suburbs, their spaciousness underlined by the 1,200 square kilometres of parks, sports reserves and open land areas that spread about the city.

Enjoying a climate similar to but drier than Sydney's, Perth radiates a similar outdoors style of life, a sun-drenched expressiveness that has come to be recognised internationally as a genuinely Australian lifestyle. Being smaller than Sydney has produced benefits. Perth has been able to cope more smoothly and retain more natural heritage in the transformations of recent decades.

In the early 1950s the city adopted a Metropolitan Regional Plan to handle the expected growth rate. Developments have been bigger than the plan's designers imagined. But the plan has always been able to adapt to handle them. Over recent years, more than $30 million has been spent annually on new city buildings. And interspersed with them are still the plazas and shopping malls that make Perth a pedestrian's delight. No matter how much it grows, Perth is determined to remain the broad-spaced, airy, sunny city it has always been.

The history of Perth, too, is different from the story of other Australian cities. In 1827 the British colonial authorities in London suspected that the French were contemplating a colony on the Australian west coast, to rival those the British had already established on the eastern seaboard. To study possible new sites in the west came Captain James Stirling. He saw the river that was named after the black swans that glided on it and was immediately ecstatic at the prospect of a settlement here. So enthusiastic were his official reports that he created what became known as Swan River Mania in London.

'The climate,' he wrote, 'appears to be delightful and must be highly favourable to vegetation, which was accordingly observed to be most luxuriant.' And sure enough, on August 12, 1829, the first white settlers arrived to begin the building of a town at the site Stirling recommended about 16 kilometres up river from the mouth of the Swan. By the end of 1829, the settlement boasted 300 residents. Stirling came too, first as Lieutenant-Governor and later, in 1831, as Governor of the new colony. He proved as popular with the new settlers as he was enterprising. Eventually he was knighted for his services and is remembered in Stirling Gardens in the city and the Stirling Range not far outside it.

But the 'mania' generated by his early reports diminished. Perth's early development was slow. One deterrent was isolation from the other Australian settlements; it was 4,000 kilometres from Sydney to the east, for instance. British authorities also used the opening up of this section of the continent to unload some of their surplus convict numbers. By 1837, only 350 houses had been built in Perth. In 1848, the population was still only 1,148. And another 1,400 people were living in Fremantle and other nearby settlements. By 1858 Perth's population had struggled to 3,000 and Perth City Council was inaugurated. But residents' numbers still lagged: 5,000 in 1871 . . . 8,400 in 1890. Then . . . gold! Major discoveries were made in the harsh desert areas east of the city. By the end of the 19th century, the population of Perth had jumped to 27,000—and kept going.

Already by that time the awesome problems of distance and isolation were fading. Shipping services, the main transport and communication link, improved with every year. A telegraph service to the east coast opened in 1877. Ten years later Perth's telephone service began operating. But it was not until 1917 that a rail link with the east was made.

This century has witnessed Perth's most spectacular leaps: 200,000 in 1929, with that figure more than doubling to 500,000 today. Civic authorities estimate that by the year 2000 the population will reach 1.5 million. Although 'the eastern States', as they are known, are only a few hours away now by modern aircraft, a sense of isolation, of being a little away from it all, remains a major part of the city's special charm. It has given Perth an independent spirit that was displayed, for instance, in a popular vote taken in the whole State in 1932 to secede from the rest of Australia. That vote, fortunately for the nation, was never acted on. But similar sentiments continue to exist today.

Australia's first free university was in Perth. This, too, was one of the first capitals to stage a civic festival of art, music and drama that attracts international

Harry Seidler—transforming suburbia

Visionary. Missionary. Pragmatist. In little more than 20 years, Harry Seidler's architectural expertise has re-shaped the physical profile of Sydney. To a lesser extent, it has also added some useful plastic surgery in other capital cities.

Back in 1955, when Seidler was just beginning to enrich Australian architecture with his work, Robin Boyd wrote of him with typical Boyd reservation: 'Harry Seidler is primarily an artist rather than a technician'.

But the respected Boyd could already describe Seidler's work as 'architecture of excitement'. And it has been that quality that has most underlined his achievements to that time, and since.

Sydney is Seidler's base and his monuments there surround him: the circular Australia Square building, the MLC tower, the flat block at Blues Point that was Australia's highest residential structure when it was built. In the Sydney suburbs, his house designs still stand out for their originality. Interstate, his new office block for the Conzinc Rio Tinto company enriches the Melbourne skyline. Overseas, he is represented by buildings in Washington, Singapore, Mexico and, in Paris, the new Australian embassy building.

Slim, crinkle-haired, his calm personality neatly contained behind mod gold-rimmed glasses and a selection from his bow tie collection, Seidler came to Australia by way of Vienna, England, Canada, the United States and Brazil: 'There aren't many countries where a 25 year old architect who is new to the place would have been given a chance as I was.'

His father, a Viennese shirt maker, took the family to England in 1938 as Nazism began to infect Europe. Harry Seidler had just begun studying architecture in England when war broke out and he was interned, first on the Isle of Man and then in Canada. There he was able to get a security clearance, continued his studies at the University of Manitoba and graduated in 1944. He worked briefly for a Toronto architect before winning a scholarship to Harvard where he studied under Walter Gropius. Other influences in this expanding period were Marcel Breuer and the artist Josef Albers: 'Albers taught me visual fundamentals. He showed me why our eyes react to visual phenomena, why certain things are beautiful.'

After a few months in Brazil and more study with Walter Niemeyer, Seidler moved to Australia on the urging of his parents who had migrated after the war.

His first look at a Sydney suburb produced a shock reaction: 'My God, what have I done?'

But his first commission, a home for his parents in suburban Turramurra, began a transformation of suburbia he believed could happen. His design astonished the conservative suburbanites, disturbed other Sydney architects, and resulted in litigation with the local council before it could be carried out in the clean lined way he wanted. He won not only his fight with the council but that year's Sulman Prize for domestic architecture as well.

From 1952, when he arrived, his battles with civic authorities drew as much attention to his revolutionary styles as the designs themselves won him more commissions. But as no other architect before him, he was able to give to Sydney home design the clean, modern outlook he saw as most fitting for the rugged and outdoor nature of the city itself. From houses to apartment blocks to office blocks to town houses, always fresh and innovative designs have whooshed from the Seidler drawing board as the Sydney parameters have moved outward and upward.

Today the Sydney he first viewed with distaste has become his operational base. True to his concept that architects should not just design buildings but re-shape the cities that house them, on any day he can look around Sydney and observe the re-shaping his own amazing mind has produced.

artists and attention. With care, Perth has preserved much of its past as it forges into the future. A mill built in the 1830s to grind wheat remains as a museum. The earlier Town Hall, built in the style of an English Jacobean market hall, is kept intact and only the tulip fields of Holland can rival the riotous colour of Perth's flower displays every spring.

Mineral discoveries in the State's hinterland have yielded their own affluent lodes to modern Perth. In earlier times a major industry was whaling, with the nearby port of Fremantle its base. Still a sea-loving city, with beaches and the carefully preserved Rottnest Island within easy travelling distance, Perth has pushed industrial development to enhance its economy. Since 1955 the Kwinana oil refinery, with its $400 million of ancillary industrial complexes, has operated at a relatively pollution-protective distance of 32 kilometres from the centre. Other big cities have demonstrated the dangers that can come from industrial development too close to the centre of the city. Perth has heeded the warnings. For many newcomers by sea or air, Perth is the first Australian landfall. It is a role the city proudly accepts—a role it splendidly fulfils.

Hobart is a city that is a very special blend of riverscape and mountain vistas, a mixture of the old and the new settlement, chilled in winter but bathed in clear sunlight for most of the year. Although it is the State capital farthest from the tropics, Hobart enjoys a daily average of six hours of sunlight throughout the year. The mountain backdrop and riverside setting give Hobart a European alpine atmosphere that seems almost unreal in this antipodean latitude. It could almost be a busy market town on the Rhine or Danube.

Like Perth, Hobart enjoys its isolation from the nation's main population centres. Citizens will call the Australian mainland 'the other island' while conceding only a partnership of equality between the two.

Hobart is pleased to retain, and display, its genuine links with the past: streets named Byron, Nelson, Gladstone and Waterloo in the days when those names were contemporary. Then, from the past commemorated in those streets, Sandy Bay Road snakes its curved route out of the city and into the suburbia of modern homes huddled along the shores of the majestic Derwent River.

No other capital city waterway is as blue as the Derwent. None is so unspoiled. On both banks, sudden land rises provide memorable vantage points to watch this glistening waterway; whether its business at the time be the commerce of big ships, the weekend display of pleasure craft, or the spectacular fleet of yachts each year finishing the Sydney-Hobart ocean race. Straddling the Derwent is the humpback Tasman Bridge which, in 1965, replaced a pontoon crossing that rested on the waterway. On the river's east bank, suburbs like Lindisfarne and Bellerive with their flower-splashed streets provide spacious suburban relief from the narrow streets of the city proper.

Among Australia's major cities, only Sydney is older than Hobart. Here, on the Derwent, the first attempt at a settlement was made in September 1803 at Risdon, about eight kilometres upstream from the present site of Hobart. From Sydney, Governor King had despatched Lieutenant John Bowen with a founding party of 35 convicts and 10 officers to establish a penal post on the island that was at that time called Van Diemen's Land. But the original Risdon site proved unsuitable, so the settlement moved downstream in February 1804 to the present site of Hobart. Named after Lord Hobart, the Secretary of State for the British Colonies, Hobart began its life that year with a total of 433 residents, 281 of them convicts.

Sited at the farthermost point of the globe from the British authorities, the early history of Hobart Town, which it was called officially until 1881, abounded with confusion and conflict. Being so far away, it seemed an ideal dumping ground for unwanted convicts. At nearby Port Arthur, massive ruins of cell blocks four storeys high demonstrate the large numbers shipped in.

In 1811 Governor Macquarie voyaged from Sydney to inspect the bristling penal outpost, was horrified at the confusion he saw, and promptly sat down and **125** drew up an orderly town plan for the settlement. But it soon drew upon itself the undistinguished description of 'the Gaol of the Empire'. Between 1817 and 1830, more than 13,000 convicts were shipped in to eke out misery-filled lives in the struggling town. As a balance, the authorities also sought to encourage free settlement in the colony's rich pasture lands. Farmers were enticed with offers of free land grants, generous loans and a plentiful supply of cheap convict labour.

Fertile pastures, so similar to England's own, were soon producing high quality wool fleeces to be shipped out from the busy Hobart wharves. From the seas around came harvests of sealskins and whale oil. To collect them, ships from all over the world sailed up the Derwent. Prosperity from all this trading produced a new civic awareness among Hobart's civilian population. As this grew, public feeling increased against the continued transportation of convicts. This reached a peak by 1852 when the city established its first municipal council. A year later transportation ended. Hobart was launched as a completely free enterprise society.

Today it is a city of 145,000 people. And the Derwent, one of the nation's noblest rivers, remains its focal point. In its upper reaches, on the city's outskirts, it meanders narrowly through smoothly sloping farmlands. No other place in Australia looks so much like a piece of England transplanted; Devon, perhaps, or some of the gentler terrain of Sussex. After flowing through the city, it broadens dramatically. In some places it becomes more than three kilometres wide. Here, as in the city, it is also usefully deep. At the city docks its depth is more than 20 metres. Towering behind the city, the great bulk of Mt Wellington looms to a height of 1,400 metres. Beside it, Mt Nelson contributes another 400 metres. Capped, as they often are, in cloud or snow, they contribute picturesque strength to the mixed cityscape below. Twisting up and around the body of Mt Wellington are 20 kilometres of sealed roadway. All around the Olympian edifice are forests, preserved as they always were. Close by the river's edge, beside the white pillars of the Tasman Bridge, Queen's Domain provides another 2.5 square kilometres of parkland to the city. Here, around the imposing Government House, are public playgrounds: swimming pools, tennis courts, the Hobart cricket oval.

National Trust 'A' classifications, to be preserved at all costs, have been awarded to 77 historic Hobart buildings. Most are in the earliest settled area around Battery Point. They include a cluster of dockland warehouses in Salamanca Place built in the 1830s. Modern history nudges the early 19th century in the upper city sections. Here the ubiquitous AMP building, banks and office blocks have become new neighbours to grey stone constructions more than a century older.

But the most sweeping contrast is visible in the entertainment sector. Hobart is home to Australia's oldest surviving legitimate theatre: the Royal in Campbell Street. And just a short distance south towers the circular Las Vegas style casino, opened for business at Wrest Point in 1973. Its theatre is the sumptuously appointed Cabaret Room, which is just part of the $10 million complex of gambling areas, restaurants and 195 self-contained guest rooms.

A settlement founded on the despair of some of the world's most wretched convicts has evolved into a commercial and tourist centre. Some of the old buildings provide the tangible links in the chain of years reaching back to the past. Like the new edifices close by, they are part of the story of this now tranquil and aesthetically moving city.

CANBERRA

Canberra, from its beginnings, has always been the Pastoral Symphony among the various rhythms of different Australian cities. As the national capital, it carries the distinguished title of the nation's first city although it was, in fact, the last of them to be built. But being last built has meant also that it was more carefully planned than some of the others. Here good fortune and successive paternal governments have combined to treat the residents generously. Canberra is also a living monument to a dream that has recurred more regularly in this century: that people should be able to fashion for themselves living quarters that suitably complement the natural setting.

To this serene inland site, people transported all the paraphernalia they needed for modern living; the bitumen and glass, street signs and air conditioning, steel and concrete. With them they fashioned a modern city that rests easily in its environment. Here and there, they even helped Nature where they thought it useful. A string of lakes was created to provide an easier balance between scenery and buildings. Perhaps in the narcissism of politics they sought also to add a reflection to what had been done.

In some ways Canberra is a modern miracle. Strict civic codes have ensured that even hotels and emporiums be clean-lined and non-garish. Here even the buses purr softly as they grope through their often confusing routes. Here banks and office blocks must share space with gum trees in an unexpected arrangement that is ideal to the point of being bizarre, simply because it is so rare. Lucky Canberra was built on a giant meadow. Low mountains shelter it. A lazy little stream, the Molonglo, carelessly passes through. As a city, it belongs to this country as much as it belongs to the whole nation.

On December 7, 1820, a settler at nearby Moss Vale, John Wild, set out on a small expedition to discover what sort of land lay around where he lived. He came, before long, to the site where Canberra stands today. In his diary he described it: 'a beautiful clear plain . . . fine rich soil, plenty of grass, beautiful river'. By 1823 free settlers were fanning out from the restlessness of Sydney, pushing their sheep and cattle herds the 300 kilometres to the new pasture Wild had written about. In 1838 a sheep herder named Joshua John Moore bought 1,000 acres of the land. He paid five shillings an acre for it. A few months later he added another 742 acres to his holding. Of course he was not to know, but he had actually bought the land where one day would stand the Australian National University, Canberra Community Hospital, the city's Civic Centre, a Roman Catholic Cathedral, and a racecourse.

For the next 70 years the area cruised peacefully through its almost unnoticed pastoral existence. It went under different spellings of the name local Aborigines gave it: Canbury, Kembery, Camberry, Caamberra, Kamberra, and finally, Canberra. But, according to the Blacks, they all meant the one thing. Meeting place.

Australia's six States federated in 1901, an event that was of course known to the residents of this natural amphitheatre beside the daydreaming Molonglo. They could not have known the sweeping change that event would have on their district. The decision to federate was made before plans were initiated to establish a site for a national capital. Temporarily, the Federal Parliament met in Melbourne while studies got under way to choose a place suitable for the headquarters of the new federal administration. In the first nine years, more than 40 sites were considered. Eventually it was decided that a spot placed somewhere between Sydney and Melbourne would be preferable. And because of the potential Canberra's setting offered, it was agreed that here would be built a showplace capital.

In October 1909, the Australian Government reached agreement with New South Wales on the transfer of land within the State that would become the Australian Capital Territory, with Canberra its heart. That spelling was decided on, after it was also decided to retain the name.

Now the government had to decide what sort of city would be built in this placid meadow. An international competition was launched for a design. It drew 137 entries from all parts of the world. It was eventually won by an already well-respected architect and designer in Chicago, Walter Burley Griffin. He drafted a design of wide circles and contoured curves, with occasional long straight vistas in front of prominent buildings such as Parliament House. Anticipating the automobile age then just barely gaining momentum, he mapped out wide streets. Most important of all, his plan retained the bushland green.

In 1911 the federal authorities resumed the land Joshua John Moore had bought so cheaply in 1838 and the job of building the new city began. Work **127** was interrupted by World War I, but resumed in 1921. On May 9, 1927, the new city was formally launched with a ceremonial opening of the national Parliament in its new quarters by the Duke and Duchess of York, later to become King George VI and Queen Elizabeth. While that was all very spectacular and historic, for the next 30 years Canberra slumbered as a city.

By the early 1950s its population was only 34,000. Even politicians generally stayed only when Parliament was in session. Public servants posted there found off-duty Canberra life something to be endured more than enjoyed.

Canberra began changing in the late 1950s when the government of Sir Robert Menzies decided it should play its proper role as the nation's governmental and administrative centre. Departments with administrative headquarters in Sydney and Melbourne were moved, with suitable protests from the public servants, to Canberra. In less than 20 years the population quadrupled. New schools, shops and other facilities were provided. One thing Canberra has become noted for is the highest-rating education system in the country. New suburbs fanned out over surrounding hills and valleys. A little less suddenly, Canberra became one of the nation's major tourist centres. People actually came to see their national government in action . . . well, in debate anyway. And the city transformed from a dull bush town to a glamorous 'happening' place offering tourist accommodation equal to any in Australia.

Parliament House itself has become a major centre of interest where 'real live' politicians, who often appear on television, can be seen in the flesh. About 50 overseas countries maintain diplomatic missions in the city, their buildings often reflecting their home country's traditional or representative architecture. But the variety of building covers a wide range: from the classical National Library on the lake shore, to the igloo shaped Academy of Science. Or the church that was once a railway station.

But always the essentially rural setting lingers. This is still the typical Australia, the bush, that no architectural style has yet managed to replace. But Canberra's cleanness, openness and modernity blend with the bushland setting like an artful piece of jewellery.

AND THE REST

Opposite: Sydney and Melbourne, between them, contain more than a third of Australia's population and a large share of the problems of urbanisation—traffic snarls, congestion, a seemingly endless suburban sprawl and spiralling land costs. Public entertainment in these huge cities is often on an equally large scale. This pop concert at the Melbourne Cricket Ground drew an audience of more than 30,000 and some problems of its own—dozens were treated for heat exhaustion, dozens more for hysteria.

Australia's capitals, different as each one is, have a talented back-up group of provincial cities interspersed between them. Each, like the capitals, has its own qualities and character. No two are quite alike, even those industrial near Sydney twins Newcastle and Wollongong. Each of these has its high chimneys, blazing furnaces and the people who operate them. Each has fine sand beaches and belts of bushland around. But the flavours differ, as their histories differ. The open-neck way of life that was Darwin before it was devastated by the Christmas cyclone of 1974, will no doubt influence the rebuilding of the Northern Territory capital.

Distinctive in its mixing of styles is Geelong. Here Ford, International Harvester and Shell make their products, which are shipped out from the harbour along with the wool and wheat that are trucked in from the nearby Victorian Western District. This busy and historic industrial and commercial centre just happens to lie on slopes easing down to the broad sweep of Corio Bay, with its circle of calm beaches and lawned embankments.

Unique again is South Australia's Elizabeth, a brave new post-war experiment in satellite city building, where a transplanted community lives out a novel concept. Queensland's Townsville of the tropical north could be almost in another country from the wheat city of Toowoomba high up on the Darling Downs in the south of the State. And on the New South Wales-Victoria border yet another plan develops: the rivalrous twins Albury and Wodonga are being merged, with government help, into a larger development.

Cities large and small, all different, help form the patchwork pattern that is Australian life. Pioneers, bushrangers, epic moments in history are remembered. As tomorrows are planned and moved towards.

On the afternoon of January 21, 1788, Captain Arthur Phillip entered Port Jackson in a rowing boat 'and had the satisfaction of finding the finest harbour in the world'. Five days later the Union Jack was raised on the shore of Sydney Cove and Australia's biggest city was born. The cove lies between Bennelong Point, where the Opera House now stands, and Dawes Point, the southern spring-board for the great span of the famous Sydney Harbour Bridge. The opening of the bridge in 1932 was marred by a curious incident —the ceremonial ribbon was slashed with a sword carried by a mounted horseman, Captain F. E. de Groot, a member of the extreme right wing New Guard. In recent years the approaches at both ends of the bridge have been extended and modernised.

131

Left: The red roofs of suburbia smother the plain stretching 60 kilometres from the coast to the foothills of the Blue Mountains.

Below left: Many of Sydney's older buildings were demolished after World War II to make way for new high-rise developments. Victims of the race upwards included the handsome Royal Exchange, with its facade of golden sandstone. Belated action by conservation groups and a glut of high-priced office space have slowed the wreckers.

Below: Some of the inner suburban areas have scarcely changed in a century. Narrow houses, ornate with wrought iron, are jammed together in narrow streets that are also playgrounds.

When plans for the Sydney Opera House were made public in 1957 the new building was scheduled for an official opening on Australia Day, 1963, and the cost was estimated at seven million dollars. Sixteen years later, when Queen Elizabeth II officiated at the opening ceremony, the original designer, Joern Utzon, had long since resigned from the project, and the proceeds from huge Opera House Lotteries (first prize: $200,000) were barely stemming the flood of expenditure. The final cost, announced in May, 1974, was $102 million, but by then most people had stopped caring about the money and were flocking to see the controversial masterpiece.

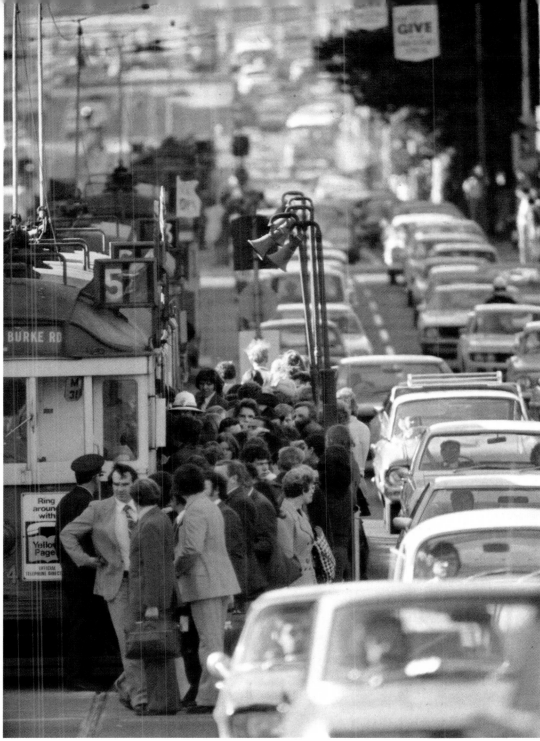

Spotlights on the tower and cupola of Flinders Street railway station emphasise a style of architecture that raged through Melbourne in the heady boom days of the 1880s when the city's growth and wealth outstripped that of its arch rival, Sydney. A disastrous slump in the following decade hit the city hard, but it maintained its pre-eminence as capital of the Commonwealth from 1901 until Canberra was inaugurated in 1927.

Sydney has been described as a whore with her skirts up, Melbourne as a prim and conservative Victorian spinster—but the conservatism (often more imagined than real, especially in the field of the arts) has paid unexpected dividends, for when other cities scrapped their trams Melbourne's were retained, and they are a highly efficient alternative to the motor car. What's more, tourists love them.

Above: The alchemy of evening light turns glass and steel into ingots of gold, appropriate enough in Melbourne's high powered commercial district.

Right: Another kind of light filters through the mosaic glass ceiling designed and made by Leonard French for the Great Reception Hall of the Victorian Arts Centre.

Far right: Some of Melbourne's old markets have fallen to the wrecker's hammer, but the Victoria Market still pulses wiith vitality.

Migrants of many nationalities, accustomed to the boisterous, jostling markets of their homelands, injected new life into Victoria Market, a huge emporium where bargaining is accepted, prices are competitive and business is brisk. Old Australians, perhaps prompted by tourist memories of bazaars and Old World markets, or perhaps by sheer economic necessity, are once again among the regular customers.

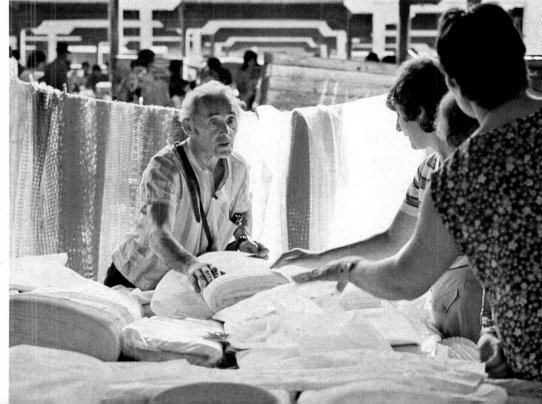

Brisbane, Australia's only tropic capital, is a curious anomaly—a commercially sophisticated frontier town. The lifestyle is relaxed, the climate is soporific, and a booted-and-spurred cowboy can (occasionally) be glimpsed in Queen Street, the city's main thoroughfare. But Brisbane is also a financial focus for the enormous pastoral and mineral wealth of Queensland, and its headline-conscious sons — Mayor Clem Jones, Premier Joh Bjelke-Petersen—are among the country's most aggressive and controversial politicians. It is also the nearest city to the Gold Coast, a strip of glorious surfing beaches marred by Miami-style developments. A new southern expressway, complete with flyovers and underpasses, is cutting travelling time from the city to Surfers Paradise.

Adelaide, precise, compact and somewhat demure, is the only Australian State capital named after a woman—the consort of William IV. It is also the only capital that developed (with few exceptions) along the lines laid down by its designer, Colonel William Light. The good colonel expected to be, and was, denigrated by his contemporaries in the 1830s, but his faith in the judgement of posterity has been vindicated. The city's clean grid layout, embraced by parklands and 'green belts', has survived virtually intact. Additions, such as the centre for the important biennial Adelaide Festival of Arts, have merely added to its attractiveness (*right*). The grand porch of Parliament House (*opposite*) is the finest of its kind in Australia.

Adelaide is sometimes described as 'small-town smug'. It can afford to be. Its superb Festival Centre—a multi-purpose theatre, two drama theatres, an open-air amphitheatre, and seating and catering facilities for 4,200 people at one time—cost only $15 million. Sydney's Opera House, almost seven times the cost, and certainly more dramatic visually, has yet to develop a reputation for consistently high standards of imagination and production. Sydney's cultural dream began with the thought 'we can be as big as . . .'; Adelaide's magnificently designed and co-ordinated centre grew out of the need to house a proven, successful cultural event.

Australia ought to have begun as a Dutch outpost. Willem Jansz made the first recorded landing, on the east coast of the Gulf of Carpentaria, in 1606; more Dutch landfalls occurred; and in 1616 Dirck Hatichs (Dirk Hartog) left an inscribed pewter plate on a coastal island only 750 kilometres north of what is now Perth. The Dutch saw, and rejected, a barren land—and missed the fertile valley of the Swan River where Captain James Stirling named and established Perth in 1829. As the capital of a State worth thousands of millions in mineral deposits alone, Perth keeps up with the building mania of the eastern States (though secessionist movements occasionally make the headlines). But it has a benign Indian Ocean climate to induce a nice feeling of satisfaction, and anachronistic quarters like London Court shopping arcade (*right*), the result of an eccentric millionaire's bequest, are easily accommodated.

Hobart was founded by Captain David Collins on the west bank of the Derwent estuary under the shadow of Table Mountain (later Mount Wellington) in February, 1804. The second oldest and the most southerly of the State capitals, it developed slowly but became one of the most charming cities in Australia.

Far left: The temperate climate produces 'English' complexions and magnificent strawberries.

Left: Pop groups, antiques, modern jewellery and jars of luscious preserves are among the attractions of the Salamanca Place street market, a high spot of the summer tourist season. This quiet backwater is lined with old warehouses dating from the 1830s.

Below left: A modern casino and hotel complex towers upward from Wrest Point.

Below: The nearby penal settlement at Port Arthur was established in 1830, and held 30,000 convicts during its existence. The last convict transport ship docked at Hobart in 1853. Today, Port Arthur's cell blocks, prison yards and watchtowers, and the ruins of its fine church (built in 1837), are major tourist attractions.

Canberra replaced Melbourne as the capital of the Commonwealth in 1927 after 17 years of planning and building—and the building still goes on. Originally conceived as a showplace city, with plans calling for complete harmony of architecture and landscape, Canberra suffered to some extent from official caution and indecision; despite lavish expenditure and lofty ideals, it still smacks of bureaucracy. It has neither the homeliness of haphazard growth nor the regimented grandeur of a Brasilia—but it fared much better than New Delhi (another 'planned' capital), and enjoys an unscarred setting and a sense of spaciousness, both unique attributes among Australia's major cities.

Above: A modern expression of classical Graeco-Roman architecture, the National Library stands on the southern shore of Lake Burley Griffin behind *Two Piece Reclining Figure*, a Henry Moore sculpture cast in bronze.

Top right: Three tapestries by the French artist Mathieu Mategot, depicting Australian subjects woven in Australian wool, and a series of stained glass windows by the Australian artist Leonard French, dominate the main foyer of the National Library.

Centre right: The Australian War Memorial and Museum commemorates those who died in every battle fought since Australians first went to war in the Sudan campaign of 1885. The museum

houses a superb collection of mementoes, and dioramas of famous actions.

Bottom right: About 40 per cent of Canberra's people are employed by the Federal Government; another 25 per cent work for the CSIRO and the Australian National University, just visible in the foreground.

153

WAL EASTON (WOMAN'S DAY)

Cyclone Tracy hit Darwin, the administrative capital of the Northern Territory, in the early hours of Christmas Day, 1974. The wind gauges were blown out at 260 km/h. By daylight, when the worst of the cyclone had passed, nearly 50 people were dead, hundreds were injured, 10,000 homes had been damaged or destroyed, and most of Darwin's 37,000 residents had no roof over their heads. It was Australia's worst natural disaster. Food, clothing and medical supplies poured in to the stricken city as communications were re-established, and 26,000 people were flown south in a massive airlift. The task of rebuilding began slowly, but the new city promises to be better designed, better built and better able to stand the brunt of cyclones. Hopefully, too, it will be as cosmopolitan, tolerant and easy going as the old Darwin.

The problems of big cities are the same everywhere: traffic congestion, drab overcrowded inner-city areas, high land prices, a suburban sprawl, pollution in all its forms, and the erosion of individual rights, privacy and identity.

Above: Terrace houses, The Glebe, Sydney.

Above right: Cars crawl along the northern approaches of the Sydney Harbour Bridge during the morning peak-hour 'rush'.

Right: The old frequently find themselves the lonely victims of expediency and callous neglect in the self-seeking city bustle.

Far right: Some old timers do win battles. Mary Ann Campigli, aged 84, fought the Camberwell Council to a standstill when the council wanted to resume her house and land for a supermarket car park in suburban Melbourne.

Cultural and artistic festivals have taken a strong hold in Adelaide, Perth and Melbourne, and draw large attendances from within Australia and from overseas. Other entertainments also abound, keeping pace with greater leisure time and demands for an antidote to big city boredom.

Above: The giddy whirl of Sydney's Luna Park funfair competes with the offerings of the Opera House just across the water.

Opposite, top and centre: Thousands of Chinese poured into Australia during the gold rush days in the middle of the 19th century, and their numbers reached 50,000 in 1888. Today there are still large Chinese communities in Sydney and Melbourne, and Chinese New Year is celebrated with firecrackers and traditional acrobatic displays.

Opposite, below: Moomba, Melbourne's boisterous March festival, derives from an Aboriginal word meaning 'backside', though the city fathers claim it means something like let's-get-together-and-have-fun—which most Melbournites do, whatever the word means.

159

POLITICS

Malcolm Mackerras

**'The frequency of elections
has one beneficial effect.
It reduces the amount
of ballyhoo.'**

The governmental system of Australia may best be described as a cross between those of the United Kingdom and the United States, leavened by some features unique to Australia.

The basic conventions by which the ministry is chosen from the party (or coalition) enjoying the confidence of the lower house are derived from the British model. However, the United Kingdom has a unitary system with all other levels of government subject to the will of Westminster, whereas Australia is a federation in which a written constitution lists the powers of the Common-wealth Parliament but leaves other, or residual, powers in the hands of the six 'sovereign' States. This model is more like that of the United States. Indeed, in some respects the Australian Constitution is based on the Constitution of the United States.

This cross-breed was the result of historical development. The settlement of Australia took place in a number of separate colonies. By the end of the 19th century there were six such colonies, each with its own two chamber parliament, but 'Australia' remained a geographic expression like 'Europe', with no political entity.

In the last decades of the 19th century public opinion increasingly favoured one Australian nation. As Edmund Barton, later to become Australia's first Prime Minister, proclaimed it: 'For the first time in history, we have a nation for a continent, and a continent for a nation'.

After a series of Convention Debates in the 1890s the colonial politicians thrashed out the Constitution which came into force in 1901. The 'Common-

Opposite: Outback Australians, like most isolated rural people, are blunt, earthy and politically conservative; city politicians and their ways are viewed with suspicion and hostility. This piece of ambiguous symbolism is a typically Northern Territory gesture.

161

wealth of Australia' was thus created and the six colonies became the 'Original States'. Though the politicians who wrote the Constitution were in many ways far-sighted, there were many contentious questions which could only be settled by compromise. It is also a conservative document that has become an anti-socialist device—and the bane of Labor governments. Where the post-war British Labour Government met no legal or constitutional difficulties in nationalising a number of key industries, the Australian Labor Government found that its nationalisation plans were declared illegal by the High Court. Where British and New Zealand Labour governments had no difficulties in introducing their universal health schemes, Australian Labor has had much difficulty.

A particular way in which the Constitution has become conservative has been in its formal amendment. The Constitution can be amended if most voters in a majority of States agree to an amendment proposed by the Federal Parliament. Although 32 proposals to alter the Constitution have been put to the electors at referendums since Federation, only five have been approved. But although the people have refused federal governments extra powers there has been a substantial *de facto* increase in federal power. This has been caused mainly by the financial dominance which the Commonwealth enjoys over the States, and has been assisted by the changing legal climate in the High Court which has interpreted the Constitution in a manner more favourable to the Commonwealth.

At the time of Federation the main political dispute was over 'free trade' or 'protection', but by 1910 the free traders and protectionists had united against a new enemy, the Australian Labor Party (ALP), which won the election that year for the first time with a majority in both houses of the Federal Parliament. Since 1910 the contest at all elections, federal and State, has been fundamentally between the ALP and various conservative parties which may be lumped together under the title 'anti-Labor'.

THE FEDERAL PARLIAMENT

In the Constitution there are two houses of the Federal Parliament, both of which are elected directly by the people by universal adult franchise.

The upper house is known as the Senate and represents the six States equally, regardless of population. At present there are 10 senators from each of the six States of whom five are elected every three years for six year terms in a rotational system. From the next election there will also be two senators for each mainland territory.

The lower house is known as the House of Representatives and is elected for a term not exceeding three years. According to the Constitution: 'the number of such members shall be, as nearly as practicable, twice the number of the senators' and 'the number of members chosen in the several States shall be in proportion to the respective numbers of their people'.

Whereas senators for each State are elected with each State as a single electorate, members of the House of Representatives are elected from single member districts, the boundaries of which change at each redistribution. The present boundaries were drawn in 1968 and (with two minor adjustments) have applied for the 1969, 1972 and 1974 general elections.

TABLE 1
The position in May, 1974

State/Territory	Electors	Senators	Members
New South Wales	2,835,191	10	45
Victoria	2,161,591	10	34
Queensland	1,156,273	10	18
South Australia	750,144	10	12
Western Australia	613,120	10	10
Tasmania	246,453	10	5
Australian Capital Territory	101,757	-	2
Northern Territory	36,980	-	1
TOTAL	7,901,509	60	127

162

At the general election for the House of Representatives held on December 2, 1972, the ALP was returned to office for the first time in 23 years. Its first term of office was marked by clashes with the Senate which resulted in a 'double dissolution' (with both houses dissolving) followed by a general election on May 18, 1974. Table 2 sets out the percentage of votes polled by each party, and the numerical strength of each party in the House of Representatives, after the general elections of 1972 and 1974:

TABLE 2

Party	1972		1974	
	%	Seats	%	Seats
Australian Labor Party	49.6	67	49.3	66
Liberal Party	32.1	38	34.9	40
Country Party	9.4	20	10.8	21
Democratic Labor Party	5.2	-	1.4	-
Australia Party	2.4	-	2.3	-
Other	1.3	-	1.2	-
TOTAL	100.0	125	100.0	127

These were the two most recent general elections at the time of writing, and serve as a basis for a discussion of the various parties and their sources of strength and weakness. The next few years will probably see another change of government and some changes in the shape of the conservative parties, but the basic choice between Labor and 'anti-Labor' is not likely to change.

Australia, like the United Kingdom and New Zealand, has a party system based on social class. However, it differs in having more than one anti-Labor party. Where the United Kingdom has the Conservative Party and New Zealand the National Party, Australia has a coalition of the Liberal Party (representing the urban middle class) and the Country Party (representing the rural middle class) —a difference mainly caused by Australia's electoral system.

While the United Kingdom and New Zealand elect their lower houses by the 'first-past-the-post' counting of votes, Australia elects its House of Representatives (and all lower houses of the mainland States) by 'preferential voting'. The geographical nature of the House of Representatives resembles other democracies in that single member districts return one MP. However, whereas 'first-past-the-post' gives the voter only one choice and the winner is the candidate with the most votes, 'preferential voting' requires voters to place a number, in the order of their choice, against the name of each candidate on the ballot paper. A candidate is not elected unless he or she has more first preference votes than all other candidates combined. Where no candidate has such a number, the candidate with the fewest first preference votes is excluded and the second preferences as nominated on the ballot papers are distributed among the remaining candidates.

Under 'first-past-the-post' voting the anti-Labor forces are generally organised as one party behind one candidate to avoid fragmenting and wasting the anti-Labor vote. Under the Australian system, however, it is possible for both a Liberal and a Country Party candidate to oppose a Labor candidate because they can exchange preferences against the ALP.

Table 2 shows that the three main parties are Labor, Liberal and the Country Party. Labor represents 'the working class' and draws much of its organisational strength from its association with the trade union movement. The Liberal and Country Parties act as a coalition because they hold fundamentally similar views of society.

Political history since 1910 points up the conservatism of the Australian electorate. Labor has been in office at the federal level for a total of 17 years, while the total for non-Labor is 47 years. Short periods of Labor government have been typically followed by long periods of non-Labor government. And the ALP has never won more than two consecutive elections, while non-Labor has won as many as nine consecutive elections.

After the 'free traders' and 'protectionists' merged in 1908 the dominant non-Labor party was known variously as the 'Liberal Party' (1908-16), 'National Party' (1916-31), and 'United Australia Party' (1931-44). When, in 1944, Robert Gordon Menzies founded a new LIBERAL PARTY from the ruins of the defeated United Australia Party, he put together an organisation which was to lead the longest-lived government in federal history. After an initial defeat in 1946 it went to a landslide victory in 1949 (in coalition with the Country Party) and remained in office until 1972.

The party was formed, in Menzies's words, 'to produce unity of organisation among those who do not support socialism as a solution to Australia's political and economic problems'. The Liberals, holding the reins of federal government for 23 of their 30 years, have been the most successful party in Australian history. And yet, except in the Victorian State Parliament, they have always needed the support of a coalition with the Country Party.

The Liberal Party claims to be the only true 'national' party. In its view the Labor Party is a 'class' party, the Country Party is 'sectional' and only the Liberal Party stands for the nation as a whole and 'the freedom and importance of the individual'.

In reality the Liberal Party's representation in Parliament is largely from urban middle class districts. This has been a source of great disappointment to many who would like to see the Liberals win a substantial number of country seats—to promote their status as a national party and rid themselves of dependence on the Country Party. In the 1949 election the Liberal Party won as

Menzies, Whitlam, Dunstan

Sir Robert Gordon Menzies and Edward Gough Whitlam had (and have) little enough in common: the one a basically conservative Liberal, a royalist knighted by his sovereign, the holder of record terms in office as Prime Minister and party leader now retired from active politics; the other Labor, a pragmatic socialist, a somewhat hesitant republican, a current leader whose achievements cannot yet be assessed historically. Yet despite these differences, there are parallels in certain events in both men's political lives—and these are interesting to compare.

Robert Menzies won seven consecutive elections (1949, 1951, 1954, 1955, 1958, 1961 and 1963) before retiring undefeated in January 1966. Gough Whitlam is the most successful election winner on the Labor side, with victories in 1972 and 1974 making him the first Labor Prime Minister to win two consecutive elections.

Both men also spent similar periods (approximately six years) as Leader of the Opposition before achieving victory. The greatest election debacle for Australia's conservative forces occurred in August 1943, when they were decimated by Labor under the triumphant leadership of John Curtin (who died in office during his term). Menzies became Leader of the Opposition immediately after the 1943 disaster, improved the Liberal vote but failed to win at the next election in September 1946, and went on to victory at the historic election of December 1949. Labor's

greatest election setback took place in November 1966 when Harold Holt triumphed (only to die in office). Whitlam took the Opposition helm shortly afterwards, in February 1967, improved Labor's standing but failed to win at the October 1969 election, and gained a memorable victory at the election of December 1972.

In each case, six years as Leader of the Opposition involved rebuilding the party. For Menzies it meant transforming the outmoded United Australia Party into a modern and more representative Liberal Party. For Whitlam there was no change of name, but there were fairly important changes in the party's structure and image. It is perhaps interesting to note that during the election campaigns which preceded their own elections as Opposition leaders, both men were accused of disloyalty: Menzies to his Leader, Fadden, in 1943; Whitlam to his Leader, Calwell, in 1966.

In December 1972, after receiving a telegram from Sir Robert congratulating him on his election victory, Whitlam sent a reply which said: 'You would, I think, be surprised to know how much I feel indebted to your example, despite the great differences in our philosophies. In particular, your remarkable achievement in rebuilding your own party and bringing it so triumphantly to power within six years has been an abiding inspiration to me.'

But perhaps the greatest similarity between Menzies and Whitlam is that they are the only Prime Ministers to have

survived a double dissolution.

Menzies in 1949 won a large majority of 27 seats in the House of Representatives. He waited for the Labor dominated Senate to commit suicide. The Senate was aware of its weakness and, through a series of humiliating climb-downs and devious manoeuvres, tried to avoid giving Menzies the ground for a double dissolution. But it made an error. In March 1951, it gave Menzies the ground without realizing it was doing so, and to its consternation Menzies immediately seized the opportunity. The Labor Senate realised its error at the moment the double dissolution was announced, for Labor knew it could not win against Menzies's majority of 27 seats. In the ensuing election that majority was reduced to 17, but Menzies could afford such a loss.

In 1972 Whitlam won a majority of only nine seats in the House of Representatives. Unlike Menzies he could not be confident of surviving a double dissolution (to have lost the same number of seats as Menzies did in 1951 would have cost Whitlam the election in 1974).

The 1972-74 Senate behaved as though its position was one of great strength. In August 1973, it gave Whitlam grounds for a double dissolution which he declined to accept. Then, in April 1974, the Senate used its power to reject Supply (an unprecedented event) and forced a double dissolution. At the time, the Liberal-Country Party Opposition were convinced that they many country seats as the Country Party, though not enough for outright victory, and has steadily lost country seats ever since despite the steady growth of the urban middle class community and a thinning out in country areas. Not only have the Liberals failed to gain ground from their coalition partners, but the reverse has happened and they now hold only a handful of country seats: in 1949 the Liberal Party had 55 seats and the Country Party 19, yet by 1972 the Liberals had only 38 seats and the CP 20. Liberal dreams of government in their own right now seem further than ever from reality.

'City-based' is the Country Party view of both the Liberal and Labor Parties. In Labor's eyes the Liberal Party is the party of 'the vested interests of wealth'. Whatever the claims, this much can be said: in all Australian cities support for Liberal and Labor varies directly according to the affluence of the suburb. Wealthy suburbs such as Vaucluse in Sydney and Toorak in Melbourne can be relied upon to provide a voting preference for Liberal over Labor in the ratio 5:1. Conversely, very poor suburbs such as Redfern in Sydney and Richmond in Melbourne give similarly strong support to Labor. It is the suburbs in the middle of the scale, such as Bondi in Sydney and Dandenong in Melbourne, which are finely balanced and determine the fates of governments.

There are, I believe, four reasons for the success of the Liberals in maintaining office. In order of importance they are: divisions within the Labor Party; the political skill of Sir Robert Menzies; fairly successful economic management; the ability to maintain reasonably harmonious relations with the Country Party and thus preserve the image of a united government.

The COUNTRY PARTY was formed in 1919. Its growth was made easy because of the introduction in 1918 of preferential voting which meant that supporters could afford to vote for the Country Party without letting Labor win.

would win the election that followed. They misread the signs. Whitlam emerged from the May 18 election, still as Prime Minister, with a working majority of five seats in the House of Representatives.

In 1951 and 1974, economic blizzards started blowing immediately after the double dissolution—but there were critical differences. Menzies had won control of the Senate by a narrow margin in 1951, and with a majority in both Houses he had a full three years in which to cope with the crisis. Whitlam, in 1974, narrowly failed to win the Upper House and was thus still threatened by a hostile Senate with the power to force another premature election.

Menzies, of course, was a nonpareil when it came to winning elections. He led Australia longer than any other Prime Minister (a record unlikely to be surpassed) and was one of only three Prime Ministers to have made a comeback, the other two being Deakin and Fisher.

Menzies's first term as Prime Minister lasted just two years and four months, to August 1941, and ended in humiliation. He left office not because his government was defeated in a general election, but because elements within his own government were disloyal. For the next two years Menzies was merely a private member of the House of Representatives. He did not become Leader of the Opposition until September 1943, and failed to regain the Prime Ministership until December 1949. Unlike Deakin and Fisher, whose periods out of office were short-lived, Menzies had more than eight years in the wilderness before returning as Prime Minister for a record term of 16 years one month, more than twice as long as the term of Hughes, the next longest serving Prime Minister.

For Menzies, the period out of office required great courage. The manner in which he lost office did not encourage faith in his leadership. There were many who said: 'You will never win with Menzies.' How wrong those voices were!

The length of Whitlam's term in office is not yet known, but some predictions can be risked. It is very likely that his will be a single term without any comeback. He is likely to retire after he has lost office, when he will be able to look back to a list of accomplishments—and setbacks—out of all proportion to the length of his term. And, if the present House of Representatives lasts its full term and he lasts with it, Whitlam will have enjoyed a longer single term than any other Labor Prime Minister.

Length of tenure is just one of the many differences that outweigh the few, and perhaps coincidental, similarities between Menzies and Whitlam. The major differences are to be found in each man's approach to government. The Menzies attitude could be summed up thus:

Leave well alone. Where changes must be made, they should be achieved through concensus, not confrontation.

Powerful vested interests must be placated and kept on side.

Decisions made in a hurry are decisions made badly. Quiet, calm deliberation disentangles every knot.

Traditional institutions and ties of kinship must be preserved.

There can be no false doctrine of equality between the productive and the unproductive. The hard-working productive people are the most deserving.

Whitlam's approach could be said to be:

Reforms must be carried out, and carried out with determination.

Powerful vested interests must be confronted and defeated.

A radical politician must look for, and find, short cuts to achieve his objectives. Otherwise he will be defeated by the stalling tactics of those who have an interest in preserving their positions of power or privilege.

Traditional institutions should be preserved only where they assist change.

The promotion of equality is the principal aim of government.

But perhaps the over-riding difference is that Whitlam is a reformer in a hurry while Menzies believed in doing things at a carefully considered pace, and for this reason it is unlikely that Whitlam's term will be long. Machiavelli aptly described the difficulties of the radical politician:

It must be remembered that there is nothing more difficult to plan, more uncertain of success, nor more danger-

There is no doubt that the Country Party has been very successful in gaining concessions for Australia's rural communities, especially farmers. The problem for the Country Party has been that although rural Australia continues to contribute more than half of Australia's export earnings its share of the total population is shrinking. Keeping pace with this fact has been the Country Party's greatest challenge—and so far it has succeeded.

In the first place it has taken several seats from the Liberals. The CP can obviously hold or even improve its position if it can gain seats from other parties at a faster rate than its own seats are eliminated in redistributions.

Second, it has persuaded the Liberal Party (and, therefore, the Parliament) to agree to changes in the Electoral Act permitting a 'rural bias' to the seats. For many years it has been the practice of Australian mainland State parliaments to have fewer electors in country constituencies than in city constituencies, a practice which did not exist in the Federal Parliament until recently. When the Liberal-CP coalition came to office in 1949 it did so on a set of electoral boundaries in which there were practically equal numbers of electors in all seats. But as a result of amendments to the Electoral Act in 1965, electoral boundaries at the end of the coalition's term in 1972 contained a 'rural bias' of 15 per cent (ie, for every 100 electors in urban seats there were 85 in rural seats) . Hence, over a 23 year period of urbanisation the CP kept its redistribution losses to only one seat, and this has been compensated for by gains from the Liberals.

Third, the Country Party has tried to 'broaden its base' in a number of ways. The principal of these has been the promotion of tariffs for manufacturing industry to win city support. In Labor's eyes the CP has changed from 'the party of wealthy graziers' to 'the party of wealthy graziers and manufacturers'.

ous to manage than the creation of a new order of things. For the initiator has the enmity of all who profit by the preservation of the old institutions, and merely luke-warm defenders in those who would gain by the new ones.

I cannot imagine that Menzies would ever have been party to the Gair appointment to Dublin. It was the kind of chicanery which would have earned his contempt. Suggestions of similarities between the Gair appointment and some made by Menzies are false, for Menzies appointed members of his own government and not opponents whose seats he wanted.

Whitlam could justify the Gair appointment because it offered reasonable hope of finding a way out of the Senate impasse. The Senate was holding up legislation which Whitlam regarded as important to the welfare of Australians, so why not buy off a willing, venal old politician like Gair for the greater good of the people?

On the other hand, Menzies for years resisted the proposal that Federal Parliament be given power to make laws regarding Aborigines. He offered a number of specious reasons for his resistance, but at heart he was content to leave such difficult problems with the States.

In Whitlam's eyes this was straight-out neglect of a major national problem. The States, short of money, were in no position to do anything for Aborigines and, in any event, Queensland and Western Australia (where most Aborigines live) were in-

fluenced by racist attitudes unsympathetic to Aboriginal welfare. [Harold Holt's decision to reverse the Menzies view on this subject was probably his major contribution to changing Liberal Party thinking. The Aboriginal referendum, put to the people in May 1967, was carried overwhelmingly.]

Concessions made to the Country Party, such as the 1962 decision on the redistribution of seats, illustrate how Menzies placated powerful vested interests. The electoral commissioners' proposals, reflecting increased urbanisation, would have reduced country representation, but the Country Party Leader, McEwen, said 'no' and although the Constitution called for a redistribution in 1962 nothing was done until 1968.

Whitlam would regard this as unjustified pandering to rural interests and contrary to the Labor doctrine of equality.

Of all the State Premiers now in office, South Australia's Don Dunstan has probably made the greatest long-term difference to the politics of his State. And, as a State Labor man, he offers interesting comparisons with the Labor Prime Minister at federal level.

From November 1938 to March 1965 South Australia was ruled by the iron hand of Sir Thomas Playford, Premier and Leader of the Liberal and Country League. It was a record of continuous service as

First Minister without parallel in the British Commonwealth.

Playford kept his power through an electoral system more biased towards the country than any other in Australia. Two thirds of the seats in the House of Assembly were reserved for the one third of electors who lived outside the capital. Even in the last term of the Playford regime, when metropolitan Adelaide held 70 per cent of the State's population, only four of the 20 government members in the House of Assembly and only one of the eight ministers represented metropolitan seats. The Legislative Council had a restricted property franchise in addition to its substantial rural bias.

Surprisingly, Labor accepted this situation with little complaint. But Labor was led throughout the 50s by M. R. O'Halloran, a country man representing the State seat with the largest area and fewest voters, and with such a leader Labor was inclined to concede some justification for the system.

When the young lawyer, D. A. Dunstan, wrested the marginal metropolitan seat of Norwood from the Liberals in 1953 he soon emerged as one of the most formidable critics both of Playford and of the electoral system. He kept up the attack throughout his term in Opposition, sometimes to the embarrassment of Labor members in country seats.

Late in 1960, O'Halloran died. Frank Walsh, the new Leader of the Opposition

In its own eyes the CP is 'the party which represents the productive people in the community' and 'those who live outside the capital cities'. In 1975 the party changed its name to the National Country Party.

Ranged against this Liberal-CP coalition at every election is the AUSTRALIAN LABOR PARTY. Its party policy is to contest every seat at every election. The coalition parties generally offer the voter either a Liberal or a CP opponent to Labor—few seats are contested by both Liberal and CP candidates.

Labor, the oldest of the three parties, was formed in the 1890s when the unions realised that industrial action had to be supplemented by political action. Since its first victory in 1910 its history has been one of splits and recoveries depending on the phases of the electoral cycle.

The Labor Party is nominally a socialist party. As long ago as 1921 the Federal Conference of the ALP adopted the 'socialisation objective' which stated as policy the 'socialisation of industry, production, distribution and exchange'. However, to accommodate every shade of opinion the same conference adopted the 'Blackburn amendment' which made exceptions of all industries that were socially useful and not exploitive. With the notable exception of the Chifley Government (1945-49) which attempted, unsuccessfully, to nationalise Australia's banks, ALP governments generally have shown little enthusiasm for the nationalisation of industry.

Labor's problems in the period since World War II have attracted a great deal of notice, but they must be seen in the context of Labor being out of office for most of the period.

Though Labor is predominantly an urban working class party, it does win a few country seats in constituencies with mining communities or large railway

and a stonemason by trade, represented a metropolitan seat. At the 1962 election Labor won 54 per cent of the vote but failed to topple Playford. Finally, in March 1965, the Playford Government fell and Walsh became Premier.

Walsh was 67 years old. Dunstan was 39, the only minister under 50, and by far the ablest. As Attorney-General he pursued a remarkable legislative programme which had the South Australian Parliament sitting for more days than it had done since 1931. High on Dunstan's priority list was legislation in the fields of Aboriginal affairs, town planning, legal reform and industrial regulation.

When Labor came to office South Australia was the most conservative State in its laws on liquor, entertainment and gambling. It is now one of the most liberal, and most of the credit for this must go to Dunstan in his role of Attorney-General. He was recognised as the chief newsmaker and driving force of the government, which was commonly referred to as 'the Dunstan Ministry'.

But the Labor Government was undermined by an economic recession in South Australia, and the Labor Party fared so badly there in the 1966 federal election that the blame fell on the State Government. Walsh retired in May 1967, and Dunstan became Premier.

Dunstan was at the mercy of the electoral system which Labor had been unable to change, all its attempts to do so having been blocked by the Legislative Council. When he first went to the polls as Premier, on March 2, 1968, he had had less than 12 months to restore the battered fortunes of his party—and he lost one of the most extraordinary elections in Australian history.

There had been no redistribution of seats for 12 years. At one extreme, 4,988 electors in Frome elected one member; at the other extreme, 45,510 electors in Enfield also elected one member. The result was every bit as peculiar as these figures might suggest: Dunstan's Labor Government won 52 per cent of the vote and lost; Steele Hall's Liberal Opposition polled 44 per cent of the vote and won.

The result caused a minor scandal. The new government felt that it had to do something to reform the system, and this was one of Hall's major achievements: he persuaded his party to carry out a necessary but suicidal reform. It is difficult to allocate due credit for the 1969 electoral redistribution. Hall's admirers naturally praise him for a measure which led to his defeat, but in my view more credit must go to Dunstan who had dramatised the inequity of the old system for so long that Hall had no real alternative but to change it. With the new boundaries in force, Hall was defeated at the general election of May 1970, and Dunstan returned to office with a 27-20 majority in the House of Assembly.

The second Dunstan Ministry was unlike the first. In the first, Dunstan, the only member under 50, presided over a cabinet of old men who had spent many years in Opposition; in the second, he collected a younger and more able ministry, and turned his attention to the Legislative Council. He was determined that the franchise restrictions should be removed so that the Council would be elected by the same voters on the same day as the Assembly. It took three years to achieve this reform, but it came into effect in July 1973.

At present Australia has a federal Labor government but only two States (South Australia and Tasmania) have Labor governments. In that context, the two senior Labor leaders are Whitlam and Dunstan.

Both come from the urban middle class— probably the first time that Labor has had two senior leaders of such origin. In both cases their predecessors were older men with working class backgrounds: Arthur Calwell exercised all his influence in trying to prevent Whitlam being his successor, and Frank Walsh did the same to Dunstan.

Dunstan was a man in a hurry during his first two years as Attorney-General but he seems to have slowed down since becoming Premier. In many ways he has been all the more effective for that. His term at the top of the political heap in South Australia has certainly coincided with the greatest change in political alignment ever seen in that State, and it could be argued that Dunstan has been the architect of that realignment.

Market research and public relations play an increasingly important role in Australian politics. Parliamentary leaders are carefully coached and groomed in the projection of a sympathetic, favourable image—especially at election time, when party policies are showered on the public. Here, a Labor devotee pays homage to party leader Gough Whitlam during a pre-election rally at Blacktown, Sydney, in 1972. (Rick Stevens, *Sydney Morning Herald*)

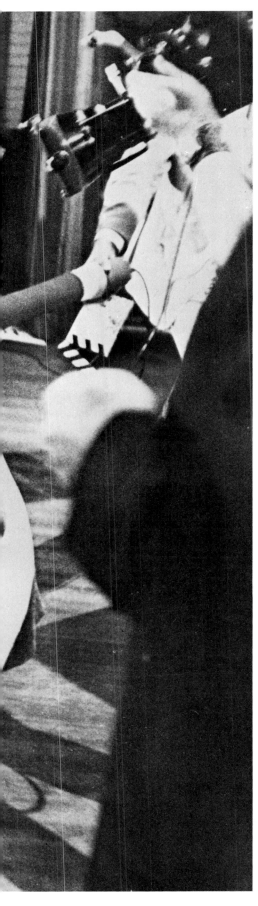

towns, or where it has an unusually good candidate. Barriers to its electoral success have been:

- Australia as 'a land of opportunity and prosperity' does not provide fertile soil even for mild forms of socialism. It is widely believed that differences in wealth are due not to privilege but to hard work.

- Labor's opponents have had some success in portraying Labor as being subject to undue communist influence.

- The electoral boundaries are mildly gerrymandered against Labor.

- Internal divisions, sometimes resulting in splits. Since 1910 three major splits (the first two occurring while Labor was in power) have kept the party out of office for long periods: the 1916 'conscription split' which brought it down and kept it out until 1929; the 1931 'depression split' which toppled Labor and kept it out until 1944; the 1955 'communism split' which kept it out until 1972.

The damage caused by the first two splits has long since been repaired. The effect of the 1955 split, however, was the establishment of the Democratic Labor Party which polled between 5 per cent and 10 per cent of the vote at each election it contested between 1955 and 1972.

This, in essence, is what happened. From the mid 40s onward the fear of communism was such that an organisation led by Mr B. A. Santamaria, indirectly associated with the Catholic Church, attempted to infiltrate the trade unions and the Labor Party with anti-communist members. The organisation, popularly known as 'The Movement', was so successful that some of the party's more left-wing members became afraid of its power.

Late in 1954 the Leader of the Labor Party, Dr H. V. Evatt, attacked Santamaria and the Movement, and in 1955 the entire Victorian Branch was suspended because it was regarded as being under Movement domination. The 'old' Victorian executive and anti-communist members in other States (not all of them, incidentally, members of the Movement) then left the Labor Party and formed the DEMOCRATIC LABOR PARTY.

The DLP believed that the Labor Party was dominated by communists and the 'pro-communist left', and recommended that its voters should give their preferences to the Liberal-CP coalition and not to Labor unless Labor abandoned its left wing. Since Labor has so far refused to oblige, DLP preferences have been a critical source of support for the Liberal-CP coalition. The DLP vote is too evenly spread to win seats in the House of Representatives, so DLP preferences have effectively become Liberal-CP votes.

Formed in anti-communism, and with religious overtones, the DLP has tended to move further and further to the right and is generally regarded at the most right wing party in the political spectrum. The retention of the word 'Labor' in its title is a misnomer, but serves as a reminder that some of its present members were in the Labor Party 20 years ago.

Since the primary objective of the DLP was to keep Labor out of office until it came to terms on the left wing question, the election of a Labor Government in 1972 was, for Labor, a recovery from the 1955 split, and for the DLP, ultimate defeat. It had to look for a new home and proposed a merger with the Country Party. The proposal was given a trial run in Western Australia at the 1974 election as the 'National Alliance', but proved disastrous for both parties.

At present it looks as though the DLP will die and the CP will adapt by changing its name (which it has already done in Queensland, where it is now known as the 'National Party').

A fifth political grouping, the AUSTRALIA PARTY, had its origins in the Vietnam War. In 1966 a Sydney businessman, Mr Gordon Barton, inserted in Australian newspapers an advertisement calling for opposition to the war. Within weeks he had formed the 'Liberal Reform Group'and was running anti-war candidates in Liberal seats at the 1966 federal election. After its first electoral foray Barton's group changed its name to the 'Australian Reform Movement' before becoming the Australia Party in 1969.

169

The Australia Party draws most of its votes in Liberal seats though it generally recommends that supporters give their second preference to Labor. Approximately 70 per cent of its voters follow this advice. The AP vote, like that of the DLP, is too evenly spread for it to win seats.

THE AUSTRALIAN ELECTORAL SYSTEM

With the exceptions of the Federal Senate, the New South Wales Legislative Council and the Tasmanian House of Assembly, all parliaments are elected by preferential voting from single member constituencies. Electoral boundaries have a rural bias.

To illustrate the preferential system, there is a suitable example in the 1972 election for the Victorian seat of Bendigo in the House of Representatives.

There were four candidates. Thus, each voter was required to number his ballot paper 1, 2, 3, 4 against the candidates' names in his or her (the voter's) order of preference.

Because no candidate received an *absolute* majority on the first preference votes (see Table 3), the lowest polling candidate (Mr Brennan, DLP) was eliminated and his second preferences were distributed *as full votes* among the remaining candidates, with 3,417 votes going to the Country Party, 592 to the Liberal Party and 258 to the Labor Party. Once again there was no absolute majority. The lowest poller of the three (Mr Pearce, CP) was eliminated and his second preferences, along with the third preferences of the 3,417 votes he had received from Brennan, were distributed between the two remaining candidates —with 11,375 votes going to the Liberal Party and only 855 to Labor. The Liberal candidate, Mr Bourchier, squeezed home with a majority of 165 over Labor's Mr Kennedy.

TABLE 3
BENDIGO 1972

	Bourchier (Lib)	Brennan (DLP)	Kennedy (ALP)	Pearce (CP)
First Preferences	13,637	4,267	24,326	8,813
Brennan votes transfer	592	-	258	3,417
Total	14,229	excluded	24,584	12,230
Pearce votes transfer	11,375	-	855	-
FINAL TOTAL	25,604	excluded	25,439	excluded

This example shows why Labor so heartily dislikes the present system. Although Labor does receive some preference help from the Australia Party it otherwise relies on 'leakages' (such as the 1,113 from Brennan and Pearce) from anti-Labor candidates. It is common for Liberal or CP candidates to come from behind to beat Labor, but rarely does the reverse occur.

My view is that Labor somewhat overdoes allegations of unfairness in the preferential voting system. While it is certainly true that Labor's opponents exploit the system it is not clear that the result would be very different under 'first-past-the-post'.

For example, had there been a 'first-past-the-post' contest in Bendigo there would have been only one anti-Labor candidate (presumably Mr Bourchier) competing in a straight fight with Labor. The result, I believe, would still have been a narrow Liberal victory.

Another common objection to preferential voting is that it permits excessive minority pressure, although this view depends largely on whether the voter likes or dislikes the minority in question. There is, however, no doubt that the Liberal Party by depending on the CP has had to make concessions to rural interests.

Equally, Liberal dependence on DLP preferences gave the DLP disproportionate influence over Liberal policy in the past. This influence has waned considerably since the disastrous decline in the DLP vote and the Labor victory

Opposite: Up to March, 1975, the Liberal Party had had four leaders since the retirement of Sir Robert Gordon Menzies in 1966; three— Holt, Gorton, McMahon—had been prime ministers. The fourth, Billy Mackie Snedden, was deposed as party leader and leader of the Opposition by a former minister of defence, Malcolm Fraser, seen here on his 3,250 hectare property, Nareen, near Hamilton in the heart of Victoria's wealthy Western District. (Alan Birtles, *Herald-Sun*)

The leader of the National Country Party, Doug Anthony (seventh from left) and members of the party executive cheer the result of a bye-election for a marginal seat. (Peter Wells, *The Australian*)

in the 1974 election. It now appears that the Australia Party is trying to use the influence of its preferences on Labor and, indeed, on the Liberals as well.

Labor has a stronger case in the matter of electoral boundaries. In every Australian house elected by single member constituencies the boundaries are loaded against Labor in three ways.

Since country districts are usually more conservative than city districts, 'rural bias' favours the conservative side of politics. This benefits the Country Party.

Although boundary lines are drawn by supposedly impartial electoral commissioners it is claimed that some commissioners favour the party in power. In practice this has meant the Liberal-CP axis, and Labor governments in recent times have not had their redistribution proposals accepted by conservative upper houses.

Finally, in some cases the geographical distribution of voters hurts Labor because Labor wastes votes in impregnably safe seats while Liberal strength is spread more economically.

However, before agreeing too wholeheartedly with the Labor proposition that 'the boundaries are crook', two points should be made.

There are degrees of unfairness. For example, the anti-Labor bias of the federal, New South Wales and South Australian boundaries is relatively mild and Labor can win a workable majority of seats when it wins a sufficiently large majority of votes. On the other hand, the boundaries for the Queensland Legislative Assembly and the Western Australian Legislative Council are such that Labor has little chance of achieving a majority of seats no matter how large a majority of votes it might receive.

Also, in my view, Labor's remedy for this situation is in itself of dubious fairness. Labor wants to create federal and State electoral districts that are 'equal in population', with total population rather than enrolled electors as the basis of distribution. It so happens that many non-electors are congregated in working class districts containing large communities of migrants who have not been naturalised and a higher ratio of children than in middle class areas. In practice, if all seats were equal in population, Labor seats would have fewer electors. The system would favour Labor.

Some countries have developed bi-partisan agreements on their electoral systems. In the United Kingdom the Conservative and Labour parties (but not the Liberal Party) agree that the system is fair. In New Zealand the process is officially bi-partisan. Unfortunately, however, there seems little possibility of a bi-partisan approach in Australia while the Country Party demands some rural bias to which Labor is opposed, and Labor demands 'first-past-the-post' voting to which other parties are opposed. The prospect for Australia is a continuation of the party struggle over the electoral system, and of gerrymandering in particular.

The Senate, the NSW Legislative Council and the Tasmanian House of Assembly are exceptions to Australia's prevailing tradition of single member constituencies.

The Senate and the Tasmanian House of Assembly are elected on the basis of proportional representation from multi-member constituencies.

In the case of the Senate each State returns 10 senators altogether, with five normally being elected every three years for six year terms. To be elected a candidate needs to win a 'quota' (usually one sixth) of the votes. This produces a party composition in the Senate different from that of the House of Representatives. Whereas the House is composed entirely of members of the geographically concentrated parties (Liberal, CP and Labor), the Senate offers prospects of election to minor parties or independents whose evenly spread vote can obtain a quota. The most successful of these minor parties has been the DLP which held the balance of power in the Senate in the last decade. During the last term of the Liberal-CP government, the DLP was able to use its position in the Senate and the power of its preference votes to press the government to favour DLP policies, especially in foreign affairs, defence and State aid to private schools.

173

The Tasmanian House of Assembly is elected by the same system as the Senate except that seven members are elected from each of the five federal divisions in the State. Interestingly, the system has not produced a proliferation of parties.

The Legislative Council of NSW is the only chamber in Australia which is not elected by the people. It is indirectly elected by current members of both houses of the parliament and its members enjoy the luxury of 12 year terms. As a body it has been attacked by the Labor Party in recent years, though the 1961 Labor attempt to abolish the Legislative Council was overwhelmingly rejected by the voters. Labor is currently committed to reforming the Legislative Council so that it is elected by universal adult franchise—a reform that must eventually come.

ELECTIONEERING IN AUSTRALIA

The most distinctive feature of Australian electioneering is the sheer frequency of elections. Australians are compelled to go to the polls on an average of once a year. Voter turnout at these polls is always over 90 per cent—due to voting being compulsory—but there can be no doubt that the frequency of polls causes boredom with the electoral process.

The basic reasons for so many polls are the three year parliament and the separate elections for the House of Representatives and the Senate. Hence the electors of New South Wales have voted for the House of Representatives in 1961, 1963, 1966, 1969, 1972 and 1974, for the Senate in 1961, 1964, 1967, 1970 and 1974, and for the State Legislative Assembly in 1962, 1965, 1968, 1971 and 1973, which has meant that the people of New South Wales have been compelled to vote once every year since 1961. In addition there have been separate federal referendums in 1967 and 1973 and a separate State referendum in 1961. In the other States the frequency of elections has been very nearly as great, though fortunately for them State upper and lower houses are elected on the same day.

This frequency of elections probably has one beneficial effect. It reduces the amount of ballyhoo. Australian elections are not the national events they are in the United States, and many State elections, at least, pass with scant attention.

Australia has no laws compelling parties to disclose the state of their finances either in a general sense or in relation to the amount each spends at an election. Bits of information are published, but nothing more. For example it is known that Labor's national budget for the 1969 election (which Labor lost) was $50,000 but was $250,000 in 1972 (when it won). It is commonly believed that party leaders have their own 'slush funds' existing separately from the party organisation.

There seems no good reason to doubt that the Liberal and Country Parties are better endowed financially than Labor since they represent the wealthier part of the community, especially business interests. Undoubtedly these interests have more money to spend than the trade unions, which are Labor's power base.

The Labor Government has been attempting to change the law so that parties are compelled to disclose their sources of funds, but the proposal has been resisted by the Liberal and Country Parties which clearly wish to protect the interests of their donors. However, one consequence of the lack of proper laws relating to party finance is that each party is open to wild accusations by its opponents.

ORGANISATION OF PARTIES

Australian parties are organised on a federal basis. Even the ALP, which is dedicated to a unitary system of government and the abolition of the Senate, organises itself on an essentially federal basis. Each State has a branch of the ALP and each is equally represented at the Federal Conference (the party's supreme policy making and governing authority) and on the executive.

The Federal Conference normally meets every two years and consists of: six delegates from each of the six State branches; the Leader and Deputy Leader of the ALP in the House of Representatives and the Senate; the six State ALP parliamentary leaders; a representative from the ACT; a representative from the

Northern Territory; and a representative from the Young Labor organisation, for a total of 49. It last met in February 1975 at Terrigal, NSW.

The basic principle is equality for each State delegation even though the States have enormous variations in population and party membership.

The Liberal Party's Federal Council is similarly organised except that it meets annually and does not bind the parliamentary party.

Each of the three main parties is made up of separate State branches or divisions which run their own State affairs—including the selection of candidates. There are wide variations in the procedures through which candidates are chosen by the parties in the various States. Each main party also maintains a Federal Secretariat in Canberra to carry out research and co-ordination between the States, together with a fair amount of public relations work and the servicing of members of the Federal Parliament, but the bulk of organisational work is carried out at State divisional offices.

The government of the day exists by maintaining the confidence of the House of Representatives through total party discipline, and each vote is virtually a foregone conclusion in favour of the government majority. Political bargaining is thus at a discount in the House.

The situation is more interesting when the governing party does not control the Senate—and this has been the case, in an acute form, since 1972. During the first term of the Whitlam Government the numbers in the Senate were as follows: ALP, 26; Liberal, 21; CP, 5; DLP, 5; Ind 3.

Although the combined Liberal-CP-DLP numbers constituted a majority, the numbers of any one group added to Labor's gave Labor a majority. Most proposed legislation was either passed without opposition or blocked by the combined Opposition, but there were a few cases of wheeling and dealing between the Labor Government and individual Opposition parties.

For example, in November 1973, the Opposition parties were threatening to hold up the States Grants (Schools) Bill because the government was proposing to abolish grants to certain well-to-do schools, contrary to a promise given by the Prime Minister when he was in Opposition. The impasse was broken only when the Leader of the Country Party, Mr Anthony, arranged with Labor a compromise solution which seemed to meet some of the objections. Thus the bill was passed with CP and DLP senators voting with Labor against the Liberals.

A similar incident had occurred in September 1973, when the government brought in legislation to amend the Constitution to give the Commonwealth Parliament powers over prices and incomes. The Labor Caucus (the Parliamentary Labor Party) had resolved to gain power over prices, but it would have taken six months to present the matter to the people at a referendum unless legislation was passed by the Senate. Accordingly, a deal was made with the DLP by which the five DLP senators would support the legislation if power over incomes was also sought.

The first term of the Whitlam Government was marked by explosive clashes between the Senate and the House of Representatives. It had been speculated almost from the beginning that a double dissolution would inevitably result if, as expected, such clashes occurred—the double dissolution came as no surprise.

In essence, the Senate can cause a double dissolution by *twice* rejecting, refusing to pass, or passing with amendments unacceptable to the House of Representatives, any proposed law which has been passed by the House.

By August 1973, Mr Whitlam had the technical grounds for a double dissolution when the Senate, for the second time, rejected the *Commonwealth Electoral Bill* (No. 2), 1973. He did not, however, seek an immediate double dissolution: there was too much evidence of the government's unpopularity, and many felt that Whitlam would be defeated at the election following such a dissolution.

The Opposition parties, at the same time, began discussing whether they should force a double dissolution through the Senate's power to refuse 'Supply'.

THE 1974 DOUBLE DISSOLUTION

(The term 'Supply' refers to the passage of money to keep the government running.) The power of the Senate can be used to extract concessions from a government, and in this case meant agreement by the government to dissolve the House of Representatives.

There was a stand-off period during which neither side took action to force the situation, and it was announced that a normal election for half the Senate would be held on May 18, 1974. But there was an unexpected development. Senator V. C. Gair, former leader of the DLP, was appointed Ambassador to Ireland—a move designed to enable Labor to take his seat at the normal Senate election.

All hell broke loose, and ultimately the Opposition senators forced the double dissolution. Thus Mr Whitlam became the third Prime Minister to fight a double dissolution election, the second (after Menzies) to win such an election and the first to be forced to the polls by a hostile Senate.

THE CURRENT POLITICAL OUTLOOK

The composition of the Senate, in early 1975, was: ALP, 28; Liberal, 24; Country Party, 6; Independent, 2. Although some people speculated that the Opposition might force another premature election, the political outlook changed in March 1975 when the Liberal Party deposed its leader, B. M. Snedden, and installed Malcolm Fraser.

The Liberal Party's main weakness in recent years has been instability in its leadership. Since the retirement of Menzies the Liberals have had four short-term leaders, H. E. Holt (1966-67), J. G. Gorton (1968-71), W. McMahon (1971-72) and B. M. Snedden (1972-75). Fraser is only 45 and he might well dominate Australian conservatism for a full two decades as Liberal leader and probably as Prime Minister.

In the short term the main consequence of his accession to the leadership has been to reduce the prospect of a premature election. An election before mid-1977 now seems most unlikely.

Opposite: Parliament House, Canberra, has been the 'provisional' seat of the Federal Parliament since 1927 when the Duke of York officiated at the opening ceremony. The final site for a permanent building has not yet been determined; the National Capital Development Commission had recommended the shore of Lake Burley Griffin, but recent developments suggest that Capital Hill, the hub of the city plan, may be chosen.

RELIGION

Dr Rudolph Brasch

**'It could have become
a most powerful force
from the beginning.'**

From the beginning, religion in Australia was neglected and ignored and, at most, used and abused by the establishment for its own advantage.

The colony was established without a prayer and the first service on Australian soil seems to have been an afterthought. It did not take place until the second Sunday, eight days after the first landing.

Australia also has the distinction of having been the only 'Christian' country whose earliest parliaments had no divine invocations. Attempts in 1843 and 1844 to change the situation were defeated. Indeed, when in 1851 a renewed effort to put God into the Victorian Parliament, as it were, was again rejected, W. Westgarth praised this defeat of religion as a victory for the spirit of progress. It was a fortunate sign of Australian maturity, he said, to confine religion to 'its proper place' and refuse the obsolete tradition, the 'old remnant', of the British House of Commons.

It took another 11 years, until 1862, for the New South Wales Legislative Assembly to open its session with a prayer. It was the first Australian Parliament to do so but the action was not welcomed unanimously. Far from it—members resented the intrusion of religion and some left the Chamber in protest. Eventually, the government was forced to change the text of the invocation and reword it in a form more innocuously 'neutral'. Religion could have become a most forceful power in Australia from the beginning. Leaving behind its divisiveness elsewhere, it could have, from the outset, proved a uniting, dynamic spirit in the building of a nation.

The very newness of the colony, even taking into account the disadvantage of its penal start, offered infinite opportunities. Merely to transplant institutions

Opposite: Perhaps because of its inauspicious beginnings, and an essentially tolerant, easy going attitude towards matters of faith, religion in Australia has largely escaped the schisms and doubts that have limited or even reduced congregations in other parts of the world.

179

and inapplicable traditions from the 'old country' showed lack of understanding and imagination.

But despite everything that was against it, religion made its presence felt and through the initiative of individual ministers, it pioneered significant features which have contributed greatly to the life of the nation, and indeed the world.

It was from Australia that missionaries went out to Christianise islands of the Pacific. Moreover, they did so unsupported by the authorities, neither following the flag nor linked with aspirations of trade, but urged on solely by their consciences.

Another factor gave Australian religion a unique aspect. Although certainly Protestants were fostered for many years, they were never given the status of an established church. Gradually but inevitably, every denomination, as it was imported into the country, received equal rights to exist and even to ask for financial support from the government.

ANGLICANS

The Church of England has always been the largest denomination in Australia. At the 1921 census it constituted 44 per cent of the population, in 1954, 31 per cent, in 1966, 33.6 per cent, and in 1971, 31.2 per cent. As distinct from the Church of England in Britain, the Church of England in Australia, in spite of some attempt at the beginning to achieve such supremacy, never became an 'established' church

In a letter Governor Bourke warned the Home Government that in this 'new country, to which persons of all religious persuasions are invited to resort, it would be impossible to establish a dominant and endowed church without much hostility'.

Certainly, in the early days, the authorities fostered the Anglican Church. Yet, slowly and inevitably, it had to take its place within the Australian community of religions without ever gaining the power it had in Britain. It took a long time, however, to become indigenously Australian. To start with, Australia was regarded as so insignificant that it was attached to the diocese of Calcutta, thousands of kilometres away. Not until 1835 was a first 'Bishop of Australia', William Grant Broughton, with his newly established See of Australia, nominated.

For many years, strong links with the home church continued to influence and determine Anglicanism in Australia. The first Australian-born Archbishop, the Most Reverend Marcus Loane, was installed only as recently at 1966. It was then realised that Australia no longer needed (or even appreciated) an imported hierarchy and to confirm the new independence the 27 dioceses of Australia agreed to replace the old name 'Church of England' with 'The Anglican Church in Australia'. Its head was not the Queen but the Primate of Australia.

The decision was taken after much deliberation and against the wishes and advice of the Archbishop of Sydney who saw the change of name as a most regrettable break with history. But his being overruled was indicative of the democratic government of the church in Australia. That Australian Anglicanism has never produced an historically eminent figure, might well be explained by its synodal government. With its strong lay representation it greatly reduced the possibilities of individual initiative and excellency.

As in almost all denominations, emphases of belief and practice differ within the Anglican Church. As in England there is a distinct division between Anglo-Catholics (also known as the High Church) and the conservative Evangelicals most strongly represented in the Sydney diocese. The ultra-orthodoxy of the latter led critics to describe it as 'so low' that it was almost 'underground'.

In order to stress its new Australian orientation, the Anglican Church, in conjunction with Presbyterians, Methodists and Congregationalists, is to publish a new, interdenominational hymn book. Significantly, this hymnal eliminates metaphors and expressions that make sense in the Northern Hemisphere, especially Britain, but have little meaning to Australians. No hymn refers to a snowy Christmas! The language used is clear, contemporary, and of literary merit; even the tunes suggested seek to replace the traditional chants.

Taking up the modern trend of women's lib, the Church also found no theological reason to deny women an office in the Anglican ministry. However, so far it has not gone beyond the verbal declaration. Yet in a lesser field Australia has been the first in the world, so it is claimed, to appoint (at St David's Cathedral, Hobart) a female verger.

No church can survive this modern age if it disregards its social duty. The Anglican Church in Australia, well aware of this, has been instrumental in not only fostering but actually pioneering essential social welfare. In 1960, it was among the first, with the Salvation Army, Methodists and an independent group, to establish a hostel exclusively caring for unmarried mothers. Until then, any work of that type was looked upon as so delicate that it was conducted, if at all, clandestinely.

In a youth-oriented and youth-worshipping age, the Psalmist's petition 'cast me not off in the time of old age' has acquired an almost tragic connotation. That is why the Anglican Church inaugurated retirement villages. Financed by the Commonwealth and administered by the Church, they provide comfort, dignity and a meaningful life for more than 2,500 old people.

Equal in importance and need is the work done for the chronically sick among the aged, those most neglected and least regarded of people. Nine geriatric hospitals, with more than 1,500 beds, attend to their welfare. Hardly ever understood, but symbolic, is their name: Chesalon. It is the name of a site from the Book of Joshua meaning 'Hope'.

Inevitably, however, these tasks will be reduced as more are surrendered to the government. Meanwhile, the Anglican Church has resumed yet another, and the most ancient, religious duty: to act as the conscience of the community, to make its voice heard on issues of national and international importance and, no matter what the cost, speak up. In the words of Marcus Loane, the Anglicans are trying to fulfil a contemporary role by making Australians 'wake up and grow up'.

Roman Catholicism has always played a prominent role in Australian life and many factors and prejudices combined to create militant antagonism, intense animosity and distrust.

CATHOLICS

At first there was the fight for its very existence and for the right to worship 'the Catholic way'. Then came the drawn-out battle for an independent State-supported education. Additional causes of conflict through the years were the ethnic background of priests and people, the inferior social position of Catholics and their resulting association with a specific political party and particular circumstances of the administration of their church. No wonder extremists claimed that Australia's two major religions were Catholicism and anti-Catholicism.

Some challenges for Catholicism in Australia were almost inevitable. The Irish origin of its early majority caused a vocal and active sympathy with their oppressed brethren in the Emerald Isle. Its implicit antagonism against the Protestant British, in turn, immediately aroused further anti-Catholic feeling. Suspicions of disloyalty were increased by the fact that most of the priesthood came from Ireland and were Rome-trained. In a request to the Colonial Office in 1826, Governor Darling said that if, against his wishes, more priests were to be sent to the colony, they should be Englishmen as, regrettably, 'the Catholics here being, I believe, nearly all Irish'. Catholic leaders themselves argued at the time that you could never make a good priest out of convicts. And so grew the accusations of a Papal plot to create a hegemony in Australia to control people's minds and the entire national life.

Even Catholics began to resent the alien influence of their hierarchy and the battle for the 'Australianisation' of the church was not easy. Indicative was the establishment of the theological seminary at Manly, St Patrick's College. Its purpose was to break the monopoly of the Irish and foster an indigenous **181**

priesthood. Yet significantly, the first two bishops there were given positions in the distant and minor dioceses of Townsville and Geraldton! Equally telling was the choice of the name for the Catholic students' university societies. Very pointedly they honoured (first so in Melbourne in 1910) the English intellectual Newman, a choice hardly welcomed by Irish priests!

Catholics, who had started in Australia as convicts, for a long time continued to belong in great number to the labouring class. It was not surprising, therefore, that they also played an eminent role in the growth of the Labor Party. This, Catholics maintain, was the only reason why at times a majority of Catholics filled the main Cabinet positions in State governments.

When Australia stopped its financial support of the Church, and its schools, Catholics took it as an outright attack on their faith. Their fight for subsidy of their own educational system became a rallying point. On the other hand, non-Catholics viewed Catholic schools with much suspicion. Wild allegations were made (and strongly denied) that these schools encouraged pupils to enter the public service to gain further influence in Australian politics . . . another Papal plot!

But even the Catholic-dominated Labor Party eventually suffered from the influence of non-believers and communists. Two schools of thought split the Catholic community. One was adamant that Catholics should 'stay in and fight' and thereby continue to exert their Christian influence from within. The other faction, fostered by Mannix-inspired Santamaria, regarded such a policy as futile. Abandoning 'a hopeless situation', they separated to form a new Catholic party that would stress Roman Catholic social principles.

The heated battle for government funds for church education fanned anti-Catholic antagonism and then the great paradox! Political vote-catching caused, not a Catholic-dominated Labor government, but a Protestant Liberal Cabinet to give Catholics their wish. It instituted State support for *all* non-government schools, and a fight that had raged from the 1830s suddenly was at an end.

The world-wide decline of religion has made its inroads into Australian Catholicism as well, but compared with other countries, fewer priests have resigned their office. Within the congregations incidents of disturbance are comparatively rare. This may not so much be the result of deeper religious feeling among Australian Catholics as the Australian temperament which, perhaps lethargically, is not disposed to crisis situations. Its cause might also be found in Australia's remoteness from the ferment of European and American thought and a general apathy towards things spiritual which in this instance would strangely work to the advantage of Roman Catholicism.

A small but significant characteristic of Australian Catholicism concerns the relationship between priests and the people, which lacks the traditional aura of awe and fear. Although not over-familiar, the relationship nevertheless reflects the typical Australian tendency towards mateship.

Australia has been one of the first countries to follow Papal directions for further education of its ordained priesthood. Australia thus became one of the first countries to introduce a pastoral year of practical training for newly graduated priests as well as refresher courses for those having served congregations for some time.

Catholicism is the major Australian religion to show a considerable increase in numbers in proportion to the rest of the population. This is due to immigration. According to the 1971 census Catholics had grown to more than a quarter (27 per cent) of the people. This compares with 22.6 per cent in 1901; 17.5 per cent in 1935; 20.7 per cent in 1947 and 26.29 per cent in 1966. In fact, some authorities suggest that the Catholic Church may eventually overtake the Anglican.

Opposite: Many post-war migrants arrived in Australia with little more than hopes for a better future—and the support of a strong religious faith.

Many significant features have distinguished the Jews' place in Australia, almost from the very beginning. Contact between Jew and Christian has largely been one of mutual trust and friendship. Until recently, anti-Semitism as an organised

JEWS

force had been unknown and alien to the Australian people. With few exceptions, widely exaggerated through the publicity they received, Australia has practised little discrimination against the Jew.

Typical is the fact that many synagogues throughout the country were built with financial help from Christian friends. Certainly unique in the world was the occasion when the New South Wales Parliament adjourned for Yom Kippur in deference to its Jewish Speaker! Jews have belonged to all parties and sections of the community and at no time have they tried to act as a pressure group or a political force.

Religiously the average Jew, like Christian neighbours, has become increasingly indifferent and apathetic towards faith. Affiliations to the synagogue and active participation in religious life are diminishing. The influence of spiritual leaders has been minimal. In spite of the Jews' presence in Australia ever since the establishment of the colony, only two of its rabbis serving the community are Australian-born. And even these had to go overseas for their rabbinical studies.

Communities once flourishing in country centres have died out, their former synagogues empty shells, some being used as a furniture store or a garage. Almost 90 per cent of Australian Jewry now live in Sydney and Melbourne. Mixed marriages are increasing with at least 20 per cent of young Jews said to 'marry out'. Although the majority of non-Jewish partners used to seek conversion to Judaism, now many couples no longer care.

The opening of Jewish denominational day schools (only completely successful so far in Melbourne, whose 'Mount Scopus' is regarded as the largest and best of its kind in the world), is an attempt towards stemming the flood of this Jewish disintegration.

Liberal Judaism, the progressive interpretation of Judaism, was established in Australia, first in Melbourne, in 1936. Since then it has spread to the other capital cities. Its synagogues are known as 'Temples'. Although Temple affiliations are still in the minority, this is attributable for the most part to a lack of available ministers. Orthodoxy's membership majority is only nominal since most members no longer observe the orthodox Jewish traditions. In fact, many an 'innovation' of liberal Judaism is now practised by orthodoxy, most conspicuously the confirmation of girls, known as Bat Mitzvah.

Perturbing for the future of the Australian Jewish community are the figures of the 1971 census. This showed an actual decline of the number of Jews in Australia from just over 63,000 in 1966 to under 59,000. In relationship to the total population this further lowered an already small percentage— from 0.54 per cent in 1966 to a mere 0.46 per cent.

METHODISTS

It could be said that a snake was responsible for the foundation of Methodism in Australia. After his discharge from the New South Wales Corps, John Lee had settled in Castlereagh on a grant of land he received in 1804. Religion meant nothing to him. Like so many others in the colony, he much preferred gambling and drinking.

One day, so the story goes, while collecting firewood, he grabbed a poisonous snake which instantly bit him. Terrified he might die, he vowed that should he be saved he would mend his ways. More so, he would do everything in his power to turn others from debauchery to a Christian life. Lee survived, and kept his promise. At the back of his home, he built a timber slab church— Methodism had started in the antipodes.

Mere chance again gave the young church its first minister. The small group of Methodists into which Mr Lee's venture grew, felt the need of a spiritual leader. Far from ministering merely to their own needs, he would be of great benefit to the 'thousands of souls perishing for lack of knowledge, both in high and low life'.

They requested the Wesleyan Missionary Society in London to send such a man and wisely stipulated that he should be broad-minded enough to serve 'not in hostility against the (Anglican) Church but rather in unison with it.' Only a man not 'radically a Dissenter' would do.

At that time the Reverend Samuel Leigh was waiting in London to take up duties in North America. But just before he was due to sail, his appointment was cancelled because of the 'disturbed state' of that part of the world and immediately the Society asked Leigh to switch his destination—to Australia.

Economics and politics played a part in the new appointment. Aware that government approval had to be obtained, the Society cleverly pointed out that Leigh's erudition would in fact enable him to serve in a dual capacity and thereby save the government money. He could act both as a minister and a schoolmaster. And that consideration decided the issue. Leigh, who was a man of principle, however, made it clear that he would never stoop to act 'as the hired agent of the colonists'. And when on his arrival in Sydney in 1815, the Governor offered him a much more lucrative position 'under the government' with the promise of a comfortable living and future wealth, Leigh reiterated his determination to stay independent.

That is how he set to work, sparing no effort. He did not wait for people to find him but sought them out. His circuit at times extended to 240 kilometres, and there were times when he got lost in the bush. Within 10 days he might preach at 15 different places. In 1820 ill health forced him to return to England. He could, however, do so knowing that Methodism was firmly grounded in the new country.

PRESBYTERIANS

Presbyterians came to Australia in 1802, not as convicts or goalers. They were Scots among the first 'assisted' free immigrants who were offered attractive grants of 40 hectares of rich alluvial land. Theirs was the first church to be built in the colony—at Ebenezer on the Hawkesbury River in NSW in 1809—solely by voluntary contributions. It still stands today.

Perhaps the greatest gift the Presbyterian Church made to Australia was that of one of its most outstanding clergymen: fiery, freedom-loving, undaunted John Dunmore Lang. He arrived as the Ebenezer congregation's first minister in 1823 and, with some interruptions and controversies, served it for 55 years.

Lang took a prominent part in the political life of the country. Representing Port Phillip, he became a member of the Legislative Council. This caused much stir, as some objected to a clergyman meddling in politics. But to Lang's mind a churchman's vital duties included affairs of State.

Numerous indeed were his contributions to Australian life. He agitated for the creation of Victoria as a separate colony. Equally enthusiastically he supported the separation of Queensland from New South Wales. When W. C. Wentworth tried his hardest to introduce an Australian peerage, his scheme was defeated not least by Lang's vehement opposition which he expressed with biting sarcasm.

Above all, Lang was convinced that Australia's future depended on the right type of settlers. In numerous visits to the 'old country' he fostered and popularised migration, pioneering family settlement as a totally new endeavour. In pamphlets and books he expounded his thoughts of a greater Australia. Using the American model but improving on it, he outlined his dream of a 'golden land', no longer tied to Britain but totally free and independent, the United States of Australia.

His is the typical example of the role of religion in Australia—how it never played a significant role as 'the Church', but left its important mark on the life of the nation by the zeal and dedication of individuals. And not the least of them was John Dunmore Lang.

Following page: The Easter observance of the Stations of the Cross, a major event in the Roman Catholic calendar, draws as many as 30,000 worshippers to the annual open air service at Campbelltown, near Sydney.

LUTHERANS

If Australia had its own Pilgrim Fathers, they were Lutherans who came from Prussia seeking freedom of worship. The Prussian government at the time tried to force the Lutheran Church to toe the national line and those refusing to do so were mercilessly persecuted.

One of the leaders of the ostracised Church was Pastor August Kavel, of a Prussian village, Klemzig. He realised that his congregation's only hope for survival was emigration and resolved to lead his flock, just as Moses had once done, out of this modern 'Egypt'.

In 1838 they settled in South Australia and, sentimentally, called their first village Klemzig. From there they proceeded to the Barossa Valley, and out of the small seed grew the Lutheran Church of Australia.

That same year Lutherans also arrived, hundreds of kilometres away, in what is now Queensland. Yet they came there for an entirely different reason. John Dunmore Lang, the famous Presbyterian leader, was responsible for their migration. It was not because of any interest in the Lutheran Church on his part, but out of concern for the Aborigines!

In 1836-37, Dr Lang took up the cause of the Australian Aborigines during a London visit. Their abject condition, he claimed, could only be alleviated by Christianity. His agitation resulted in a government grant to subsidise the posting of three Presbyterian missionaries. But no volunteers came forward.

Having failed with his own people, Lang contacted a Lutheran friend in Berlin, Pastor Gossner, who gladly agreed to supply the men. However, there was one condition. To send individual missionaries to pagan people, he was convinced, was futile. The only effective method of conversion was by the example of an entire community. Their way of life would prove the supremacy of their faith and thus win converts.

If Dr Lang would submit to this condition, Gossner promised an entire colony of Lutherans. It was an unprecedented type of selected migration with a spiritual purpose.

Dr Lang accepted and the German Lutheran contingent settled at Moreton Bay. Their missionary reserve covered an area of 260 hectares on both sides of a creek which, biblically, they called Kedron Brook. Their purpose, however, was never achieved and the colony soon petered out. But the story of their settlement, like that of their South Australian brothers, added a colourful note to the pattern of religion in Australia.

BAPTISTS

A church which was to take a leading part in the fight against drink in Australia held its first service at a hotel: the Rose and Crown Inn in Castlereagh Street, Sydney, in 1831. The Reverend John McKaegh, the Baptist Church's foundation minister, did not stay long with his congregation. Discarding the 'cloth', he became a tobacconist and eventually settled in Tasmania.

Without a spiritual leader, the young community felt completely lost. An urgent appeal they sent to their Missionary Society in London remained unheeded. Its charter, the desperate Sydney Baptists were told, specifically restricted its work (and ministers) 'to the heathens of the world'. And, after all, Australia was not considered a pagan country.

But all was not lost. One member of the committee approached the Reverend John Saunders, a fervent young man, who was anxious to spread the Gospel, no matter where. His first impressions of Sydney were predictably discouraging: 'It appeared as if we had landed among a set of the most degraded and uncomfortable beings we had ever thought of,' he wrote. To top it, many of the men were 'so drunk'.

Undaunted, however, he took up his task. Soon he realised yet another regrettable feature of the colony's religious life. Constant bickering among the various denominations did not contribute either to its status or stature. Above all, Saunders felt the need for Christian unity and, more than a century before modern ecumenism, he spoke up for 'Christian fellowship'. Thus he can be considered a pioneer of interfaith work in Australia.

When poor health forced him to resign in 1847, he had made his mark not only in his own church but in Australian religious life. Son of a London alderman, he had lived up to the inscription of his family crest, 'Nothing without God'. He is remembered as 'the first Baptist missionary to Australia', 'the Apostle of Temperance', and as a dauntless fighter against transportation.

Congregationalism was responsible for the first boarding school on Australian soil. It was opened by the Reverend William Pascoe Crook who, with four other men, organised the first Congregational community in 1810. The fact that he, a Congregationalist and not an ordained minister of the Anglican Church, administered the sacrament, led to a clash with Governor Macquarie. Crook was threatened with expulsion from the colony, should he continue to celebrate what was the privilege and prerogative of the Anglican Church alone. His reply was typical of the courage and independence of many of Australia's early churchmen. Even if he had to suffer death, he stated, he would go on holding Communion services the way he had done.

Only towards the end of the 1840s did Congregationalism begin to play a role in Australian life. Its pioneers then, among them David Jones and John Fairfax, have their prominent place in Australian culture and commerce.

Aborigines have an indigenous place in the history of Australian religion. In their pristine state, unsullied by manipulation and exploitation, religion was their very basis of life and the cement that held together their social structure. Their various myths, and particularly their belief in a 'dream time', endowed them with values they cherished and served as the very foundation of their existence. They closely linked individual Aborigines with their ancestors' past, their own totem group and the territory they occupied. But going far beyond, into the spiritual sphere, they also accepted the existence of an immortal soul. This not only survived the death of the the body (returning to its ancestral home) but pre-existed their birth. A system of kinship taught the Aborigines a social gospel: to share possessions and to take care 'religiously' of the orphan and the aged.

There was also, to be sure, much in their pattern of beliefs that was primitive, fearful and repulsive to the Western mind. But to them it gave deep satisfaction and a meaningful way of life. The Aboriginal faith imbued their life with beauty, affection and profound belief. Their initiation rites gave each individual a permanent feeling of belonging and an awareness of social obligation.

Much controversy has raged as to the merits or crimes of Christian missionaries. No one can deny that among them were most dedicated and selfless people and that they gave the hungry blacks nourishment and some sort of home in their mission stations. On the other hand, they destroyed much of the indigenous Australians' proud heritage and social integration. No wonder that thinking members of their race could ask white people, in the words of their poet Kath Walker, what difference it truly had made to 'change our sacred myths for your sacred myths'.

Aboriginal Doug Nicholls who, through one of the mission stations, became a Christian pastor himself, once confessed that 'perhaps our people—our great people—were really close to God'. In most cases when their tribal beliefs were taken from the Aborigines nothing was put in their place, with the resulting deterioration, degradation and loss of self-respect. And for this Nicholls bitterly accused white people and the Church.

At times there was an invidious competition between the various mission stations in the conquest of souls. Almost possessively, some tried to enforce their specific brand of Christianity on their charges. The effect was not greater happiness but confusion. Anxious not to go hungry, the natives adopted the new faith, not for the sake of their souls but that of their body. What they really needed was a knowledge of a loving God and its application in everyday life. But they became the victim of an atomised Church with divisive dogmas and doctrines.

Nevertheless, in the present mood of putting all blame on 'the Church', it should be remembered, and acknowledged, how, from the earliest days, some of its institutions and representatives showed great concern for the original Australian and went out of their way to help. In great loneliness they carried on their little appreciated work. They were undaunted by the small response of the Aborigine and even less encouragement on the part of the authorities. They were further handicapped by their rudimentary knowledge of Aboriginal values, beliefs and languages.

It is interesting to note that Richard Johnson, first in line of all Australian clergy, was already greatly worried about the Aborigines' spiritual welfare and morality—for a very specific reason. He was afraid that the white settlers' debauchery would act as a bad example and that all chances of conversion would be spoilt by so-called Christians showing hardness of heart, obscene living, and an altogether blasphemous existence.

And that is why in one of his early sermons, he implored the inhabitants of the colony, especially for the sake of the natives, those 'poor unenlightened savages' to change their own way of life. Because if they became 'more and more acquainted with our language and manners, hear you, many of you, curse, swear, lie, abound in every kind of obscene and profane conversation; and if they observe that it is common with you to steal, to break the Sabbath, to be guilty of uncleanliness, drunkenness and other abominations; how must their minds become prejudiced and their hearts hardened against that pure and holy religion which we profess? Oh beware of laying stumbling-blocks in the way of these blind people, lest the blood of their souls be one day be required at your hands'.

His words, spoken so long ago, seem almost prophetic and certainly are most apposite in our time. With the general sense of guilt caused by the injustices done to the Australian native, the present-day church in Australia is trying hard to remedy the dismal neglect of the Aborigine. It does so, however, mostly not by its spiritual teaching but by fighting for their fundamental rights.

THE ORTHODOX CHURCH

Greek sailors, who first visited Australia around the 1850s, told their folks at home of the great country in the antipodes. No doubt, their story started the first migration of Greeks, and towards the end of the 19th century their number had grown to form the first Greek Orthodox communities, in Sydney and Melbourne.

However, the Orthodox congregation did not form a local diocese but placed themselves under the ecclesiastical jurisdiction of the Church of Greece. But in 1923, now strong in numbers, the Orthodox Church of Australia was established to become—with New Zealand and all Oceania—a 'Holy Metropolis'—under the Ecumenical Patriarch of Istanbul.

By 1927, with new refugee migrants from Asia Minor, the number of members of the Greek Orthodox Church had grown to 10,000 with communities extending to Brisbane, Perth, Port Pirie and Darwin.

A further influx of migrants from the Mediterranean region and other countries in which the Orthodox Church prevailed, vastly increased its members (and diversity) in Australia. Though sharing the identical spiritual outlook, doctrinal tenets and major ritual, the various groups established churches which reflected their ethnic and cultural background. They included the Greek, Russian, Ukranian, Rumanian, Lebanese (Antioch) and Serbian Churches.

Strong family life has always been one of the distinguishing marks of the Orthodox community. This was linked with a deep pride in their ethnic tradition, which has enriched Australian national life. That only marriages solemnised in the Orthodox Church were recognised in Greece, enabled the religious community to maintain a special link with all its adherents.

However, throughout the years Orthodoxy has gravely suffered from factionalism which gave the Orthodox community extraordinary publicity—not for its religious message but political squabbles. At their very basis is the peculiar organisation of the Orthodox Church in Australia. Legally, its various houses of worship are not recognised as religious communities but as 'limited companies' with, as it were, their boards of directors. This opened the doors of the Church and its administration to political interests which could overrule spiritual endeavour.

Opposite: Australia's reverence for sport can reveal itself in curious ways. This tombstone is in a cemetery at Whyalla, SA.

Australia experienced an unprecedented immigration of members of the Orthodox Church after World War II. It now occupies the fifth place among the country's major religious groups (2.7 per cent of the population according to the 1971 census).

CREEDS AND CULTS

Australia certainly has been, and still is, the target of numerous old and new cults, philosophies and religious faiths, brought to this country either by migrants or special emissaries. The Salvation Army began its march into Australia with a conspicuous open air meeting in the Adelaide Botanic Gardens in September 1818. Its two founders, Saunders and Gore, had been trained under William Booth himself. To begin with, their operations met tumultuous opposition. Larrikin gangs joined their meetings to cause disturbances, often pelting the 'soldiers' with all types of unpleasant missiles.

Quakers quietly started their work and way of life as long ago as 1832, when two English Friends, James Backhouse, a botanist, and his companion George Washington Walker, came to Tasmania specially to meet other Friends already settled there and to join them 'under concern' to aid convicts and Aborigines. Their efforts went much further. Quakers, in fact, established in 1887 Australia's first co-educational boarding school in Hobart, more than half of its pupils being non-Quakers.

The only connection of the Liberal Catholic Church with Roman Catholicism is historical. It was founded in Holland, in 1870, when it severed its link with Rome, refusing to recognise Papal infallibility. In Australia since 1916, its clergy serve in an honorary capacity and, receiving no stipend, must earn their living outside the church.

Bahais, proclaiming the brotherhood of all people in their syncretistic system of faith, established themselves in Australia in 1920. Their nine-sided domed temple on the outskirts of Sydney is one of the only five shrines in the world outside Haifa in Israel.

A strong migration from many Arab countries has established Islam. Moslems are about to build a mosque in Sydney, as their second Australian sanctuary, the first being in Canberra.

Mormon missionaries, always in twos and travelling the world at their own expense, have also reached Australia in recent times to teach their message.

Two Americans started the Hare Krishna Cult in Australia, at Kings Cross in Sydney, in 1970. Its yellow-robed, shaven-headed followers, as elsewhere, roam the cities or stand on street corners. With odd chants, cymbals and drums, they add their own colour and sound to city life. Few people, however, know or ever care to find out, what it is all about. They are not aware of the devotees' totally dedicated life which demands the sharing of everything (with no private possessions), complete abstention from alcohol, coffee and tea, and the restriction of sex to marriage, and then only for the purpose of procreation.

Scientologists, on the other hand, would probably have gone on unnoticed had their group not been declared illegal as inimical to society. However, again legalised since 1973, they are now recognised as constituting a 'proper' religious denomination with authorised marriage celebrants.

Jehovah's Witnesses, Pentecostalists, the Radio Church of Christ, Christian Scientists, Seventh Day Adventists and since 1850 at least, the Unitarian Church, all have a place in Australian religion, battling for minds and souls.

RELIGION IN ACTION

Never interested in the speculative, Australians were, and are, concerned with the practical aspect of religion alone. However, its social task has been greatly restricted by the modern welfare State. Many of the former vital functions of the church have now been appropriated by the government. On the other hand, the impersonality of bureaucracies gave religion a new and important meaning. Well aware of the opportunity, imaginative and enterprising ministers discovered a new lease of life for an otherwise dying faith. If they did not actually invent them, they ingeniously applied innovations from overseas and adapted them to the Australian scene.

The Lifeline

Today the Lifeline has become not only an accepted Australian institution but has been adopted, though sometimes under different names, in many parts of the world. It all began in the mind of one man.

In 1958 the Reverend Alan Walker of the Central Methodist Mission, Sydney, was well-known through radio and television programmes. Countless men and women in distress thought of him first, and his telephone rang day and night. It became impossible to be on call for 24 hours each day, yet to have a silent number in these circumstances was out of the question.

One of the calls Mr Walker received, on a Saturday night, came from a man who identified himself as Roy, who said he was going to take his life. In fact, he had written Mr Walker a letter, and by the time it reached him Roy would be dead. Alan pleaded with him. If only they could meet face to face he might still change his mind. Eventually the man seemed to give in. They made an appointment. But before the time came the police found the body of a man, identified as Roy Brown. A letter attached to his chest was addressed to the Reverend . . .

The experience prompted Mr Walker to start the project. Aware of a similar effort made in England by the 'Samaritans', he convened a meeting of 30 members of his congregation. On explaining to them his plan to save by telephone people from despair and death, a committee was formed and after three years of deliberations Lifeline was established in 1963. It was to be served by voluntary, but thoroughly trained, Christian men and women. It assured everyone, of whichever denomination (or none), that help was as close as the nearest telephone at any time.

Within the first 10 years of its existence, Lifeline received 157,000 calls. Other Australian capitals took up Mr Walker's venture. International *Time Magazine* gave it world renown and from Australia the idea spread first to New Zealand, and then to more than 60 cities in the United States, Latin America and South East Asia.

In 1966 Lifeline became an officially recognised international institution, and by 1972 the calls for help exceeded one million.

The Wayside Chapel

The Wayside Chapel began in a dilapidated four room house in one of the side lanes of Sydney's Kings Cross red light area. Ted Noffs, nominally a Methodist clergyman, had totally rejected what he regarded as antiquated and valueless ritual. He refused to abide by the parochialism of an institutionalised faith in the face of humanity's life and death struggle..

'Let us not talk but act,' Noffs said. People were right to despise meaningless 'verbal Christianity'. They longed for basic, unembellished truth.

Noffs embarked on his ambitious project, the Wayside Chapel, which was to be a vital and dynamic centre of religion, but with a difference. The building was comparatively tiny, but its smallness, far from being a disadvantage, bestows a special intimacy. In this 'church' a minister can never 'preach' or talk 'at' people. He must speak 'with' them and is closely involved with each and everyone.

But the very pivot of the Wayside 'Chapel' became its round-the-clock coffee house. It welcomes anyone who, in the solitude of modern life, is yearning for company; who, in the perplexity of present-day problems, is anxious to meet someone to talk to.

The Wayside Chapel became a crises centre and a 'watchtower' for the many, and ever-changing, social issues that confused the community. Certainly, it did not cater for orthodox religion. Experimental in kind, it tried to act as a catalyst to every problem of the moment, to the deepest need of the hour. No social issue was ignored as too dangerous or too political. The Wayside Chapel led the first anti-Apartheid action. It was the first to protest against the French nuclear tests in the Pacific when the rest of Australia still showed no concern. **193**

The Wayside Chapel, among the first to take up the question of Aboriginal rights, was responsible for the establishment of the Foundation for Aboriginal Affairs. Paradoxically, it was this Methodist minister who demanded that the New South Wales government abolish the law which banned the black race from drinking in hotels. Aware of the attitude of his Church towards drink, Noffs took the action for the sake of attaining absolutely equal rights for the Aborigines. Similarly, the Chapel initiated a systematic fight against drug abuse leading, in May 1967, to the creation of Australia's first Drug Referral Centre. And the Chapel is certainly youth oriented. It inaugurated the world's first employment bureau for long-haired youths!

Noffs felt that in crisis situations it was not enough to give advice over the telephone or on the air. A person to person encounter, an eyeball to eyeball confrontation, was essential.

The Wayside Chapel has no members in the traditional sense. Its funds come from outside supporters. Within the first four years of its existence, one million people passed through its ever-open doors. Ten thousand couples were married at the Chapel during the first 10 years. Children are not baptised there or christened but 'named'. Debates and discussions are held regularly in the Wayside theatre. Only a dialogue between people, Noffs is convinced, will elicit truth. No opinion is barred, no speaker excluded.

Many people continue to frown on the work and worship practised in the small Wayside Chapel at the Cross. But it might well prove a pathfinder in modern faith. By its very nature, the Chapel does not claim to have all the answers. However, as Noffs explains, it is merely 'experimental religion', a first rung of the ladder.

Opposite: Roman Catholic congregations, alone among the major Christian churches, have benefitted from the massive influx of southern European migrants.

THE ENVIRONMENT

Peter Cowan

'If conservation were a public company, its growth would have made it the glamour stock of the last decade . . .'

For as long as there is an island mass known as Australia there must, inevitably, be an Australian environment: in a broad sense, the enclosing sky and the surrounding sea; in a finer sense, the land itself which we inhabit—desert and creek, forest and pasture, mountain and plain—and which we share with many unique species of flora and fauna; and in a still narrower sense, assuming humanity avoids the holocaust, the hamlets, villages, towns and cities.

There will always be some kind of Australian environment. The question, of course, is whether it will always be the kind of environment we want (if, indeed, we really *know* what we want).

Does our environmental future hold promise of efficient pollution control, clean air to breathe, maintenance of the country's delicate ecological balance, survival of our wildlife, preservation of our often magnificent scenic beauty, retention of the visible signposts of our history? And with these as presumably desirable goals, has Australia got an 'environmental future'?

As the scent of the refinery wafts in on the southerly, with just that tang of leaded petrol from the crawling freeway, and the thunder of V-8 motors drowns out the Western on television, the short answer seems to be—no, it hasn't.

The conventional wisdom confidently predicts that the greatest challenge to Australia in the next decade, and even to the end of the century, will lie in maintaining the successful exploitation of the country's resources, a strong position in world markets, rising growth rates, and an increasing population.

But the *real* challenge may not lie in these things at all (at this stage of Australia's development they seem, for better or for worse, to be self-generating). What is likely to be far more difficult is to retain a country where there

Opposite: Although huge areas of Australia are arid, on a per capita basis it is the wettest country in the world. Much of the rain falls on the eastern slopes of the Atherton Tableland on the tropical Queensland coastal strip near Cairns, and nourishes such beauty spots as Ellinja Falls.

197

is some point in having them, to retain something of the individuality and difference that still remain after nearly two centuries of the fits and starts, the fears and euphoria, of economic advance.

'Retain' is something of a suspect word in a country so clearly oriented towards the future. It is overwhelmingly a country of city people. They are people a shade reluctant to part with legends of the Outback, with images of a simple manual labouring proletariat, with their dreams of the 90s; today they even dress occasionally in what passes for colonial gear. But they keep the dreams, and the gear, for the city pavements and the wine bars and the trendy taverns.

Eighty-five per cent of the present population find security in urban centres. There they are safe, it seems, from the strange wilderness beyond, from the great silence, from what is sometimes still called 'the real Australia'.

If home, for most Australians, is the sight of endlessly repetitive streets and buildings, the kilometres of freeways, the blocks of carparks, the noise of traffic, then perhaps any consideration of Australia's future environment should be limited to the cities; limited to the suburb, the car, the beach, those pre-requisites of the Australian dream. And if the dream, with such aspirations, were to see Sydney stretch from Wollongong to Newcastle, to see Perth stretch from Bunbury to Geraldton, would it really matter?

A visitor, taking a hard look at the urban tide engulfing segments of the coastal plains, might well imagine that this is what Australians want, that this is what they might attain, that this is where the future lies.

Should our visitor push inland, seeking the mythical 'real Australia', that first, coastal impression might well be strengthened by the sight of a landscape scarred by a series of rural expansions and retreats: the treeless hectares of the wheatbelt, the sparse shade of dairy and cattle country, the often despoiled tracts of pastoral leases. It is a landscape often seen on calendars of the more respectable kind, often beautiful in its way—but as controlled, and essentially as artificial, as any city landscape.

And so the visitor in search of the 'real' landscape would have to go beyond this again, out to where the air-conditioned buses and the four-wheel-drive safaris ply, ending up perhaps at Ayers Rock only to find that others on a similar quest had already filled the night's tourist quota for the camping area.

Every accessible corner of Australia bears, in some measure, the stamp of people. Sometimes it is no more than a smudgy fingerprint—a solitary ring-barked tree, a beer can in the wilderness, the charred remains of a campfire or a burnt out post-and-rail fence; at other times, it is eight fingers, two thumbs

The Hagboom Brothers—lovers of wildlife

Dowerin was an early settled area of the Western Australian wheatbelt. To pass through it is to see land extensively cleared for wheat and sheep, and it is hard to imagine what the country looked like even 50 years ago.

Bill Hagboom's family had been in the district a long time, and when he and his brothers, George and Eddie, took up land in 1939 their properties were among the last selected in the area. They followed the pattern of extensive clearing, but some of the lighter sandy soil was subject to erosion and they decided to let this regrow.

It was an area of york gum and mallee, with jams, banksias, ti-tree and wild pear; varied and beautiful sandplain plants had grown all over the light soil country. As this vegetation regenerated and began to reclaim an area of about 200 hectares (some

of which still had natural bush on it), the Hagbooms saw possibilities for encouraging animal and bird life.

Animals that had become rare in such a settled district began to reappear. The kangaroos were the most obvious (as many as 50 or 60 grazed in the area), there were signs of the almost forgotten echidna, and the lizards (once a feature of sandplain areas) were returning. A lake began to form, and became a centre for a wealth of bird life. Parrots, crows, magpies, hawks, wrens, rainbow birds and swallows could be seen about the bush land and water; swans, mountain duck, teal, wood duck, water hens, dabchicks, stilts and dotterels were seen on the lake; even cormorants and seagulls have occasionally appeared. With the rapid reclamation of so much swamp and wetland in the coastal plain area of the

State, lakes such as this provide refuges for a wide range of bird life—refuges that are likely to become essential if some species of waterfowl are to survive.

The Hagbooms had the area declared a fauna sanctuary. The kangaroos who have adopted it do not damage their crops; they merely eat pasture, which the Hagbooms do not begrudge them. Some of the area extends into adjoining farms, and neighbours such as the McMorran brothers and K. T. Maisey and Sons also encourage areas of natural land which become wildlife reserves.

The work and foresight of Bill Hagboom, his brothers and their neighbours have brought back something of the interest and beauty of the natural countryside to these areas, something to be enjoyed not only by themselves but by many others.

and the palm prints as well—urban smog, open-cut mines, power-line pylons striding across the land.

Where, then, is the 'real' Australia? Our visitor might conclude, as many Australians have done, that it is where one looks for and finds something of absorbing or special interest: the surfing beach, the city freeway, the red sand-hills of the desert country. But the conclusion might also suggest that *all* of Australia is where the real Australia can be found—and if this is so, *all* of it must be the concern of those who are concerned about our future environment: the city lovers, the country lovers, and those who respond equally to both.

It is seldom like that, of course. The person who would defiantly face a bull-dozer moving in to wreck an old city building might barely notice the over-night clearing of a thousand hectare paddock of marginal land. The person who tries to defend an untouched beach against the ravages of rutile mining might simply pass by the shire bulldozer at work on the verges of the road. We see what we want to see, and our vision is limited.

In theory, even the environmental problems of rapid urban expansion should not be too difficult to solve. Cities no longer just grow (says the theory), they are planned; there is no dearth of planners; and it would be pleasant to imagine that modern planning could produce places free from traffic congestion, polluted air and water, noise, unsuitable buildings. But in practice modern planning has produced the freeways ringing our major cities, the highways choked with traffic, the buildings that turn city streets into sunless wind tunnels.

MORE CO-ORDINATED PLANNING NEEDED

The problems are evident. Not the least of them has been the fragmentary, unrelated consideration given to the many factors involved in industrial and urban expansion. In the last two decades it has been admitted that this kind of piecemeal expansion should be replaced by co-ordinated planning concerned with the environment. State and federal governments began to develop ministries of conservation and environment. This may have seemed like a classical red-tape approach—laying plans for planners—but at times the pressure for this kind of legislation came directly from openly expressed public concern, from street marches and protests; people were demanding something better than short-term goals in the expansion of industry, housing and recreation; they were questioning the wisdom of indiscriminate exploitation of apparently 'limitless' resources. There was growing concern not simply for isolated pockets of the 'real Australia', as identified by individuals, but for the whole Australian environment.

Legislation for environmental planning varied from State to State. And although environmental authorities made reports, there were obvious doubts about their value: the reports were purely *advisory*, and the cynics wondered about the effectiveness of government departments reporting on government projects to other government departments.

The power of the Commonwealth Ministry of Environment and Conservation lay only in areas of Commonwealth control, and there were few enough of these. Where its actions in any way coerced the States they could be bitterly resisted. Some States and local government authorities approached hysteria over the federal Ministry's decision to ban the sale overseas of kangaroo products in the interests of conservation and of Australia's image abroad; loss of revenue and the apparent infringement of State powers were among the arguments against the ban.

Confusion over aims, powers and goodwill seems to be built into the whole matter of Australian conservation. In the cities the trend towards the new, towards the future, suggested that there was very little to retain and everything to achieve. The need to 'advance' over-rode most other concerns—concern for human scale, for intimacy and variety, for relics of the past; these became victims of the trend towards size, uniformity, impersonality. But as the dead air, noise, crowded streets and repetitive buildings spread across once quiet timbered hillsides and over scrub covered dunes along the beachfronts, a counter-current developed. Older urban areas listed for destruction became **199** valued because they were old, different, individual—links with a past that could no longer simply be evaded. All the capital cities discovered their own examples of areas that had survived to see fashion turn in their favour.

A delayed appreciation of older building styles was one thing. Power to retain examples was another. The National Trust had in its care buildings acquired through purchase (rarely enough) or gift, and ranging from old farm houses to Georgian mansions. But in the property boom of the 60s older city buildings fared badly, victims of the value of their sites. The Trust, with authority to classify buildings worth preserving, could only parallel the environmental protection authorities in the pointlessness of recommendation without power. Legislative power to protect buildings and whole city areas of historic or architectural interest would require some federal and State co-operation, and that had not been particularly noticeable.

Ironically, the most effective expressions of public demand and public frustration have been offered by those called on to do the actual wrecking: the workmen on the sites, and their unions. Sydney and Perth have seen union black bans on city buildings listed for demolition. Melbourne saw the ban on the gas pipeline under Port Phillip Bay. Such bans rarely, in the long run, save a building or site, but they help support the growing number of conservation groups who believe that an advisory role is a waste of time. Public concern for the future of the cities and their urban areas is now obvious, and growing.

The landscape beyond the cities has seen an immense ebb and flow of humanity. In 1933, 35 per cent of Australia's population tolerated rural residence; in 1947, the figure was still high at 31 per cent; but by the beginning of the 70s it had shrunk to only 14 per cent; even allowing for the vagaries of statistical methods, it is obvious that a lot of people lost interest in the rural areas. If the millions of hectares of farming and grazing country now seem remote to city dwellers, their distaste may be reasonable enough. Clearing has been ruthless, often total. It has been determined by short-term convenience, by the development of large-scale machinery operations—and perhaps even by a kind of distrust, an emotional fear, of the once surpassingly beautiful natural vegetation. The effects on rainfall and soil salinity are still being determined, but if one effect turns out to be the loss of city water supplies the irony is unlikely to be appreciated.

SOME MISTAKES ARE SELF-PERPETUATING

Again, as with the cities, it would be pleasant to think that all the mistakes had been made, that somehow they had been due to a lack of ecological knowledge back in the bad old days. Yet, just as city planning mistakes often seem to be self-perpetuating, so water catchment areas are still threatened by adjacent farm clearing, by mining, and by every rise in the price of wheat which leads within months to the clearing of new land. Thousands of hectares of marginal land, with low rainfall and low soil fertility, are being ruthlessly cleared as if the frontier were endless. Nothing seems to have been learned.

On existing farms, what little tree cover remains may be cleared (even from hillsides) simply because such clearing is an allowable tax deduction. Small wonder that the city dweller has a distaste for all but inter-city highways; small wonder that the traveller asks if there is anything left to conserve.

But something could still be reclaimed from this increasingly featureless and often increasingly sterile area of over-clearing and over-grazing that takes in most of the inhabited land beyond the cities. It has been suggested that all farms should retain 10 per cent of their natural cover in the interests of rainfall and soil fertility, of birds and native animals. Many travellers, most naturalists and all soil scientists would agree. But to most farmers and agricultural protection boards, to bushfire boards and shire councils, native fauna is vermin, native plants are a fire hazard, and it's posterity's job to worry about rainfall.

Once again, a confusion of aims and practice. Conservation groups would suggest legislation to force the retention of some natural cover, but no State government is likely to hang on that rope. Replanting is possible, and some farms have planted wind and sun breaks and have encouraged small areas of regrowth; on trial salt lands there have been experiments with regrowth patterns; and a few (very few) farmers have declared their properties fauna reserves.

It can also be strongly argued that Australia could now halt any further alienation of Crown lands. The exploitation of new land now means taking agriculturally marginal land or reserves. These marginal lands, mainly in the light rainfall mallee and sandplain areas, have their own beauty and interest, They hold plant species found nowhere else in the world, they are a refuge for rare marsupials and reptiles, and are themselves a factor in rainfall and erosion patterns. Some of these areas are still only partly classified botanically, and we are thus destroying plants we have never known and which we never will know. The clearing of this land can produce near-desert areas which, ironically, are invariably abandoned when the periodic decline of farm prices draws back the frontier. The light lands of NSW, South Australia and Western Australia suffer this treatment—but so too does what little remains of the Queensland rainforest.

It would be entirely possible for Australia to say it had cleared enough agricultural land, that it would conserve what was left, and farm what it had more efficiently. This is not a popular doctrine, and in those political areas where the frontier mentality lies entrenched it is anathema. But it is not a doctrine of whimsy and sentimentality: it can be justified on the grounds of the unique interest of these remaining areas, on their now limited extent, and on the economic grounds that the conservation of these lands may benefit everybody in terms of rainfall and soil retention.

Unfortunately, if all further expansion of farm and pastoral land was halted tomorrow, the threat to Crown land would not halt entirely.

The mineral boom of the 1950s and 1960s created a situation extraordinary not only on the stock exchanges but on the land as well. Mining exploration moved into areas forgotten or never travelled, and the small claim pegs with their fluttering ribbons of colour seemed to be everywhere. Mining suddenly became the great threat to the Australian environment. Yet the fact emerged that most mining caused less damage than farming. Much of the country had been mined before, and one could walk in apparently virgin bush only to find old mine shafts and dumps of the previous century. Vast areas of salmon gum, gimlet and mallee in the Kalgoorlie-Coolgardie region were felled more than 60 years ago for mines using up to 100 tonnes of timber a day for fuel. Today, thanks to regrowth, there are extensive stands of new trees virtually indistinguishable from the few remaining original stands of such timber. There are few areas of agricultural land that offer a parallel.

MINING IS NOT THE MAIN OFFENDER

Jack Mundey—the 'green ban' man

Jack Mundey has a deep concern for Australian cities, and part of that concern is for the older buildings that developers have so little regard for. His claim that the buildings of different eras should be preserved if the character and charm of Australian cities is not to be lost is shared by many in Australia today; so is his conviction that claims about the final purpose of a building being functional have become an excuse for uniformity.

Jack Mundey was secretary of the Builders Labourers Federation until his term ran out in 1973 and he returned to labouring. As secretary he organised support for the placing of 'green bans' on the destruction of historic buildings which were worth $3,000 million to building companies around Sydney.

His concern did not stop with Sydney. In Perth he addressed a public meeting called to protest the destruction of the Palace Hotel in St George's Terrace. He announced a union green ban on the old hotel, now one of the few remaining buildings of an earlier age in a street that has become a wind canyon of contemporary high rise office buildings. He announced, too, the decision of the Builders Labourers Federation at its national conference in Hobart in November 1973 to place an Australia-wide demolition ban on buildings classified 'A' by the National Trust.

Jack Mundey's conservation views alone might not have made him a controversial figure—they are becoming increasingly shared in the community—but translating those views into action certainly did so. He is outspoken on the subject of developers and their gospel of 'progress' and the links between government and developers, which he says can destroy cities, citing Sydney as a case.

His concern for the cities of Australia is not restricted to retaining their historic buildings; he is as opposed to the motor car in modern cities as to thoughtless development, and is a member of the Federal Government Cities Commission as well as a council member of the Australian Conservation Foundation.

Today's mining is as much above ground as below. Two types in particular, bauxite and mineral sands mining, can permanently change the face of the land. Both remove top soil and subsoil, and alter growth conditions for vegetation; when the areas are re-established (as the leases demand) the natural vegetation is rarely replaceable. Both are often carried out near population centres and thus may have a variety of consequences.

Bauxite mining in the Darling Range close to Perth was opposed on the grounds that it would destroy the limited areas of jarrah forest, change the visual nature of the landscape, destroy the flora and fauna dependent on the forest association, and affect the main water catchment areas of the city and coastal plain with a quite unknown effect on soil salinity. The mining leases were granted. Some of the original objections remain to be decided, but it is obvious that eventual re-establishment of the areas, even if carefully carried out, will not bear much resemblance to the original landscape.

Sand mining tends to destroy small regions of great beauty, displacing estuaries and beaches as well as limited areas of timber. Near the coast these are often places of great tourist and public interest, and the threatened areas range from Augusta to the Cooloola Sand Mass. Finding a compromise acceptable to the opposing commercial and conservation interests is more difficult than it is with bauxite mining: commercial and shire pride may be satisfied, but the nature of the re-establishment may be unacceptable with the unique quality of the locality gone, the ecology disturbed, and many people finding themselves inhabitants of a new world.

The general lease pegging of the 60s was often in areas remote from any human use and was often unlikely to go beyond the pegging stage, but its intrusion into reserves and parks focussed attention on the existing mining Acts—and on the diminishing natural areas of Australia. The threat to national parks had never been clearly stated before, the outright contradictions of Acts establishing parks and granting mining leases had never been obvious. It became clear that relatively little land was reserved as parks in the national interest, and that even these had no security. A declared reserve or an established national park could be pegged, and an application to mine could be granted at the discretion of a warden (following a hearing in a Warden's

John Iggulden—writer turned conservationist

John Iggulden had written four novels, *Breakthrough*, *The Storms of Summer*, *The Clouded Sky* and *Dark Stranger*, which had been published in England and America, and was slowly freeing himself from his family engineering business in Brighton, Victoria, so that he could devote his time to writing. He was working on a book of political philosophy, *The Modification of Freedom*, and on plans for a fifth novel when his concern for environmental issues began to slow his literary work.

His involvement started in 1969 with his concern for a piece of his local environment when he helped organise a successful protest against Mordialloc Council granting approval for a boat marina at Beaumaris. By 1970 he had become president of the Port Phillip Conservation Council, a coalition of 19 conservation groups concerned with a wide range of issues around the bay. All this was time-consuming, but the major issue was to come in 1972 with the Esso-BHP proposal to place an ethane gas pipeline in the bay.

The affair became a complex series of moves and countermoves, and grew to a dramatic confrontation when the laying of the pipeline began. Part of the beach at

Mordialloc was fenced off from public use. The police armed guards and dogs were used to keep people off the site; a local councillor was manhandled by guards; and John Iggulden, walking onto the beach to examine the work, had a cocked, loaded shotgun pointed at him.

The day after the shotgun episode John Iggulden asked councillor Charles Falkiner of Frankston, president of the Environment Action League, to join him in an inspection of the beach. They parked their cars in the public parking area and went to look at the beach. Police told them their cars were obstructing the path of the pipeline and would have to be moved. They refused, on the grounds that the cars were properly parked on the public area. Both men were booked for refusing to move their cars.

The following day there was a strong protest meeting at the site, and trade union support against the laying of the pipeline was announced. Here John Iggulden and four others were arrested on various charges, and some of the protesters were bodily removed from the area.

For John Iggulden and many others this was the area in which they lived, an area in which they believed they had normal

public rights. They found themselves forced off their own beaches and recreational places, and were subjected to threats, violence and arrest for protesting against the use of the bay for ethane gas and crude oil pipelines.

The obstructing and trespassing charge was heard in Mordialloc Court. Iggulden was found guilty and placed on a bond without a conviction being recorded. In a review of the decision sought by John Iggulden and Rodney Knowles, one of those arrested and charged with him, the Supreme Court of Victoria dismissed the convictions and upheld the right of the public to enjoy without restriction the use of land reserved by statute for the public.

They were vindicated. But it was not the end of a struggle which had revealed very grave issues. It put a stop to John Iggulden's literary work—temporarily, he hopes. 'In the beginning,' he says, 'I tried to avoid involvement, knowing what would happen. But I'm afraid I allowed myself to be overcome by a sense of moral outrage at what was going on all around. So it happened that three years of my life were involved in ways I had never intended.'

Court) or at times by the minister for lands or mines. The new confrontations sharpened public concern for the national parks cause.

For a country so generous in giving away its land to farmers and graziers—400,000 hectares a year was the boast in WA even as late as 1967—there might have seemed little difficulty in establishing large areas of national parks. But enough confusion arose to make the issue of parks and reserves obscure even now.

Serious consideration of reserves for anything other than agriculture or mining, and State legislative attempts to bring some order to the chaos, are recent. In 1970, the *National Parks and Wildlife Act* of Tasmania placed the control of parks and reserves, flora and fauna, under a single authority, the National Parks and Wildlife Service. The South Australian *National Parks and Wildlife Act* of 1972 repealed previous Acts to form a National Parks and Wildlife Service. The New South Wales *National Parks and Wildlife Act* (1967-69) set aside national parks, State parks, and historic sites reserved under earlier Acts. Victoria with the *National Parks Act* of 1958 set up a National Park Authority from earlier Acts. In Western Australia the *Parks and Reserves Act* (1895-1963) appointed a National Parks Board to control certain parks and reserves.

The growth of national parks has reflected growing public concern. Parks controlled by the National Parks Board in WA increased from 130,000 hectares in 1960 to 1.7 million hectares in 1973, a dramatic increase even allowing for any reclassification of reserves to Park Board control; NSW areas rose from 810,000 to 1.2 million hectares; SA from 1.2 million to 3.6 million hectares.

The increased classification of land as parks and reserves illustrates a change on the part of most State governments in their attitudes towards environmental conservation and also towards solving Australia's share of the world-wide problem of over-use and overcrowding of national parks. Large increases in visitors threaten to change the character of most parks near major cities, and even those as distant as Ayers Rock. The States are now trying, but for some of them further increases in park and reserve areas will be difficult because most other existing land has been sold or leased.

In the whole of Australia less than 2 per cent of the land area is set aside for parks and reserves—a telling figure when one realises that about 32 per cent of Australia is alienated Crown land (that is, land originally controlled by the Commonwealth or the States but now sold). The percentage of each State area devoted to national parks ranges from a low of 0.5 per cent in Queensland to a high of only 6 per cent in Tasmania. Many factors influence interpretations of such figures, including the type of land reserved and (perhaps as important as area) the security of the declared reserves.

NSW seems to offer the most protection for parks and reserves. Land within a park is exempt from occupation under the *Mining Act*, and an application for a lease or appropriation of land within a reserve must go before Parliament. But existing parks can be threatened, as shown by applications to mine limestone at Bungonia Gorge, near Marulan, where mining menaces a limestone gorge area of outstanding interest.

In Tasmania the Lake Pedder controversy became national, finally involving the Federal Government. Lake Pedder, though a central feature of a national park, is being flooded as part of a hydro-electricity scheme. No other single act within a national park or reserve has aroused so much controversy. Against all persuasion and argument the Tasmanian Government stood firm, finally rejecting the moratorium offer of the Federal Government to compensate Tasmania for losses it would incur through a reversal of its decision to proceed.

In the Northern Territory the newly formed Kakadu National Park faces possible exploitation because of uranium deposits within its boundaries. In WA, an application to mine within the new major national park at the Fitzgerald River was made but was later rejected.

The list could be extended, as could a list of areas proposed for inclusion in reserve schemes but which already have mining claims against them (including **203** the magnificent wilderness area of Precipitous Bluff in Tasmania). Security is plainly a continuing struggle until State governments accept the simple principle that declared national park areas cannot be subject to conflicting uses. Slowly, and with apparent reluctance, State parliaments are moving towards such legislation.

The problems don't go away at the water's edge. The beaches and the sea itself, such important features of the Australian way of life, have received little concern or interest. Industry is still being sited on the coast, raw sewage finds its way into the sea off Sydney beaches, industrial effluent is emitted from Botany Bay to Cockburn Sound; heavy population pressures have led to the continuing subdivision of scarce coastal land, and over-use of limited recreation areas is producing marine deserts along all the suburban coastlines; temperature changes, effluent and mineral dusts all affect marine growth and sea life; the colours of the weeds and reefs are changing, and the very clarity and beauty of the water are being dulled.

The Great Barrier Reef itself has been threatened by oil drilling and mining. It has achieved some security, late in the day, because of public protest, but on the other side of the continent coral from the north-west reefs is being taken for sale in the eastern States.

The idea of marine national parks is only now becoming any kind of reality, and while the whole business of State and Commonwealth sea-bed rights remains unresolved they may present as much confusion as national parks have on the land, though Queensland, with its wealth of coastal attractions, has passed legislation to provide for the reservation of selected areas as marine parks.

That all these issues involve public concern can be seen most clearly in the growth of conservation groups. Unheard of a few years ago, they have now mushroomed. Local groups have formed to protect a local area or dispute a local issue—the Yunderup Delta Society, the Yarra Valley Conservation League, Save Lake Pedder Committee, the Cooloola Committee—while on a national scale the largest organisation is the Australian Conservation Foundation.

Founded in 1965, the ACF began as an advisory body, promoting a wider understanding of conservation and with a wide range of activities. Any brief summary of the Foundation would be inadequate and unfair since it has done so much, but the inherent problems faced by an advisory, fact-finding organisation were highlighted by two issues. First, the Federal Government set up its own Ministry of Conservation with its own experts, and cut the federal grant to the ACF (which, happily, was restored almost at once). Second was the criticism within the Foundation of the role it played (or did not play) in the Lake Pedder dispute. Some members felt that the ACF was in danger of becoming a kind of semi-governmental institution, receiving funds from and offering advice to the Federal Government, and would therefore ultimately suffer from the fact that governments do not lack documentation and recommendations on projects, but frequently lack any intention of abiding by the proposals and recommendations. The Australian Conservation Foundation may now take a more active role in trying to get facts and points of view not only presented but accepted as well, just as the smaller societies have done.

Confusion and problems! In an economy dedicated to growth, to the expanding development of limited resources, neither the problems nor the confusion will disappear. Yet if conservation, if a real concern for the intelligent shaping of the environment, were a public company its growth would have made it the glamour stock of the last decade . . . which is an irony some elements of business may not appreciate. Yet there are fewer such elements, fewer newspapers and politicians branding the person with a serious concern for the environment as a lunatic or an invader from outer space. Nothing in the last decade has matched the growth of concern among people everywhere for an environmental future in which they have some voice, and the organisation of that concern to make it effective.

So . . . an environmental future for Australia? There has to be.

Opposite: Jutting from the coastal plain north of Brisbane is monolithic Mount Beerwah, one of a group of ancient volcanic plugs which form the Glasshouse Mountains.

204

The land's extremes of environment are dictated by variations in latitude and by the effects of its geophysical structure on the prevailing weather patterns. The fertile eastern slopes of the Atherton Tableland (*above*) draw the nation's highest rainfall from the moist south-east tradewinds; on the same latitude, and a thousand kilometres to the west, a cow and her calves (*right*) shelter from the 38°C heat on the Barkly stock route.

MICHAEL MORCOMBE

The lush tropical to temperate rainforests of the north-eastern seaboard are the habitat for hundreds of unique species of fauna.

Left: In the mountains of the Atherton Tableland the Green or Striped Ringtail Possum, *Pseudocheirus archeri*, is effectively camouflaged by its mottled greenish fur and two stripes down its back.

Above: Farther south, in the New England Ranges of NSW, mossy, fern-grown gullies attract bushwalkers and naturalists.

Following page, left: Less accessible areas of the Great Dividing Range are home to the Tiger Cat, *Dasyurops maculatus*, whose long claws and wide opening jaw are reminiscent of the extinct Tasmanian Tiger. The Tiger Cat is Australia's largest marsupial carnivore, measuring up to 1.5 metres in length, and is found only on the mainland.

Following page, right: The Fat-tailed Dunnart, *Sminthopsis crassicaudata*, is found in all mainland States; it feeds on grasshoppers, spiders and other small insects, and in lean times relies on food stored in its tail.

These three fauna studies were made with live animals in their natural habitat by Michael Morcombe, one of Australia's leading naturalists and wildlife photographers.

MICHAEL MORCOMBE

The kangaroo and the emu are supporters on the Australian coat-of-arms; toy koalas are souvenir-store favourites; and the 'roo and the bear are probably Australia's best known ambassadors.

Opposite: The koala is not in fact a bear but a marsupial, and the only living species of its genus. The fossil remains of the koala's ancestor, *Koalemus*, have been found—it was an animal similar in shape, living a million years ago on the Queensland coast, and weighing up to half a tonne.

Above, above left: The Great Grey or Forester Kangaroo, *Macropus giganteum*, is found in most parts of Australia. It is almost as big as the Great Red Kangaroo.

Left: Emancipation came to the female emu a long time ago—the male makes the nest and incubates the eggs for about two months. The brown and white striped chicks grow into Australia's largest birds, flightless, but with vestigial wings held close to the body.

GARY LEWIS

213

Right: The delicately hued Turquoise parrot, *Neophema pulchella*, lives in open timbered country on the New England tablelands, west of the Great Divide. It is uncommon outside of its limited nesting areas.

Opposite, top: The Spotted Cuscus, *Phalanger maculatus*, is characterised by handsome skewbald markings, hand-like hind feet and a scaly prehensile tail. This family ponders the evening programme amid a tangle of vine stems in a tropical rainforest in the far north of Queensland.

Far right, centre: The Pygopididae family of legless lizards exist only in Australia and New Guinea. They differ from snakes in having ear openings, wide fleshy tongues and, in some cases, vestigial legs. One of the most common species is Burton's Legless Lizard, *Lialis burtonis*. It is generally striped, the number and colouring of its stripes varies, and it grows to about 40 cm in length.

Far right, bottom: A Feathertail or Pygmy Glider, *Acrobates pygmaeus*, hunts for unplundered blooms among the sweet-nectared blossoms of an Erythrina tree in tropical Queensland.

Opposite, left: The ubiquitous Bungarra or Sand Goanna, *Varanus gouldii*, grows to more than a metre in length and can run at great speed on its hind legs. When cornered it assumes a ferocious pose, rearing back on its hind legs, ballooning its throat and hissing loudly.

214

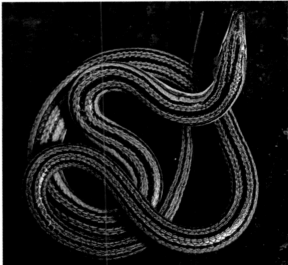

The continent's flora, like its fauna, include ancient relic species, some of great antiquity.

Above: The graceful palm *Livistona mariae* is only found beside permanent water holes in gorges (such as Palm Valley) near Alice Springs. More widespread, and far older, are members of the Cycad group which grow on the sides of the gorges. Cycads are direct descendants of fern-like palms which flourished 100 to 200 million years ago; one *Macrozamia* Cycad in Western Australia is believed to be 14,000 years old, which (if true) would make it the oldest living thing on earth.

Right: Flower heads of another primitive species, the silver-leaved grass tree, *Kingia australis*, found along the south coast of Western Australia.

Opposite: Oblivious to danger, a foraging ant wanders among the false blooms of the carnivorous Albany pitcher plant, *Cephalotus follicularis*. There are pitcher plants in north-eastern Australia and other parts of the world, but this species is found only in the Albany district of WA. Ants, flies, beetles and other insects are attracted by the nectar at the bottom of the plant's 'pitchers'; the covers close over the victims and the insects are absorbed into the plant as nutrients supplementing the normal root intake.

Much of Australia's coastline is beach, running in vast stretches of clean flat sand for up to 130 kilometres in such places as Eighty Mile Beach, between Port Hedland and Broome, WA. Roughly the same length is the sheer limestone cliff face that drops from the edge of the Nullarbor Plain into the Southern Ocean.

Above: White sand dunes and the grey-black weathered rock of Mount Barren, on the wild southern coastline of Western Australia.

Right: Two of the Twelve Apostles standing out to sea near Port Campbell, western Victoria. Millions of years of storm and weather erosion have carved a spectacular coastline from the hard, high sandstone cliffs.

PHOTOGRAPHS BY ALLAN POWER

The Great Barrier Reef runs 1,930 kilometres along the north-east coast. Its incomparable variety of marine life is rich and colourful.

Opposite, above: The delicately fleshed herbivorous Green Turtle, *Chelonia mydas*, was once harvested for its meat by canneries on several Barrier Reef islands. Now protected, its numbers are increasing, and it is again a common sight on summer nights to see the females plod ashore to lay their 50 to 200 eggs in the sand. Slow and clumsy on land, they are fast swimming reptiles, and even at a top weight of around 200 kilograms they move through the water with great speed and grace.

Opposite, bottom: The Harlequin Tuskfish, *Lienardella fasciatus*, is typical of many brilliantly coloured reef fish. Related to the parrot fish and wrasses, the tuskfish are generally pugnacious.

Above left: The long snout of the Raffles Butterfly fish, *Chaetodon rafflesi*, probes coral crevices from which its bristle-like teeth extract food particles. Rivalling butterflies in their brilliant colouring, these fish move easily through narrow coral cavities because of their deep, compressed body shape.

Bottom left: Moray eels, *Gymnothorax meleagris*, seldom leave their lairs during the day, preferring to wait in hiding for their prey. Growing up to four metres in length, and the thickness of a man's thigh, moray eels are naturally feared because of their sharp and dangerous teeth but they attack only if disturbed or frightened.

221

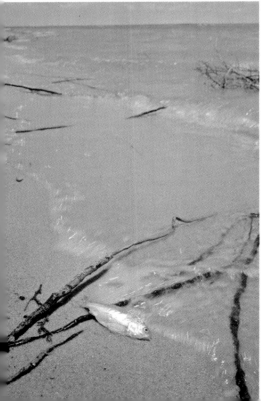

When rain comes to the dry Centre the Biblical promise of flowering deserts becomes a reality. The cumulative effect of widespread rains in 1973 and again in 1974 was the filling of both arms of Lake Eyre for only the second time since the normally dry lake bed was discovered in 1840.

Above left: Migratory waterbirds, like these waders, crowded the margins of the lake within weeks of the filling, and squadrons of pelicans cruised offshore.

Above: In a reproductive explosion, insects and their predators jostled for food and living space around Lake Eyre. Spiders shrouded the full length of the leeward shore of the main, or north, lake with a continuous sheet of web that trapped clouds of insects blown across the water by the prevailing wind.

Far left: Wildflowers along the border of the southern lake.

Left: In 1964 the late Donald Campbell set a world land speed record on the flat salt surface of the dry lake. The salt bed was 40 cm thick. Ten years later the main lake miraculously teemed with fish, and tasted slightly less saline than seawater, but within weeks of the flood peak the process was reversing—as the water evaporated and salinity increased the beaches were littered with dead fish.

Water—too much, or not enough —has been a preoccupation since man first set foot in Australia. The flatness of the land and the vastness of the ancient drainage systems are insuperable obstacles to the complete control of extremes of flood and drought.

Below: Rain is so uncertain in some areas that a drought is not said to have begun until there has been no rain for several years.

Bottom: A river gum, carried down by the last rains, hangs

from the huge causeway across the Burdekin River near Charters Towers, Queensland.

Right: A few kilometres from the edge of the Sturt Desert the Bulloo River fans out over a floodplain. The plain is normally semi-desert, and is useless as pasture in poorer years.

Below, opposite: Rich topsoil from the fertile Namoi valley washes away through the cotton town of Wee Waa, north-west NSW, during the summer floods of 1974.

Most country towns are inured to extremes. The hardships imposed are borne with patience, a wry humour and the old 'battler' spirit of mateship.

Opposite: A Wee Waa family, study the flood level for signs of change.

Above: Wee Waa cemetery under water.

Left: Some houses, built well above the ground, stayed dry. This Wee Waa couple and their friends wade to a tractor waiting to take them to the bowling club for an evening's entertainment.

Even more important than flood mitigation is the constant need to find and conserve water.

Opposite, above: Sub-artesian water brought to the surface by windmills has turned vast areas of otherwise waterless scrubland into viable pasture. Artesian reservoirs are another source of water, the largest being the immense anticlinal basin lying beneath most of Queensland west of the Great Divide; artesian water, when tapped by wells or bores, rises spontaneously to the surface.

Opposite, below: This rockhole in the Daly Waters area of the Northern Territory holds the only permanent surface water to be found for 170 kilometres in any direction. Local Aboriginal tribes have raised water here for hundreds and perhaps thousands of years—the deep grooves opposite the ladder have been carved into the rock by the continual friction of human-hair ropes to which hollow-log buckets were attached.

Above: Not a near-empty dam in a bad season, but an example of realistic water conservation. The principle is simple: run-off is modified and retarded by a long, shallow diversion channel which permits maximum water absorption by the surrounding land. It is a departure from the traditional use of storage dams, but Charlie Phillott of Carisbrooke station near Winton, central Queensland, is satisfied with the result.

In many areas where man has tamed—or raped—the natural environment, the major problems are not those of flood, drought or fire.

Opposite: Obsolescence and disposability, built-in sales appeals for many products, are creating a new Frankenstein's monster in the form of waste materials. This automotive graveyard is in a small country town in the far north of Queensland.

Left: A polluted sunset over an industrial complex at Whyalla, SA.

Bottom left: A strip of commercial jungle in Parramatta, NSW—though it could be any major Australian city.

Below: The Brisbane River at the heart of Queensland's capital city.

Above: The infamous 'lunar land-scape' at Mount Lyell, on the west coast of Tasmania. In 1881 gold was first mined here and Queenstown (left background) was established. The smelting of copper-bearing ore began in 1897, and heralded the most devastating pollution ever seen in Australia. Sulphurous fumes from the smelting plant killed off thousands of hectares of natural forest; heavy rainfall eroded the denuded slopes. The smelting plant has been closed—open-cut mining continues—but not a blade of green-ery has appeared. In Queenstown itself, some regeneration has been coaxed from the devastated land.

Opposite, top: Under the shadow of a chimney stack and a tailings dump a Queenstown resident spruces up his house.

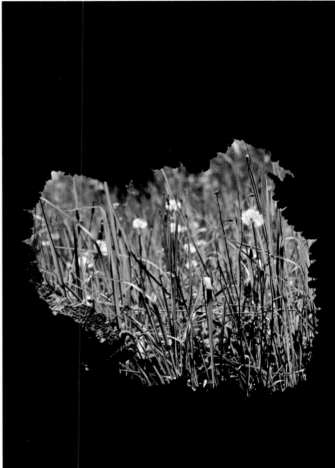

233

Above: Ayers Rock, after the exceptional rains of 1973-74, seems to float above the 'inland sea' sought in vain by the explorer Charles Sturt in 1844. Rising 335 metres above the plains west-south-west of Alice Springs, the world's largest monolith is the symbol of the 'Dead Heart' for white Australians—and for the black, the symbol of life.

Right: Farther west of Ayers Rock are the Olgas, a group of monoliths on the edge of an almost waterless desert extending 1,500 km from the southern Northern Territory across central Western Australia. The haze rose after a day of torrential summer rain.

THE ARTS

Martin Johnston

'An imitation Namatjira on the wall and half a dozen half-remembered stanzas about cattle and stockmen . . .'

The arts in Australia are in a very special position at the moment, a position from which they may possibly make dramatic advances, or from which they may follow the fate of earlier apparent Great Leaps Forward.

Some things, though, seem to have definitely changed. A number of factors that conditioned our cultural development from the very beginning do not operate any longer, or operate only in a remote and attenuated way. Others, to which we are unaccustomed, have quite suddenly become relevant.

An example: for a very long time, and for obvious reasons, the paramount factors in our history, including the cultural, were isolation and the hardships of building a country from scratch, a situation in which the artistic attitude is seen as irrelevant.

But Australia retained this attitude, by and large, well into this century, when it was no longer justified by the facts: hence, partly, a peculiar wave of expatriation by talented but frustrated Australians.

In very recent times, on the other hand, the extreme proximity of overseas cultural centres, rather than Australia's isolation from them, has become important; Australians no longer have excuses for cultural lag.

Three relatively recent events may serve to suggest 'where we are now'. These are: Patrick White's 1973 Nobel Prize for Literature; the opening, at

Opposite: Curiously, in view of the often dramatically carved quality of its landscape, Australia has elicited little response from would-be sculptors (though painters have captured its mood and form in every imaginable style). But there are signs of change. This environmental sculpture in stainless steel, the work of Adelaide artist Max Lyle, is among the major pieces on permanent display at the Adelaide Festival centre.

237

last, of Sydney's Opera House; the National Gallery's purchase of Jackson Pollock's *Blue Poles*. Most of what can usefully be said about contemporary Australian culture can be extrapolated from these 'symbolic' events and their antecedents and repercussions.

Patrick White, then. There seems little doubt that, though we have had a fair number of good writers (in the circumstances), Patrick White is Australia's first great one.

His Nobel was not only a notably well-deserved one in itself, but belated compensation for a career which seems to epitomise nearly all the qualities of Australian society, of the Australian character, that have driven such hordes of local artists to seek refuge in Stephen Dedalus's 'silence, exile and cunning'.

Again, one need not recapitulate too much. The legend of his early universal savaging by the critics *is* at least in some measure a legend. He received some good reviews, though more bad. But the interesting thing is that almost none of the hostility was directed against him as a *writer*: it was against him as someone who had impugned 'Australian values', sent up Australian verbal and social mannerisms and suburban mores, exploded the sunburnt country mythology in which the drabness of middle class life is somehow supposed to be validated by an imitation Namatjira on the wall and half a dozen half-remembered stanzas about cattle and stockmen. The review that hurt most may have been A. D. Hope's notorious 'pretentious and illiterate verbal sludge' attack, but the important ones, retrospectively, were those by people who knew nothing about the craft of writing but did realise that *Voss*, *The Tree of Man*, *Riders in the Chariot*, were dangerous. They showed too clear an ear and eye.

Anyway, White became Australia's most illustrious expatriate, perhaps, from an illustrious field. His 1958 account of Australia, published in the magazine *Australian Letters*, eloquently suggests why:

'In all directions stretched the Great Australian Emptiness, in which the mind is the least of possessions, in which the rich man is the important man, in which the schoolmaster and the journalist rule what intellectual roost there is, in which beautiful youths and girls stare at life through blind blue eyes . . . and the march of material ugliness does not raise a quiver from the average nerves . . .'

And this was written after he had returned.

Expatriation is one problem, one aspect of the Australian artist's life, that may not be unique. The great migration of American artists to Paris and London between the wars was rather differently motivated: they went more because of the excellence and excitement they anticipated when once they had reached Europe than because of the hopelessness of home, though certainly that was a factor. The Australian expatriates, in every field, from Peter Finch to Charles Mackerras to Joan Sutherland to George Johnston to Sidney Nolan to —you name them!—they went because they believed there was nothing for them in Australia and almost regardless of what they would find 'there'.

Were they right? And have things changed?

That they were mostly right at the time seems unquestionable. Quite apart from the difficulty of surviving financially, the cultural atmosphere of Australia was still pretty much the same as that exemplified in the lines, from C. J. Dennis's archetypal paean to Australian egalitarianism, mateship, etc., *The Sentimental Bloke*:

'Doreen she says he's got a poet's eyes,
But I ain't got no use for those soft guys.
I think we oughter make 'im sumpthin' great—
A bookie or a champeen 'eavyweight.'

Some cases in point from the 40s. In 1943 William Dobell won the Archibald Prize for portraiture—with a portrait, in what anywhere else in the world would have been regarded as a mildly retrospective style suggestive of Soutine, of fellow-painter Joshua Smith. He was forthwith subjected to a ridiculous trial, in which two minor artists sued the award's judges on the grounds that the picture was not a portrait at all but a caricature. *The Bulletin*, typically, apos-

trophised Archibald's shade, saying it had been 'besmirched'. General brouhaha was stirred up. The judges won the case, but Dobell himself, mocked by larrikins and gutter press alike, was forced to retire from public life—and, as it turned out, from adventurous or contentious paintings.

A trial even more after the style of Lewis Carroll was that of Max Harris the following year. Harris, then editor of *Angry Penguins*, a Melbourne avantgarde magazine, had printed a series of poems purporting to be by one Ern Malley but which turned out to have been concocted for Harris's confusion by James McAuley and Harold Stewart, poets of a somewhat more classical temper. This was bad enough, since it exposed poetry in general to even more contempt and mirth than it already had to put up with, and made anything 'modern' even harder to get across. The climax came when Harris was sued for having published 'indecent advertisements'—to wit, the Malley poems. Harris assembled the battery of experts customary for the defence in such cases (*Lady Chatterley*, London *Oz*, *Last Exit to Brooklyn* and the like); the sole prosecution witness was a policeman who admitted not understanding the poems, but felt that 'something was going on' in them. Harris lost.

Taken in conjunction with Patrick White's general statement on the Australian malaise, these events do suggest that for many artists there was no other way of getting the job done, of establishing a context in which they could work, than expatriation. Some, it's true—such as Russell Drysdale in the 30s—went overseas primarily to study; others have never returned to this day, or evinced the slightest desire to. The poet Peter Porter came out for the last Adelaide Festival after many years of exile, read his poems, wrote an article which seemed to indicate that he was quite impressed by the changes that had taken place, and went straight back to England. Art critic and semi-professional *enfant terrible* Robert Hughes has done much the same. And so on, and so on.

What is there for them to return to?

The question is not a rhetorical one, because at least on the face of it there have been dramatic changes in the last few years.

IS IT REALLY AN OPERA HOUSE?

The Opera House, for instance. It finally opened in 1973, with the Queen, much splendour and fireworks, and an ornate production of *War and Peace*—and, an absolutely apposite touch of the preposterous, an Aborigine done up as Bennelong declaiming from the topmost sail.

Indeed, if ever the sublime and the ridiculous came together in the history of a single enterprise, is was in that of Sydney's magnificent new landmark. The story would take up—indeed has taken up—whole books; but some points might be noted here. Joern Utzon's design, which won the 1957 competition, was a masterpiece: a composition of outward-sweeping curves that seemed itself to move almost across the borderline of architecture and into music. As it stands now, superb though it still is, the curves are blunter, the whole effect squatter. The reason is, of course, the long history of sordid squabbles which resulted in the State government taking over, Utzon returning to Denmark, and the project being finished by local architects.

Then there was the question of costs, the spirals of which, traced out, might well show the same elegance as the arcs of the building itself, although of rather more angular momentum. Fortunately, and in typically Australian fashion, it was financed by a public lottery, a lottery still in operation. How many people, one wonders, buying their weekly ticket, had any clear conception of where the money was going?

And then, when the Opera House was finished, it turned out that it wasn't really going to be an Opera House at all. Opera was relegated to the second hall (which hadn't an orchestra pit large enough for a full-scale orchestra, and looked incapable generally of dealing with the large and ornate productions that so many people seem only to go to the opera for). The bars and restaurants and, indeed, most of the appointments throughout the building came in for all manner of criticism. John Coburn's great *Curtains of the Sun and Moon* were hardly ever hung; a lot of public opinion didn't know what to make of

John Olsen's *Homage to Five Bells*, the central artwork; and for the final touch of the utterly bizarre, the brilliant expatriate pianist Roger Woodward, upon returning for a series of concerts, discovered that the management wouldn't allow him to use the resident grand piano, on the grounds that the type of modern music he sometimes played would damage or destroy it. It's gratifying, if additionally absurd, to note that upon Woodward's return a year later his touch had apparently lightened to such an extent that not the slightest suggestion was made of quarantining the instrument.

It is not the English who muddle through; it is us. And at the time of writing, after all these years of bungling and trying to make do and tragicomic crises, the Opera House seems to be serving its purpose well. It may, indeed, not be an Opera House at all; but that is surely all to the good? Chamber music, rock and roll, films, lectures, art exhibitions, Sunday pops for 'the mums and dads': something that's supposed to be the cultural centre for a city like Sydney can hardly afford *not* to accommodate as much diversity as possible, rather than restricting itself to befurbeloved first-nighters. The same, incidentally, would seem to be true of the new performing arts complex in Adelaide, which cost a good deal less money and took a good deal less time to build, and, though unostentatious, looks to be a singularly harmonious piece of architecture and landscape blending. Adelaide has long needed an adequate setting for what shows signs of becoming a really major Festival of Arts; it would appear that it now has it. Similar developments, again, have been occurring in Perth and Melbourne. Victoria's Arts Centre, in particular, growing out from its superb bluestone National Gallery, is developing into something to challenge the Opera House itself, despite being less picturesque.

That the Sydney Opera House, despite its unexpectedly populist character, should be mainly known to the majority of Australians (as it surely is) firstly as a name which prefixes lists of lottery results, and secondly as something that nicely sets off the Harbour Bridge on postcards, need not surprise anyone: that, largely, is how it has been presented. And in a country whose population, although no longer consisting entirely of pioneers and diggers, tends to be hostile or, much more commonly, simply indifferent to the arts (at least, of the 'high art' variety) it is hard to see how else it could have been. And, although they may not have thronged to the outstanding Australian Opera production of Janacek's *Janufa*, the people of Sydney know that Joan Sutherland returned and sang there—which is something.

The Opera House, although certainly a symbol, is equally surely becoming something more than a symbol—which is mildly surprising and tremendously encouraging. And perhaps one day the sandwiches will improve and the beer get cheaper. Meanwhile, people like Bernstein and the New York Philharmonic seem happy enough with it.

We must, at this point, return to money: because it is in financial terms that the current Australian experiment in the arts has been conceived, and a great deal depends on whether the gamble will come off.

Patronage of artists is probably as old as art itself: one imagines that the Neolithic painters who could best imbue their bison and reindeer with the sympathetic magic that would ensure catching them were spurred on by the promise of extra marrowbones, a spot nearer the fire, exemption from the actual hunting.

And it has always been contentious. 'Is not a Patron,' thundered Dr Johnson, 'one who looks with unconcern on a man struggling for life in the water, and, when he has reached ground, encumbers him with help?' And I well remember being warned by the poet and painter Jurgis Janavicius, when the current munificent system of Arts Council grants was instituted, that artists were liable to become, here as in communist countries, vassals of the State, subject to thought control and even intimidation.

It is too early, of course, to know whether this has happened: though if it does it will only be reminiscent of the good old days when novelist Frank Hardy, author of the once sensational *Power Without Glory*, was vetoed for a grant

Following page: The sculptural purity of the roof shells of the Sydney Opera House has won world wide acclaim, despite considerable modification of Joern Utzon's original prize-winning design.

because he was a member of the Communist Party. In those days awards were, in fact, overtly subject to political scrutiny.

Still, there was a little patronage, here and there. A handful of writers, producers, musicians were able to get on with it for a year or so; and the big theatre and opera companies were attended to, from 1954, by the Elizabethan Trust. There were isolated institutions like the Australian National University's annual fellowship for a creative artist—the sort of thing, of course, that has existed since time immemorial in almost every American university or college. There was the odd handout from industry: a painter or sculptor here and there would be commissioned to jazz up some new 30-storey monstrosity; a film-maker would be paid, handsomely enough, to celebrate some other company's depredations.

The Australian Council for the Arts was founded in 1968, the initial idea being partly that the job of patronage was getting too big and too complex for the Elizabethan Trust, which was in any case concerned strictly with the performing arts. The impetus came in large measure from the 1951 Massey Commission on the arts in Canada, which had resulted in lavish government patronage and a tremendous burgeoning, at least in quantity, in Canadian art—though the only actual results most Australians were aware of was the flood of Canadian documentaries that at one time seemed to precede every film shown in Australia. Still, that in itself contrasted strikingly with the Australian film industry, since the latter did not then exist.

In its first year the Council for the Arts worked on a grant of $1.66 million. By 1972 it had $5.7 million, and it has been able to disburse this money not only to organisations—theatre companies, musical groups, Aboriginal art societies and so on—but to hundreds of individuals. Thus, at least two people, Richard Tipping and John Collings, have been given grants with which to work as, in essence, wandering minstrels; Stan Ostoja-Kotkowski, in the avant-garde of the avant-garde, has been able to move on from his complex and spectacular electronics to experiments in creating imagery directly from the brain itself; Graham Bell, our leading jazzman, has been able to go to America and study the field at first hand; novelists have at last become free to attempt the Big Novel (which has only eventuated from Patrick White, who is reputed not to accept grants); publishers have been able, in theory, to publish such unsaleable matter as poetry, knowing that the government will help cover the almost inevitable losses. And the developments in theatre and cinema have been particularly encouraging.

EMERGENCE OF THE AUSTRALIAN THEATRE

Ten years ago there was no Australian cinema bar the odd documentary, and no theatre to speak of. The National Theatre in Melbourne and the Old Tote in Sydney, the senior companies, were lavishly subsidised; the little theatres were mostly told to go hang, and did. Although Robin Lovejoy at the Tote did what he could to promote Australian drama, organising workshop performances and promoting seasons of Australian plays, there was little encouragement for young writers trying to make their way in drama; there just was not the room for them.

Two things have altered this grisly situation, to the point (which would have been unthinkable a few years before) where an Australian playwright, David Williamson, can win English awards against English competition, not to mention English prejudice.

One is the grant system in itself: the fact that money now flows in some quantity not only to the old established theatres but to such vital centres of new Australian drama as the Nimrod Theatre in Sydney, the Hole in the Wall in Perth and, particularly, the Pram Factory and the Australian Performing Group in Melbourne. The other, interlinked, or rather perhaps another aspect of the same process, is precisely the work done by such organisations: the boldness and originality that have enabled Williamson, Alexander Buzo, John Romeril, Michael Boddy, Bob Ellis and others to create a local theatre which shows signs—for the first time since the isolated success of *Summer of the Seventeenth Doll*—of acquiring a more than local reputation.

Opposite: Although photography has long had a place in the art galleries of Europe and America, only recently in Australia has it gained a wider audience than that catered for by family albums. Now, in many cities, one-man exhibitions vie with painting for public attention, and newspapers run regular reviews of the latest work.

This theatre is of particular interest because, far more than poetry or the novel, it shows a remarkably well-defined set of attitudes, a cohesion which, at this stage, is probably very useful. It could be loosely defined in terms of the old *Bulletin* slogan: 'Temper democratic, bias offensively Australian' (and certainly some of the London and New York critics have been very much offended).

'Australian history,' writes Geoffrey Searle, 'has been ransacked for subjects and, among others, Macquarie, several explorers, Henry Parkes, Archbishop Mannix, John Norton and King O'Malley have lived again.'

And not only the subjects have been 'offensively Australian'. At last the demotic Australian language has found its way into the theatre, mercilessly pilloried in *Dimboola*, accurately and dramatically rendered in *The Removalists* (a ferocious post-Pinter affair that may be the best of the lot so far), celebrated in *The Last of the Knucklemen* and the plays, such as *The Chocolate Frog*, written in prison by the highly talented and rapidly improving Jim McNeil. And Australian mores, long and lovingly dissected by satirist Barry Humphries, now have a host of other chroniclers, vivisectors and expositors.

All this is very well, at present, because it gives the nascent Australian theatre a discernible direction and sense of identity, makes it possible to speak of a school or a movement; a very useful thing if you are dealing with such things as overseas critics.

Beyond a certain point, however, this all-Australian attitude becomes a danger, as it has, historically, in other fields: it turns into cultural chauvinism which in turn brings about isolation, and the whole by-our-bootstraps process has to be gone through again, perhaps 20 years later. This is all so much speculation, of course, but the emergence as a tremendous popular and considerable critical success of *The Rocky Horror Show*, even though it is in the now well-worn convention of the pop musical, seems promising.

All of this is true, possibly to a lesser degree, of the cinema. Australian films have a very long and honourable history, but the industry had been dormant if not extinct for a couple of decades until recently. In the 60s such organisations as UBU, with Aggie Read and Albie Thoms, made a number of self-consciously 'underground' films, of varying derivativeness and merit, and catering largely for a university type audience. But it was not really until the 70s that a feature-film, general-release industry got going, and so far the fact that is has got going is very nearly all that can be said for it.

Certainly it seems impossible to discuss the doings of Barry McKenzie (a coarsening and dilution of Barry Humphries' caustic wit), Alvin Purple or Petersen under the rubric 'the arts'; nor do such sensationalistic local commercial efforts as *Stone* inspire much excitement. There are signs, though: the industry has come up with a very good horror movie in *Night of Fear* (and do not sneer at horror—think of *Nosferatu* and *Caligari*: it can be a great medium for expressionist directors), an outstanding exploration of the grimmer side of Australian society and the Australian character in *Wake in Fright*, and a rather masterly evocation by Michael Thornhill of the eponymous subject of *Between Wars*, from a Frank Moorhouse text. The Australian film industry is roughly where the Indian film industry stood just before the appearance of Satyajit Ray, or the Greek before that of Michael Kakoyannis. If the money keeps coming in, things look promising: all the more so because of such recent instances as the award of 10 grants to schoolchildren to make films—not simply generosity but enlightened generosity.

If Australia's film industry is still fairly primitive, its television is thoroughly sophisticated: at least in the arts of cupidity and pandering too often to what appears to be something slightly lower than the lowest common denominator of public taste. The controversial 'points' system introduced by the Ministry for the Media, whose intention, avowedly, was on the one hand to increase the Australian content on Australian television, and on the other to improve its quality, has not had the slightest discernible effect on the commercial channels. Australian television might improve if something could be done about the hysterical chase for ratings.

If the current developments in the Australian theatre are interesting, they are particularly so when compared with the position in painting. Here the problems seem to be of almost exactly the opposite kind: the development, here as elsewhere, towards an 'international' style. This may not be bad in itself, but it is depressing to see one overseas art movement after another (French until roughly the end of the war; American afterwards) slavishly taken up by scads of Australian artists who then devote themselves (mostly in all sincerity, I should note) to reproducing what has already been done somewhere else five, 20 or 50 years ago. It may stem, this magpie thieving, from a particularly exacerbated form of our perennial problem of isolation: certainly it has been a pattern ever since the first colonial artists endeavoured to transform the intransigent gum trees into the elegancies of familiar English landscape.

This is not to say that distinctive work is not being done in Australia, but many believe that the most impressive Australian art still resides in the mythopeias of Drysdale, Nolan, Tucker, Boyd, the unique Byzantine richness of French, the calligraphic landscapes of Williams.

All the same, the progress of Australian painting in general can be charted with surprising accuracy in terms of the influence of particular exhibitions. The Melbourne *Herald* show which introduced us (25 years after the Armoury show in New York, as Robert Hughes points out) to the post-impressionists; or the 1967 *Two Decades of American Painting*, which popularised 'colour-field' and 'hard-edge' painting—though Terry Smith and Tony McGillick have noted that, for once, these movements had already at least got under way through the Australian artists who had lived and worked in New York and London in the 50s and 60s, so that there was already sufficient basis for the famous *The Field* exhibition, of local artists, in 1968. And it seems likely that the recent exhibition of American conceptual and minimalist art will have a long-lasting effect. Again it is only fair to say that Alan Riddell, for instance, has been working in this general area—concrete poetry is very much a borderline, work-out-your-own-definitions sort of a business; as has such an artist as Tim Johnson, who caused

Sir Russell Drysdale—international master

'Life imitates art', said Oscar Wilde, citing Turner and the Thames fog. True: what we think we see is made up partly of what is there and partly of the preconceptions we bring to it.

This quirk of perception can be seen in an especially plastic form in Australians' visions of the Australian landscape. The Australia seen in the polite drawing-room canvasses of our first century is not the Australia, washed in strong light and colour, that revealed itself to the Heidelberg impressionists; and that in turn, finally become mannered and sterile, gave way to the mental landscape first captured by two very different painters, Sidney Nolan and Russell Drysdale.

Drysdale's present-day eminence should not blind anyone to the originality of his achievement (as eminence has a habit of doing)—to the fact that he saw, and painted, Australia as no-one had ever done, but in such a way that once he had pointed it out the vision became valid for everyone.

Gone, once he had started, were the ornamental arrangements of riverbanks and eucalypts, the meticulously punctuating sheep, the soft delicate pigments of a convention that had become formally pastoral; the sense of landscapes seen through a curtain of drifting pastels. Now the country —the red heart, the dusty hamlets, the

improbable configurations of rock and tree and isolated human figure—declared itself with the harsh beauty it had revealed to the explorers. The people themselves, almost stick-figures in the early paintings, meticulously interrelated with almost abstract, almost surreal elements of landscape later, gained in stature and dignity through their very smallness in such surroundings.

Like any great artist, Drysdale has developed (there's a great distance between *Moody's Pub*, 1941, and, say, the lunar but ferociously dynamic 1968 *Duststorm in the Central Desert*), but his theme, his vision remains intact. And, as always happens with great innovators, he suffers from throngs of would-be Drysdales who believe that it is sufficient to paint a contorted piece of timber in a desert, or a broken-down truck and an old windmill, to become 'of his school' and vicariously his equal. None of this seems to worry him particularly; his own achievement, after all, is intact; he is recognised internationally as a master; and, for that matter, at 63 he still has plenty of work to do.

It is curious that Drysdale and Patrick White, perhaps the two men who have most effectively redefined the way we see Australia, should both have been born (in the same year) in England; but Drysdale runs to paradoxes. Although he knows the Aus-

tralian country more intimately, perhaps, than any other painter, he has mostly lived in Sydney; to the unique clarity of his feeling for the Outback he has brought a technique in many ways based in Paris; a painter wonderful in his sense of form and balance, he only has the sight of one eye; a portraitist whose subjects tend to be characterised by naive strength and simplicity, he is a genuine polymath and pyrotechnical conversationalist; a man with a deep aesthetic intuition amounting almost to mysticism, he has always been thoroughly and seriously involved in his directorship of Pioneer Sugar Mills.

The map of Australian art can be charted in terms of paradoxes just as much as in terms of achievement; and on either criterion Drysdale is an equally central figure.

Fred Williams, John Olsen and Ray Crooke have suggested different ways again of looking at Australia's landscape; others again—Jeffrey Smart and John Brack, for instance—have developed an urban idiom that Drysdale never attempted; but Drysdale country is by now as much a climate of the mind as either actual sand and spinifex or pigment on canvas: it constitutes an achievement as definitive as that of any in Australia.

The rebirth of a vigorous, idiomatic Australian art after World War II was accompanied by a change of outlook in galleries and museums. Private galleries began to spring up in the 50s and 60s, State institutions modernised, and exhibitions became more a public entertainment and less a social exercise for the wealthy. More than 178,000 people visited the Art Gallery of NSW early in 1975 to see the 'Modern Masters from Manet to Matisse' exhibition—though in 1906, in only 18 days, 206,778 people (almost half the population of Sydney at that time) flocked to view a single painting, Holman Hunt's *The Light of the World*. The cap, trousers and pose of this young woman would have been unthinkable then.

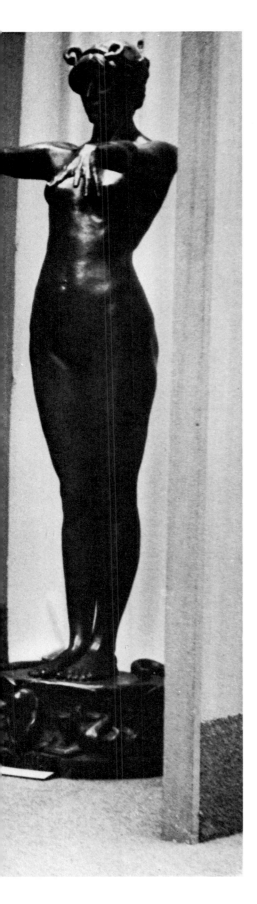

such a splendid stir in Queensland with his conceptual body-art happenings, which the ever-susceptible northerners took for orgies.

The question of expatriation, you may have noticed, has risen up again unbidden, as seems to be its way in every nook and cranny of the Australian arts scene. It is only because Australian artists have gone overseas, to 'where it's happening'—and returned—that the stupefying pre-war lag in painting styles has been partly overcome.

And this is where the third of those usefully symbolic events comes in: the new National Gallery and its clearcut but definitely controversial buying policy, as most picturesquely exemplified in the purchase of Jackson Pollock's putative masterpiece, *Blue Poles*.

The gallery's director, James Mollison, who was granted $4.5 million for acquisitions in 1974, and who is more or less single-handedly responsible for what the gallery buys, said that he was not going to send the latest big purchase, Kasimir Malevich's $1 million suprematist *House Under Construction*, on a tour of the States—'I don't want it to become a freak show like *Blue Poles*.'

The public reception of *Blue Poles* was very interesting: as interesting as, say, the persecution of Dobell.

Of course, the circumstances made it impossible to look at it just as a painting: it had already, before anyone had seen it, been blown up into a sensation. That it was abstract-expressionist in style (a mode of painting perfectly calculated to provoke the 'my four year old daughter could do better than that' type of response) was bad enough; that more than $1 million had been paid for it made it a full-scale scandal. And that, so it was put about, it was painted In Drink (and perhaps Drugs) really gave the politicians, the more mindless sections of the press, the cartoonists and writers of indignant letters something to dig their teeth into. A collection of cartoons on the subject (one could accumulate quite a fair-sized book of them) would be especially revealing. All the weary old images were dragged out again: chimpanzees sploshing canvases at random with paint and banana peel; Leonardo being rejected by Mollison; the full hysterical apparatus that was trained against Turner, the *fauves*, surrealism, anything new and different; the same reactions that drove Lionel Lindsay to write *Addled Art*, intended to prove that post-impressionism was part of the world-wide Jewish conspiracy. It will be impossible to look objectively at *Blue Poles*—or de Kooning's *Woman V*, or the works by Malevich, Brancusi, Oldenburg, Warhol and the rest that have also been bought—for years.

The dilemma in which we find ourselves at the moment is aptly acted out in this little dark comedy. It is almost (though not quite) the dilemma posed by A. D. Hope in a famous poem, 'Australia'. After first excoriating the country, its people, its history (or lack of it) and its culture (ditto), he concludes in terms which have puzzled several critics:

'Yet there are some like me turn gladly home
From the lush jungle of modern thought, to find
The Arabian desert of the human mind,
Hoping, if still from deserts the prophets come,
Such savage and scarlet as no green hills dare
Springs in that waste . . .'

This was powerfully apt, as speculation, when it was written. There can be little doubt that, for reasons having to do with the nature of its discovery and partial conquest, Australia has not traditionally been all that fertile a ground for the arts: 'Arabian desert of the human mind' will do very well as an analogy. It is possible also to suggest that the 'savage and scarlet' Hope looks for has to some degree shown itself: in *Voss* and *The Tree of Man*, in Nolan's Kelly and Mrs Fraser paintings, in Peter Sculthorpe's *Sun Music* series and his *Irkanda IV*.

But in any case things have changed since Hope wrote his poem, and what one must call the '*Blue Poles* affair' demonstrates how; and also, perhaps, how they have not.

First of all, then, the Whitlam Government is probably the only government in the history of Australia that would have bought *Blue Poles*. Another prime minister with a reputation for being cultured, Sir Robert Menzies, attempted —when he was Attorney-General in 1937—to found an Academy of Australian Art, in order to 'set certain standards' and keep at bay 'the people who call themselves modernists', who 'talk a different language'. Fortunately he failed, and in reaction the Contemporary Art Society was founded instead.

Mr Whitlam, by his very assumption of the Ministry for the Arts on top of the prime ministership itself, and by the encouragement he's given to the Australian Council for the Arts—as opposed to most previous federal, and current State governments, which run to such exotic ministries as 'Arts, Aborigines and Environment' or 'Arts, Sport and Recreation'—has shown, rightly or wrongly, something closer to the Confucian idea of the centrality of art than any other prime minister, and has been willing to experiment, and also to let the experts, like Mollison, have their say. There's little doubt that the structure of the council could be improved, that there are altogether too many bureaucrats with fingers in various cultural pies, that public relations work has not been all it could be. Still, the intention is there, as well as achievement.

What, though, of the prophets, the deserts? What seems to be envisaged today is a sort of antipodean Athens, with everyone eventually appreciating things of *vertu*. And we don't, at present, have anything like the foundations for such a society. *Blue Poles* proves it. Indeed, the only group, it could be argued, that does is the Aborigines. But their position, in the arts as in everything else, is very much up in the air at present. The most encouraging incident I've come across, so far as their traditional arts are concerned, is not one of the rather numerous grants and subsidies individuals and organisations have received, but the fact that an exhibition of Aboriginal art in Melbourne was immediately ended when a group of Aborigines, looking at it, were shocked to see secret ritual objects being shown, and protested.

Apart from a, for once, commendable attitude on the part of the whites involved, what this episode shows is that we have a long way to go (and are probably going the wrong way in any case) to achieve anything like the profound integration of art with all other aspects of traditional Aboriginal society —and, indeed, of 'primitive' societies in general. Some of our artists, in isolated works, are learning from the Aborigines. This is perhaps most evident in ballet and music, where choreographers like Sir Robert Helpmann and composers like Sculthorpe and Dreyfus have shown, in such a ballet as *Corroboree* or such a sequence as *Sun Music*, that a surprising degree of Aboriginal style, idiom and background can be assimilated without detracting from the integrity either of the original or of the new work. This is less true of writers. Who remembers the Jindyworoback poets, with their verses studded with incomprehensible gobs of Arunta or whatever? And in general, I feel, the example set by a few has not been as much followed as one is entitled to hope; but then ours is a culture that makes for 'isolated works'. That is only to be expected; we believe ourselves, still, to have better things to do.

Nonetheless, some of the auspices are good. We are, of course, almost ideally situated to become a cultural centre as great as our small population (which is rather larger than that of fifth century Athens, though; or Renaissance Florence or Siena) will allow. Urban, well off, by no means overworked (most of us), with a climate that ought to encourage the proliferation of such useful incidentals as open air cafes and theatres and exhibitions, and with the example of a few genuine major artists—I do not know what stands in the way; I certainly do not propose to plunge into the mystical obscurities of 'national character', which seems to be the main obstacle.

And meanwhile, though the reception accorded to artists here may still be very far from what one might hope for, the work itself is often exciting.

It has turned out to be impossible to write this appraisal as a sort of *catalogue raisonné*; so there is much I have only touched on, or not mentioned at all. In painting, for instance, a general point about isolation and cultural lag fails to take account of, for example, the achievement of younger artists like Michael Johnson, David Aspden or Peter Powditch; in poetry similar tendencies (the homage paid by many to Frank O'Hara, Robert Duncan, Ted Berrigan and other Americans, either of the New York or the Black Mountain persuasions, is one instance) can hardly circumscribe the achievement of poets as vital, and different, as James McAuley, Judith Wright, David Campbell among the older generation; such younger poets as Les A. Murray, chronicler equally of the countryside of his youth and of the great Western myths, or the cosmopolitan Rodney Hall, elegant or abrasive with equal skill; and the 'new' poets like Kris Hemensley, Robert Adamson (a master; 'new' hardly covers his case), Rhyll McMaster, John Forbes and a good many others. Poetry, indeed, has thrived here for decades, far more, I would think, than any other art. But the list could go on for pages: prose writers from Christina Stead through Thomas Keneally to the brilliant convolutions of thought and language in Frank Moorhouse, Michael Wilding, Peter Carey; composers like Sculthorpe, Richard Meale, David Ahern—Sculthorpe's opera/oratio/ballet/what have you, *Rites of Passage*, intended for the opening of the Opera House but, typically for that edifice, not completed and performed till more than a year after, deserves a chapter in itself. Certainly these composers, as well as making effective use of at least one aspect of the Aboriginal heritage, have also been in the vanguard of recognition for our Asian neighbours; in no way has our music been more enriched than through the infusions from Bali, Java, Japan. This is 'influence' with a point to it. Then the musicians: there was the Sydney Symphony's extensive 1974 tour of Europe, which drew a fascinating reaction (cheers almost everywhere; jeers in Vienna and Munich)—and then what about Neville Amadio, the Renaissance Players . . . well, it's impossible.

And then entrepreneurs like Michael Edgely and Harry M. Miller; administrators like Drs Coombs and Battersby—and I have not even touched on dance or opera, both forms to which I have an irrational rooted aversion, possibly due to their traditional 'society' elitist image. But that's unfair, and they have certainly

Thomas Keneally—consistent concerns

A new, vociferous and vastly talented group of fiction writers—Frank Moorhouse, Michael Wilding, Peter Carey, Vicki Viidikas, Damien White and others—has made itself felt in Australia over the last couple of years. One result of this ought to be that people will stop referring to Thomas Keneally, now 40, as 'a younger writer', as nearly everyone has been doing for the last decade or so. This in turn will make it possible to look at Keneally's work without the appearance of making allowances that clearly do not need to be made.

Keneally did not quite spring up full-grown a la Minerva, but his third novel, *Bring Larks and Heroes,* was a masterpiece by pretty much any standards. Simply as an evocation of the colonial days it was something new in our literature, neither romanticising on the one hand nor dwelling lovingly on the brutalities: it has scenes that are brutal enough, but they're both necessary and sensitively realised. What was really striking, though, was the prose. Outside Patrick White, virtually all Australian novelists had been content with a rough-hewn journeyman's prose, apparently under the impression that what they had to say was the important thing (one wonders why many of them ever took up the novel at all, rather than, say, journalism). Keneally's style gave the impression that it could do anything, from splashing on great wads of *fauve* colour to building up character or scene through the accumulation of precise, minute details. It was never crude and it was never pretty.

After this, Keneally became a dominating figure throughout the 60s and continues to be one today. His work has been both varied and uneven, but his main concerns have been consistent. With a seminarian upbringing—he came close to becoming a priest—he has always been preoccupied with cases of conscience and images of guilt. Of the latter perhaps the most direct is *The Survivor*, with the corpse slowly thawing out of the Antarctic ice to reveal—cannibalism? Perhaps. In itself it is an image as powerful as the great pike rising to the surface of the pool in Ted Hughes's poem, but in many ways the book is overdone, even oppressive. *Three Cheers for the Paraclete*, on the other hand, which is an exploration of the relationship between religion and morality, authority and conscience, is totally successful, seemingly drawing directly on Keneally's experience. The prose is tauter, less colourful, perhaps more pragmatic than that of *Larks and Heroes*, and perfectly suited to its task.

A Dutiful Daughter, an extraordinary *jeu d'esprit*, fantasy, allegory or, well, something, involving the transformation of people into cows—with life continuing substantially as usual—was followed by *The Chant of Jimmie Blacksmith*, for me Keneally's best novel. Based on the life of the Aboriginal bushranger Jimmy Governor (also the subject, at about the same time, of an outstanding poem by Les Murray), it is, while under complete artistic control, Keneally's harshest, most bitter, most violently coloured and cadenced performance. The headlong collision between Jimmie with his axe and the whole of white society is a superb illustration of the dialectics of violence. The book just failed to carry off England's prestigious Booker Prize; it may not be too unkind to suggest that they've grown unused to the hard stuff.

With his latest novel *Blood Red, Sister Rose*, on Jeanne d'Arc, and a commissioned work in progress on Moses, Keneally is keeping up what for most writers would be a killing rate of work, which doesn't seem to affect his quality.

And with all this, he is one of the rare Australian writers who finds the time to encourage younger writers, to get involved in workshops and courses and so on. He is, in fact, totally involved in the business of writing, and not just his own. Would that there were more like him.

kept Australia very much in the cultured public eye overseas; even the most hardened balletophobe must be delighted to see the Australian Ballet enthusiastically received in such Meccas as Leningrad, and honoured by Nureyev's association with it—as in *Swan Lake*, successfully filmed as well. It is equally pleasing to see in today's newspaper that Joan Sutherland is returning to Australia on a three year contract: they *are* coming back!

What I have just tried to convey is that there is a great deal going on, and of that a great deal is good and some very good. It must be asked, though, whether we are better off than other roughly equivalent countries. Certainly we are dealing, in Australia, with 'special circumstances'; so is every other country. How do we match up?

My own feeling is that, despite all attempts to bring the arts 'to the factory floor' (or, perhaps more to the point, to the bourgeois living-room, whose cultural appurtenances are liable to be a dozen *Reader's Digest* Condensed Books), Athens we will not be. The traditional Australian egalitarianism is in many ways genuine, and these ways seem to include a lot of the more pernicious ones: particularly anti-intellectualism and a stifling conformity. About this I doubt that any conceivable system of State support for the arts can do anything.

On the other hand, so far as the artist is concerned, they are better off than they have ever been. If they are mocked, at least they have a good chance of not being starved; which helps, with due respect to Dr Johnson.

What will happen, with luck, is feedback: people in distant and mysterious 'overseas' will realise with astonishment that Rod Laver and Shane Gould, admirable of course in their own fields, are not quite all we have to offer; our local media will convey this perception back to us; and we shall all chant Hosannah, turn cartwheels and realise that we have reached a position where we can *begin* to do something about the arts.

Opposite: Australian theatre flowered briefly in the late 50s and early 60s, then withered away for a decade. Among those responsible for the current resurgence of a strong, idiomatic, distinctively 'Australian' theatre is playwright David Williamson; his work has won awards—and box office success—not only in his own country but also in the fiercely competitive English theatrical arena.

Left: Australian painting came of age with its Impressionists, notably Arthur Streeton and Tom Roberts, in the late 19th century. Their concern was the catching of a momentary atmospheric effect, an ideal exemplified by Streeton's *Redfern Station*, completed in 1893.

Below: Tom Roberts finished *Bailed Up* in 1895, but worked on it again in 1927. Bushrangers' hold-ups were a normal hazard of life until the capture of Ned Kelly in 1880. Roberts' attention to the atmosphere, and the casual figure arrangement, suggest a typically Australian understatement and even a sense of pride in the event.

Opposite: A rugged, uniquely Australian idiom came to full flower during the 1940s in the work of George Russell Drysdale, now Sir Russell, the father of modern Australian landscape painting. *A Horsebreaker from the Snowy River* was completed in 1971.

Above: The 1960s saw the rise to fame of the Broken Hill painter, Pro Hart, who quickly established a large following with his distinctive style and his prodigious output of popular Australiana. He has reaped the rewards of being one of the most sought after painters in the 70s, and now owns one of the largest private collections in the country.

Above right: The mantle of Streeton, the leading landscape painter of his time, appears to have settled on the Melbourne artist Fred Williams, remarkable as the only Australian painter to have based his entire output on the unpeopled monotony of the bush. But where Streeton sought the three-dimensional atmospheric moment, Williams has concentrated on a synthesised concept employing no devices of depth.

Right: Albert Tucker, hard on the heels of Sidney Nolan, was the second major painter to follow Drysdale into the strange new Australia of harsh red deserts, tortured sculptural forms and monumental symbolism. Nolan peopled his vision of the landscape in the famous Ned Kelly series; in Tucker's series of Antipodean Heads, the gaunt, eroded faces of bushrangers, explorers and others haunted an ominous, dead land.

Two of the most successful younger painters are Tim Storrier (*above*) and Brett Whiteley (*right*). Storrier, a landscapist in the strictest traditional sense, brings a new, modern eye to the old themes of the Outback and its inhabitants in luminous, delicate and detailed paintings. Whiteley, by contrast, paints with extreme economy of detail, and has made extensive use of abstraction and symbolism.

Opposite, top: Whiteley's *Glimpse of Eden*, painted in 1974.

Although Australian drama has had a checkered career, ballet and, to a smaller extent, opera, have been richly endowed with talent.

Opposite: Sir Robert Helpmann, doyen of Australian theatre and ballet, dances the title role in a recent Australian Ballet Company production of *Don Quixote*.

Left: The incomparable operatic soprano Joan Sutherland, latest in a long line of world-renowned Australian sopranos that began with Dame Nellie Melba.

Below: Lucette Aldous, currently prima ballerina with the Australian Ballet Company, dances the role of Kitri with Rudolf Nureyev as Basilio in a performance of *Don Quixote*.

With the honourable exception of a tiny handful of anthropologists and ethnologists, white Australians ignored Aboriginal tribal art for almost 200 years. Now, almost overnight, more people are appreciating its value as one of the few keys available for unlocking the mysteries of past tribal cultures.

Above right: These relatively recent mouth-blown ochre stencils at Carnarvon National Park, Queensland, are similar to the wall art of European cavemen 30,000 years ago.

Right: Totemic funerary sculpture of the Melville Island and Bathurst Island Aborigines.

Far right: Sacred Churinga or Tjurunga stones, like this one from central Australia, are normally seen only by male tribal elders.

Opposite: Marita Narjic of Port Keats, a Roman Catholic mission south-west of Darwin, learns modern copperworking techniques at East Arm Leprosarium settlement.

262

Despite the 'great Australian ugliness' of the suburban sprawl, there is much distinctive and attractive architecture to be seen.

Opposite top: Roof shells of the Sydney Opera House.

Opposite centre: A new farmhouse in northern NSW.

Far left: A cluster of spires and towers along Melbourne's Yarra Yarra River.

Above: Leonard French's huge stained glass ceiling at the National Gallery of Victoria, part of the growing Victorian Arts Centre. Using French and Belgian glass, 2.5 cm thick, the artist chipped, ground and polished by hand every fragment in the ceiling, a task which took five years. He described the construction as 'painting with light', and the concept as 'a huge, deep, sonorous Persian carpet suspended in the air'.

Left: A verandah at the Seppeltsfield winery in the Barossa Valley, SA.

The completion in the last decade of new cultural centres in many parts of Australia, and the opening of the National Gallery of Victoria, have multiplied the display possibilities for sculpture and major works of art.

Top left: Barbara Hepworth's totemic bronze, *Ultimate Form*, dominates the upstairs plaza of the Adelaide Festival Centre.

Top right: A tourist poses for a friend's camera beside one of several pieces of sculpture displayed at the Adelaide Festival Centre.

Right: The only large, modern museum and art gallery to be built in Australia since World War II, the National Gallery of Victoria, opened its doors in August, 1968.

Opposite: Part of the extensive ceramics collection at the National Gallery of Victoria.

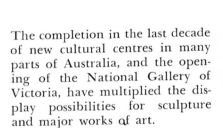

266

SCIENCE

Dr Peter Pockley

'. . . such a low level of
knowledge about local
science . . . that outsiders
are amazed.'

Australian science today is faced with a number of disparate yet related problems. Until the early 70s, science had enjoyed two decades of increasing political support—slow, steady, and essentially ad hoc, but at least it increased. Now that support has levelled off, as has the number of new students enrolling in science-based faculties in Australia's universities. In the halcyon postwar decades Australian science also enjoyed the leadership of a handful of outstanding and well known men who were highly regarded by the public and the politicians alike, and who earned what was then the valuable accolade of a knighthood.

Sir Mark Oliphant, the nuclear physicist (and later Governor of South Australia), and Sir Rutherford Robertson, the botanist, were both Presidents of the Australian Academy of Science. Sir Frederick White, the ex-Chairman of the CSIRO, Sir Ernest Titterton, the nuclear physicist, and Sir Philip Baxter, ex-Vice-Chancellor of the University of NSW and forthright ex-Chairman of the Atomic Energy Commission, all had their days as influential advisors.

Well known too was the ebullient, entrepreneurial Professor Harry Messel whose publicity campaigns for the Science Foundation for Physics successfully helped support his School of Physics at Sydney University.

In recent years, however, the advances of the 50s and 60s have been partly offset by some disenchantment with the role of science, and more specifically with the technological applications of scientific research. Many scientists now find themselves on the defensive (or at least imagine themselves to be so), an attitude not improved by less generous government financial support.

In some respects, too, Australian science suffers from the widely dispersed and largely unco-ordinated nature of scientific research and technological development in this country. We have achieved international prestige in areas

Opposite: This experimental solar furnace at the University of NSW, Sydney, is one example of the important solar energy research being conducted in Australia. A sample of tektite on a column of zirconium oxide, enclosed in a vacuum chamber, is subjected to concentrated sunlight focussed by a large concave collecting mirror; the tektite melts at just under 2,000°C, the zirconium oxide at 2,800°C, and scientists are thus able to gauge the heat generated in the experiment.

269

like chemistry, medical research, earth sciences and astronomy; and we have a sound reputation for research on our own flora, fauna and environment. But we do not have anything to compare with Germany's achievements in chemistry in the late 19th and early 20th centuries, Holland's and Japan's success in applied electronics research, Britain's trail-blazing role in unravelling the structure of the atom, or the United States' overwhelming efforts in biology, medicine and armaments.

An assessment of where Australian science stands today must therefore consider not one discipline with an outstanding continuous record of achievement, but rather a number of highlights spread across a dozen or so different fields of work.

VIRUSES, NERVES AND NOBELS

That medical research has received popular support in Australia unmatched by the other sciences is shown by the press coverage of often minor medical advances in Australia and by the existence of private foundations for the financing of medical research. Regular public appeals for medical research funds are reasonably successful (though puny by American standards); the National Heart Foundation leads the field, but is by no means alone in attracting public support.

The government gives funds for medical research, notably through the National Health and Medical Research Council which granted $16 million over the three years to 1975, and also indirectly supports academic medical research through the financing of universities where most of this research is done. Drug companies are reasonably generous, although it is difficult to estimate their contributions because many of their grants include consultancies and overseas travel for researchers.

The faith implied by such support has, in the past, been amply justified, for Australian medical science has produced three Nobel Prize winners. The first Nobel Prize awarded to an Australian-born person went to the late Lord Florey for work he did in Britain on penicillin; the first *Australian* Nobel Prize was won by Professor Sir Macfarlane Burnet; and the second went to Sir John Eccles. It is no coincidence that Burnet and Eccles earned their laureates for research at centres internationally recognised as housing the nation's two leading groups of medical scientists: the Walter and Eliza Hall Institute for Medical Research (associated with the University of Melbourne) and the John Curtin School of Medical Research (an integral part of the Australian National University in Canberra).

When he received his award in 1960, Burnet was Director of the Hall Institute, a post he held for 22 years to 1965. Although lionised by the establishment and the media, he is a shy, almost introspective person—yet 'Mac' Burnet became the most honoured Australian scientist with a knighthood and the rare Order of Merit, and a four year Presidency of the Australian Academy of Science as further recognition of his standing among fellow scientists.

Even in retirement, while writing erudite books about biological theory (while well into his 70s he has developed a refreshingly direct approach to the problem of ageing, including his own), he has retained his long-held status as the guru of science in the nation. In a rare excursion into non-scientific affairs, he was, with leading businessmen and academics, one of the influential signatories to a famous letter of support for the Labor Party which helped swing it into power in December 1972. For many people, Sir Macfarlane Burnet still *is* Australian science.

Burnet was unashamedly a scholarly scientist. He tackled major problems with a simplicity and tenacity of approach which would tie him to his laboratory bench until the solution was found, long after lesser scientists would have lost heart. He did not work with elaborate apparatus, but spent much of his time in the outwardly boring business of inoculating hundreds and thousands of chicken eggs to discover the rules of tolerance to infection by viruses, notably the elusive influenza strains. Myxomatosis in rabbits and Murray Valley encephalitis in man were two of the diseases whose fundamental patterns of transmission he helped to unravel. The myxomatosis work involved a famous demonstration of faith in his own experiments and theories when he and his colleagues injected themselves with myxomatosis virus to prove it was harmless to humans.

Burnet described himself then as a virologist, but while doing his pioneering work in this field he became fascinated by the broader problems of immunology —how the body builds up antibody and triggers immune reactions to fight infections. In probably his biggest discovery, he showed how the body acquires immunological tolerance to tissue transplants.

Australia's second Nobel Laureate, Sir John Eccles, since leaving Australia for the United States on reaching retiring age at the ANU, has become known in his adopted country as plain Dr J. C. Eccles. As a professor at the John Curtin School (a highly prized position because it does not carry the undergraduate teaching responsibilities which make other professorships only part-time research positions), Eccles achieved scientific fame for his physiological studies on the way nerves work. With great patience and experimental skill he elucidated the intricate mechanism by which nerve impulses act across the membranes separating adjacent nerve cells. Since going to America, he has expanded his scale of research from the single nerve to the massive problems of understanding the whole brain.

It would be ungenerous and incorrect to give the impression that brilliant individual researchers like Burnet and Eccles were alone in their excellence. High standards of research in immunology and physiology have become a tradition in the past two decades, and these fields are probably among the frontrunners to produce Australia's next Nobel Laureate in science—but because of the large number of expatriate and mainly British scientists in Australia, *he* may not be native-born. 'He' is used advisedly, for women are notably absent from the middle and top echelons of scientists in Australia; there are, for instance, only two female Fellows in the 180-strong Australian Academy of Science.

With the ever-increasing subdivisions of a subject like physiology into smaller specialisations, it is impossible to nominate one branch as the 'key area', but some can be mentioned briefly. At the relatively new Howard Florey Institute for Experimental Medicine at Melbourne University, headed by the enthusiastic Dr Derek Denton, big efforts are being made to understand the mechanisms by which animals adjust and become habituated to levels of salt. Through pioneering work in the use of the sheep as an experimental animal (most medical researchers stick to the traditional mouse or, if they can afford it, the monkey), Dr Denton and his team have made another contribution to uniquely Australian science.

Neurophysiology, the study of the functioning of nerves, is an exciting field of research at various universities—Melbourne, Canberra and Sydney in particular. One example was the work of English-born (but, unusually, Australian-naturalised) Professor Geoffrey Burnstock at Melbourne University in the 1960s and early 1970s. His remarkable discoveries about the structure and function of nerves led him to propose a hitherto unrecognised nervous system in the body. He termed this third nervous system the 'purinergic system' to distinguish it from the well-recognised 'adrenergic system' and 'cholinergic system' (the names are derived from chemicals of which minute traces are crucial in the functioning of each system of nerves).

Burnstock's work has generated much excitement and some scepticism—it requires further confirmation because of the virtual invisibility of the nerves he believes to have discovered—but his colleagues recognise it as a broad-ranging achievement which, if the claims are confirmed, could bring fame to Australian science. At the same time it is the kind of result which generates irresistible offers, tempting talented scientists to go overseas: Burnstock now holds a prestigious chair at the University of London.

Another fascinating line of physiological research in Australia is truly home-based in that it involves the study of nerves and the cardiovascular system through the unique, lethal venoms found in our native fauna. The blue-ringed octopus, the funnel-web spider, the sea wasp and the tiger snake secrete compounds which **271** are ferociously toxic when injected into the bloodstreams of their victims. They are not only among the most lethally venomous animals in Australia, but their venoms have been found to have particular importance for physiology because of the way they act on life-supporting functions in the body, notably nervous transmission and respiration. The sea wasp, incidentally, is the only one on this list for which a reasonably effective form of protective immunisation has so far been developed.

The School of Physiology and Pharmacology at the University of NSW has two groups of researchers, led by Professor W. E. ('Darty') Glover and Associate Professor Peter Gage, who are unravelling the secrets of these venoms and thereby learning more about the basic psysiological functions of the body which they affect so drastically. The venoms of the blue-ringed octopus and the funnel-web spider appear to paralyse nerves in a highly specific way: the basic chemical molecules in these venoms, unlike most others, are so small that the body is unable to form 'antibody', a substance to negate the adverse chemical effect of the venom. The very smallness of the venom molecules makes them difficult to purify for study of their active components. But, when this problem is solved by the chemists, it is not too far-fetched to suggest that these uniquely toxic beasts of Australia might benefit humans through showing the way to produce artificially some highly specific, and therefore much safer, anaesthetics.

THE MOLECULE MANIPULATORS

The largest branch of science in Australia, in terms of the number of full-time workers, is almost certainly the least recognised. This is the field of chemistry, the study of molecules and atoms and how to manipulate them.

Australian chemists do enjoy international recognition. Several are Fellows of the Royal Society of London, still regarded as the highest accolade in the 'British' scientific world; two of them, Professor Arthur Birch (known for some pioneering work leading to the contraceptive pill) and Professor David Craig (a top-class physical chemist) were attracted back to their Australian homeland from excellent jobs in Britain to set up the Australian National University's Research School of Chemistry. But chemists are not only well-established in the academic world. Their research and services provide the sinews and growth potential for Australian industries with outputs measured in hundreds of millions of dollars. Yet chemists, in contrast for instance with their colleagues in astronomy, get so little publicity that it would be easy to think they did not exist.

One outstandingly successful line of research must be described to correct the chemists' general failure to project their own achievements. This is spectroscopy, the study of the innermost parts of atoms and molecules as revealed by their tell-tale effects on light or other radiation. Using prisms or diffraction gratings to split light into its composite spectrum, the chemist is also able to identify and estimate the quantity of an element or a compound present in a substance, even if that substance is millions of kilometres away. What goes to make up the sun and stars has been revealed in this way.

While spectroscopic research is widespread, the most noted centre is the CSIRO Division of Chemical Physics beside Monash University in Melbourne. The Division's urbane Chief, Dr Lloyd Rees, held senior positions for years in the International Union of Pure and Applied Chemistry. The Assistant Chief, Dr Alan Walsh, FRS, is a Britisher whose jovial, provincial accent shows no sign of more than two decades in Australia.

The remarkable results of Dr Walsh's erudite spectroscopic research are now to be found in thousands of laboratories, hospitals and industries throughout the world. No analytical outfit can do without at least one of the instruments derived from his work and patents, and known as atomic absorption spectro-photometers (AAS). These instruments are used to determine how much of an element is present in anything from a drop of blood to a polluted river or a potentially ore-bearing rock. The scientific principle behind AAS cannot be

Opposite: The ray of laser light passing through this coil of optical fibre can carry a million simultaneous telephone conversations—as many as today's wide-band submarine cables. The fibre was developed by the CSIRO's Division of Tribophysics, Melbourne, and consists of a fused-quartz tube, with a bore less than the diameter of a human hair, filled with liquid tetrachloroethylene as the light-transmitting medium. Still in its experimental stage, the fibre appears to have great potential in the field of telecommunications. (Val Foreman)

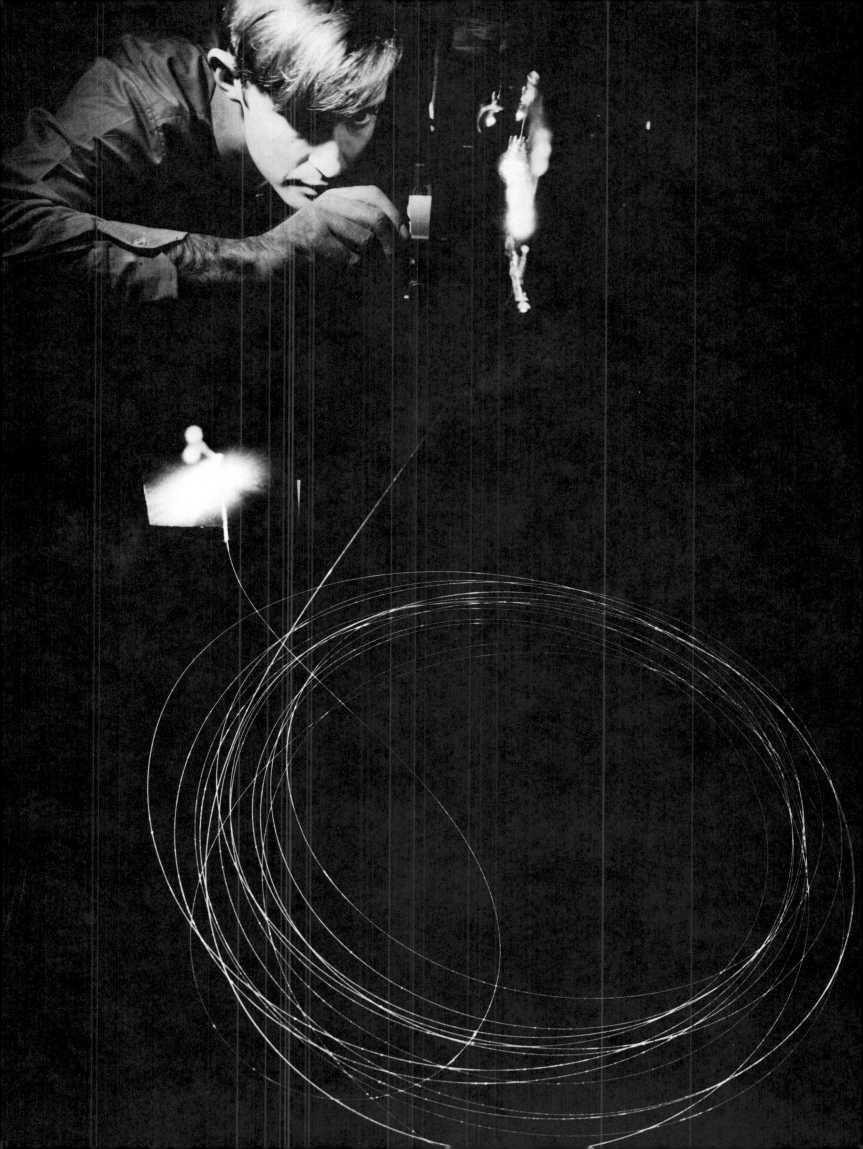

conveyed in two lines. Suffice it to say that Dr Walsh solved the very tricky problem of harnessing the enormous potential of an old but crude school science experiment in which the presence of some elements in liquid solution could be detected by introducing drops of the liquid into a flame—a bright yellow flame indicated the presence of sodium, a brick-red flame indicated calcium, and so on.

Dr Walsh designed a range of instruments which are quite staggering in their accuracy and sensitivity. As little as one-hundred-millionth part of one gram of some elements can be identified and quantified by the technique. But it is not just its sensitivity which has made the AAS method the most significant advance in chemical analysis of this century. It has also become a commercial winner because it is capable of analysing many different samples for a range of elements with great speed and reliability—and hence cheapness.

Atomic absorption spectroscopy has been described by the CSIRO as 'a long shot that paid off', but it was no shot in the dark. Faced initially by the indifference and scepticism of his colleagues, Dr Walsh was nevertheless convinced that the general idea had merit, and with determination he elucidated the basic principles by which the heated *atoms* of an element *absorb* characteristic wavelengths of light emitted separately by the same element—hence 'atomic absorption'. Those principles are now being applied in practice to at least 65 of the 90-odd elements found on earth ('at least', because the list grows annually through the continuing refinements of Dr Walsh and his disciples around the world). This is one of the signal achievements of Australian science.

The first AAS instruments were built in Melbourne under licence to the CSIRO. The firm's owner became a millionaire. Now the instruments are made all over the world, and the CSIRO has estimated the nett worth of this truly *scientific* (as distinct from technological) innovation to be $200 million over the 20 odd years for which it is realistic to expect the technique to retain its present dominance.

The CSIRO has good reason, therefore, to crow over this development, for it is a classic case of how painstaking, fundamental research can lead to profitable and socially useful applications. AAS became one of the basic tools used in the exploration for minerals in Australia, making a significant contribution to the discovery of commercial deposits of nickel, copper, silver, zinc and lead in the mining 'boom' period of the late 1960s. The detection of traces of harmful elements, and conversely of deficiencies of beneficial elements, in blood samples has led to the saving of lives. The control of purity in food, and newer AAS techniques with solid samples for process control in metallurgical operations, are among other daily applications.

One other line of spectroscopic research in Australia led to an unusual alliance between chemists and astronomers, and flourished so fast in the early 1970s that a new branch of chemistry has been born—'galactochemistry'— which to all intents is the identical twin of the new branch of astronomy, 'molecular astronomy'. While these new studies are not uniquely Australian, our scientists are specially favoured to pursue them through the facilities of the Parkes radio-telescope and the Monash University Chemistry Department.

The fusion of interests between people like Dr Brian Robinson of the CSIRO Division of Radiophysics and Professor Ron Brown of Monash came about through the astronomers' desire to observe the universe at shorter wavelengths (in the so-called 'microwave' regions) while not knowing how to interpret the signals they received. The chemists, meanwhile, had quite independently been studying the microwave spectrum of simple molecules in the laboratory, and had developed ways of identifying small, life-supporting molecules through 'fingerprints' they imposed on radiation passing through them.

It was a short jump to joint teams of radioastronomers and chemists discovering clouds of small molecules in space, many of which contain carbon and have structures like those molecules which are believed to be 'the building blocks of life'. Although structurally unsuited to the wavelengths involved, the Parkes radio 'dish' has nevertheless identified a number of these space molecules, notably methyl formate and vinyl cyanide. The CSIRO is now investing

$200,000 in a small radiotelescope specifically designed to probe radiations of millimetre wavelengths for signs of organic molecules in the centre of our galaxy. Once again, spectroscopy is big business in Australia.

In America and Europe, public debates have raged about how much government funding should be devoted to supporting a few scientists working in so-called 'big science' at the relative impoverishment of larger numbers working on more widely dispersed 'little science'. 'Big science' includes, for example, those huge atom-smashers and nuclear reactor facilities which gave Europe and America the lead in these two capital-intensive fields of research and application.

The description 'big science' now also covers astronomy. This depends for its progress on large, expensive instruments, and is the only field of 'big science' to receive support in Australia. There are few returns on investment in astronomy in terms of potential practical applications, but the Australian astronomers who have designed, built and operated their big and spectacular telescopes have been splendidly successful in achieving international and local recognition for the value of their work.

Australia is superbly positioned for observing the heavens. The Milky Way, the galaxy of which our own solar system forms such a tiny part, passes directly overhead. This provides the richest field for study of the nearest stars which are barely visible, if at all, to telescopes in the northern hemisphere. Southern hemisphere astronomers also revel in the unique availability to them of the two Magellanic Clouds, the nearest galaxies to us outside our own. Such nearness is important, for it allows study of the nature and evolution of stars in detail unobtainable elsewhere.

While these advantages of southern hemisphere astronomy were long recognised, Australia's effort in this field of research was minute until after World War II when two significant developments put our star-gazers on the world map. One was the incorporation of the existing, but small, observatory at Mount Stromlo near Canberra into the Australian National University; the resulting school of astronomy has expanded its range of instruments and research interests to the point where it has become recognised as a leading centre of optical astron-

Professor Gus Nossal—the medical man of affairs

It was not easy to follow Australia's first Nobel Laureate as Director of the nation's largest medical research institute, but Professor Gus Nossal showed no lack of confidence in making a success of it when he took over Melbourne's Walter and Eliza Hall Institute in 1965. He is the television and radio man's ideal scientist. Blessed with a striking, expressive face and an articulate confidence in interview, Gus Nossal has become a familiar subject for media 'profiles' (including this one!). Inevitably, these portray the image of a scientific achiever, a researcher on the move, a man involved in a range of medical, scientific and public affairs. But, he is more than a match for his interviewers and chooses well the ground on which he will debate publicly.

Nossal has been a consistent champion of the pressing need for scientists and public to get to know each other better. Equally, he has been concerned to promote the cause of fundamental science. It is disappointing to him, though, that so few of his scientific colleagues put as much thought and effort into the popularising and promotional tasks.

Born in Vienna in 1931, Nossal came to Australia at the age of eight when his parents escaped from the Nazis. His father was of Jewish extraction, but not religious association; his mother came from one of Austria's most prominent Catholic families; as Nossal himself says, 'Hitler was not one to bother with the fine points.' The religious influence went deep. Educated at the big Catholic school of St Aloysius' in Sydney, he is putting his four children through similar education. He has frequently debated subjects of Catholic ethics, notably in relation to such medical matters as contraception and abortion, where he has found himself moving increasingly to a liberal view.

Nossal is a busy man. He gives the impression of organising his time into strict packages: so much for research, so much for administration, so much for public relations. Although he has to be an administrator and fund-raiser (a successful one, too), Nossal is still a working scientist —he would probably be pretty miserable if he could not keep his hands on the apparatus, his eyes on the microscope and his mind on the complex problems of biological theory.

He recalls that his first big excitement came in the late 1950s and early 1960s while collaborating with the American Professor Joshua Lederberg who later went on to score a Nobel Prize. They showed that one cell makes only one antibody, the substance with which it can fight marauding antigens. This finding was important in providing one of the first pieces of experimental evidence to support Sir Macfarlane Burnet's 'clonal selection theory'. From then on, Nossal has been fascinated by the prospects which the fundamental study of immunology throw up for the conquest of disease.

With nearly 200 scientific publications to his name, he is a scientific optimist. He has not hesitated to differ in mood from his mentor and former boss, Burnet, who is basically pessimistic about medical science ever conquering cancer. Nossal believes that the lastest findings of leading immunologists, his staff at the Hall Institute and himself included, allow us to be hopeful that certain types of cancer will be controlled within their lifetimes.

As an active Fellow of the Academy of Science and member of numerous other national and international bodies, Gus Nossal remains in a strategic position to influence the development of Australian science for another two decades. In 1975 he was one of the few fundamental scientists, and the only medical researcher, appointed to the first Australian Science and Technology Council—the nation's scientific *supremos*, at least in terms of advice.

omy. The other was the formation of the CSIRO's radioastronomy group from a number of brilliant men returning from the war with skills in radar; they applied these skills to the study of the then completely mysterious radio signals emanating from space.

Today, Australian astronomers can boast a dazzling array of devices, some of them outwardly quite eccentric, for unlocking the secrets of the southern skies.

The 'big four' in Australian astronomical organisations are based in NSW —the CSIRO Division of Radiophysics, the Department of Astronomy at the ANU, the Anglo-Australian Telescope Board and the School of Physics at Sydney University. Their field stations are spread in a gentle arc from northern NSW through western NSW and back in to Canberra.

Tasmania has a modest but flourishing group of astronomers operating a very nice home-built optical telescope, a radio telescope and a cosmic ray telescope. The cosmic ray device is operated inside a disused railway tunnel, while the radio telescope beside Hobart airport looks more like a neglected hop field than an array of aerials for detecting very long wavelength radiation from space. The 'father of radioastronomy', a gentle American named Grote Reber who first detected radio signals from space in the 1930s when few would believe him, has been working quietly in Tasmania for years.

Adelaide University also nurtured a small group of astronomically minded physicists. Being the nearest academics to the rocket range at Woomera in South Australia, they naturally sought to take advantage of the high-flying rockets being launched there largely for military purposes. They piggy-backed their experimental packages on British rockets, and on one memorable occasion gained the complete use of an unwanted American Redstone military rocket with which they launched Australia's first and only artificial satellite, called WRESAT after the Weapons Research Establishment (WRE) which ran Woomera. The Adelaide physicists were among the first X-ray astronomers. With the collaboration of the University of Tasmania and WRE, Professor Ken McCracken and his team flew X-ray 'telescopes' in balloons and rockets above the earth's shielding atmosphere to pin-point the sources of intense X-radiation in the universe, such as the emissions from the centre of the well-known supernova remnant, the Crab Nebula.

The work of the X-ray astronomers typified the exciting expansion, in the 1960s, of astronomy into entirely new areas of the radiation spectrum. Until radioastronomy became respectable in the late 1940s and early 1950s, knowledge of the universe had been restricted to the information contained within the comparatively narrow band of radiation which we are biologically capable of detecting as light. Optical astronomers built bigger and bigger reflectors, almost exclusively in the northern hemisphere, to collect and analyse fainter and fainter pin-points of light from deepest space. A bewildering catalogue of facts was assembled—but their interpretation caused a degree of indigestion. As leaders in extending astronomical observations into other non-optical areas of the spectrum, Australians made substantial contributions in solving some of the puzzles posed by the optical astronomers; at the same time, the southern hemisphere astronomers—almost exclusively Australian—helped to pose a whole new set of problems through their extensive observations of hitherto unexplained and unobserved objects, such as the quasars, pulsars, X-ray stars and so-called 'black holes', which the theoretical astronomers were called upon to explain.

Since the early 1960s, the symbol of Australian astronomy—indeed, almost a symbol of modern Australia—has been the giant 'dish' operated by the CSIRO at Parkes in western NSW. This 64-metre diametre tiltable and rotatable telescope and its 18-metre companion which moves on railway tracks, also symbolise man's search into the deepest parts of space for evidence of the origin of the universe. Soon after the Parkes main dish was commissioned it featured in the dramatic identification of the first 'quasar' (short for quasi-stellar object), an intense source of radio emission in the sky, known simply by its catalogue number 3C 273. In August, 1962, the Parkes team, led at the time by Mr John Bolton, discovered the position and structure of 3C 273 by observing its signals as it was

276

eclipsed and revealed by the moon passing across it. The hundreds of quasars and other radio objects in the universe identified since then by the Parkes instrument have helped to refine our understanding of the way in which the universe began. Quasars were shown by John Bolton and others to be rushing away from the centre of the universe at incredible speeds, the higher speeds being associated with the farther objects, giving support to the so-called 'big bang' theory of the evolution of the universe.

The Parkes telescope wins in the aesthetic stakes over the Mills Cross telescope at Molonglo near Canberra, the Radioheliograph at Culgoora and the Stellar Interferometer at Narrabri (the last two are in north-western NSW), but these three telescopes are truly original in concept, design and function.

Professor Bernard Mills of the Sydney University School of Physics wanted a telescope which would observe in radio wavelengths, but which would give much finer detail than could possibly be obtained with a 'dish'. His solution was to lay two long trough-shaped aerials on the ground in the shape of a cross—each arm being nearly $1\frac{1}{2}$ kilometres long—and, by ingenious electronics, to combine the two signals to produce the same effect as a single, dish-shaped aerial of a size much larger than engineering and financial limitations would permit in practice. When the famous ticking stars or 'pulsars' were first observed in 1968, the Mills Cross proved to be the best radiotelescope in the best position in the world to study them.

Dr Paul Wild (see profile, page 278) used a broadly similar electronic principle to Mills but settled on a different arrangement of aerials for studying the radio emissions from the sun. At the Culgoora Observatory, 96 small, fixed, dish aerials are laid out in a circle three kilometres across; as each dish follows the sun, all the separate signals are electronically combined to produce a visible, moving picture of the 'radio sun', a spectacular feat of instrumentation which has resulted in a rash of discoveries about the sun's behaviour—its sunspots, flares and their manifestations as earthly weather patterns, radio communication disturbances and the beautiful aurorae.

On the other side of the quiet country town of Narrabri, British-born Professor Robert Hanbury Brown of the School of Physics at Sydney University built his weird-looking but revolutionary instrument (known as a stellar interferometer) for measuring the precise sizes of stars. Its two large mirrors mounted on a circular track collect the light from a star, like any optical telescope, but then analyse the phases of the light by techniques derived from Hanbury Brown's experience with radioastronomy at the world's first giant radio dish at Jodrell Bank in Britain. For opening up a new window on the universe, Professor Hanbury Brown's work has been hailed as a 'classic' experiment in astronomy, and in 1974 the Australian Government recognised his personal achievement with a special grant of $75,000 for a design study on a greatly enlarged version of his Narrabri instrument which has now come to the end of its useful life.

As further evidence of the standing of Australia's astronomers on the world scene, it should be recorded that Bolton, Mills, Wild and Hanbury Brown have all been elected Fellows of the Royal Society.

Mount Stromlo was once a pleasant hill near Canberra—close enough to the capital for good communications, but far enough away for the seclusion that telescopes demand. Under the successive leadership of Sir Richard Woolley (later Astronomer Royal of Britain) and Professor Bart Bok, Mount Stromlo became the pre-eminent observatory in the southern hemisphere, boasting the largest telescope south of the equator, a 74-inch reflector. But, with the rapid expansion of the public service in Canberra, Mount Stromlo became engulfed in suburbia, the lights of which at night all but ruined much of the observing programme. Under the energetic Bart Bok, the ANU decided to establish a field station for further expansion of its facilities and chose Siding Spring Mountain in the spectacular Warrambungle Range near Coonabarabran in north-western NSW. Reflectors of 40-inch, 24-inch and 16-inch diameter were established, but the success of the site in terms of weather and clarity of view made further expansion inevitable.

Siding Spring Mountain now boasts a true giant of an optical telescope—the 3.9 metre (154-inch) reflector of the bi-national Anglo-Australian Telescope Board. Formally commissioned late in 1974, under its American Director Dr Joe Wampler, the AAT was at the time the largest mirror in the southern hemisphere, but such is the popularity among astronomers of observing the southern skies that at least two other telescopes of similar size are hot on its heels in South America. The AAT cost $16 million to build, and its annual operating costs, split equally between Australia and Britain to pay for the strictly equal observing times allotted to each nation, will amount to close on $1.5 million annually. This is Big Science.

THE SOUTHERN SEAS

While astronomy has arrived and will continue to flourish in Australia, marine science is a comparative newcomer which could outstrip its rivals in its rate of growth and popular appeal. For years now, a few leading and vocal scientists have pleaded the case for a proper attack on the research problems posed by the marine environment of Australia. Our continental island has one of the longest and least understood coastlines in the world, yet it is clearly one of the richest and most diverse habitats of marine life for purposes both of scientific study and of controlled exploitation for commercial and touristic use.

Two problems on the Great Barrier Reef, oil drilling and infestation by the Crown-of-Thorns starfish, have been debated publicly with a mixture of emotionalism and sound scientific sense. The public fuss has shown dramatically how little we really know about the complex environment of the Reef, not to mention the other thousands of kilometres of Australia's coastline and continental shelf regions. There is little basic data to support conservation programmes or to give reliable guidelines to the fishing industry at a time when controlled exploitation of the sea's food potential is an urgent necessity.

The message seems to have penetrated. Australian Government money is at last beginning to flow into marine research in significant chunks, the largest investment being in the Australian Institute of Marine Science (AIMS). Distressingly long in gestation, AIMS was initiated politically by ex-Prime Minister

Dr Paul Wild—man in the sun

If anyone had asked the young Paul Wild, when he left Cambridge University in 1943, how he would end up using his physics degree, it is odds-on he would not have thought of astronomy as even a remote possibility. After all, astronomy was then largely a matter of studying the light from stars through telescopes with mirrors and other optical paraphernalia. Wild, on the other hand, was a whizz at electronics, a skill which led him straight into the Royal Navy where, like so many later leaders in the then unknown field of radioastronomy, he became a radar officer.

Fate brought him, in his ship HMS *King George V*, to the Pacific station. He liked the look of Australia, and he later applied with his eventual lifelong colleague and fellow Yorkshireman John Bolton, for the same job at the Radiophysics Laboratory of the then CSIR in Sydney. Bolton got the job, but Wild was invited to take up another post immediately afterwards. This was the beginning of a romantic story of scientific discovery about the universe through the radio 'eyes' of the new breed of electronic astronomers, a story all the more remarkable because of the persistence, over three decades, of its spate of new insights into the heavens.

Paul Wild became fascinated by the nearest star to us, our own sun. The sun's radio emissions were first identified in 1942 by a British scientist who was puzzled by some apparent jamming of radar sets scanning the skies for German raiders. The intensity of the interfering radiation, which varied irregularly, was shown to be related to the violent activity on the sun's surface known as sunspots. By 1952, Wild had so refined such observations that, on a dairy farm at Dapto, south of Sydney, he had constructed a 'radio spectrograph' which could study the radio emissions from the sun across a range of wavelengths, that is, across a spectrum.

This approach, a pioneering one in the world, was so revealing of the sun's behaviour that within 10 years Wild had persuaded his CSIRO bosses and the American Ford Foundation to invest $500,000 in an even more remarkable instrument to study the sun, the Culgoora Radioheliograph, described briefly on page 277. By taking detailed radio 'movies' of solar flares at different wavelengths, Wild's team (he is always insistent on due recognition for his colleagues) have added a whole new dimension to the understanding of the sun.

A truly modest man, Paul Wild has had a heap of scientific honours piled on him which could go to the heads of lesser people —Fellow of both the Australian Academy of Science and the Royal Society, Foreign Honorary Member of the American Academy of Arts and Sciences, recipient of the Royal Astronomical Society's first Herschel Medal, and appointment in 1971 as Chief of the CSIRO Division of Radiophysics. Although he is no limelighter and his name would be known by few of the lay public, Wild is a relaxed and accomplished speaker who seldom fails to get across the excitement of his research and the simple directness with which he has successfully tackled problems of staggering complexity. He is, for example, now turning his talents to developing a wholly new system, known as Interscan, for aircraft traffic control.

Apart from proudly fathering three children, Paul Wild's other accomplishments give some insight into the private man— a knowledgeable music lover, a deft impersonator, an expert at *The Times* crossword puzzles and chess, a social cricketer, a walking encyclopaedia on everything that has ever happened in a century of cricket (he has a complete collection of *Wisden*), and a railway enthusiast of forbidding memory (he is reputed to be able to recite every railway station, in correct order, on the old British systems GWR, LMS and LNER). Paul Wild is the antithesis of the archetypal, narrow scientist—would there were more like him.

John Gorton in a Senate election campaign in 1969, but not until 1973-74 was AIMS put on its feet with its first Director, American Dr Malvern Gilmartin, and a guaranteed $8 million for its first five years. The Institute has a site near Townsville, splendidly situated for the study of the tropical and sub-tropical waters of Australia.

AIMS, however, will not be completely dominant in marine research. Under some pressure from the Labor Government, the Australian Research Grants Committee, which gives money to individuals and small groups largely in universities, departed from its previous practice of treating all research equally by earmarking some $900,000 for marine science for the three years 1973-75. Beneficiaries include universities like Queensland and James Cook (at Townsville) with an established interest in the sea. Most of the early alarm about and resulting effort on tracking the Crown-of-Thorns starfish was mounted from the University of Queensland, with the Queensland State Department of Primary Industry organising surveys which gave a more optimistic view in the medium-term because of the observed rate of regeneration of coral reefs eaten out by the 'wave' of starfish; thankfully, this view now appears to be correct.

There are only three modest research stations on the Barrier Reef itself. The oldest is on Heron Island, off Gladstone, on the south of the Reef. Nearby is the small station on One Tree Island operated by the Australian Museum in Sydney. In 1973 the same museum began to build a station on Lizard Island on the far north of the Reef.

The Barrier Reef, though, is not the only place to do valuable marine research. There is a demand for much more study of the temperate waters where commercial fishermen reap their main harvests. This is one of the areas now delineated for the CSIRO's Division of Fisheries and Oceanography, based at Cronulla in Sydney; it spends close to $2 million annually, and at last has permission to build a 67-metre research vessel—the lack of a decent sized boat greatly retarded Australian marine research.

Physically-oriented marine research in Australia has been as slow to put to sea as has biological study of the ocean, but the School of Physics at Sydney University has joined in with its own 21-metre research vessel, named appropriately after its fund-raising head, Canadian-born Professor Harry Messel. A multi-purpose vessel, it is being used principally for hydrography, oceanography, geology and geophysics, with an occasional dash to the Northern Territory for Professor Messel's own ecological survey of crocodiles.

The commercial potential of Australia's marine life is not limited to fish meat. Scientists believe there is a very real prospect of finding useful drugs among the complex chemicals of the sea, such as the specialised venoms of the animals living on the Barrier Reef. Only a tiny fraction of our marine species have been screened, or studied in any detail, for their drug potential. To exploit this possibility, the giant Roche Company has poured $4.5 million into their new Institute of Marine Pharmacology at Dee Why in Sydney.

The marine science boys (as in other research areas in Australia, there are precious few girls in the game, more's the pity) will still have to work hard on their image with the public and politicians—and first of all among themselves —if they are to sustain their growth at an adequate rate. They have plenty going for them—a unique environment, some adventurous spirits, athletic and sometimes hazardous ways of collecting information (it is difficult to avoid becoming a diver), and problems of global importance. Yet, there are not too many marine scientists in Australia, and in the past they have not been noted for the charity of their views about each other. The late 1970s will show whether marine science will sink or swim in Australian waters.

A CRUSTY STORY

The relatively featureless terrain of Australia has long been attributed to the great age of the continent. Yet, it is only in the past decade or so that we have realised just how old the crust of Australia really is—the tough, metamorphosed rocks of Australia's Pre-Cambrian 'shield' are at least 2,500 million years old, more than half way back in time to the currently accepted date of the formation of the earth itself, 4,500 million years ago.

Because they are so old, the rocks of the Pre-Cambrian shield contain few fossilised remains of living things, the markers used by geologists to determine relative ages of younger rocks. But these old rocks are not entirely devoid of fossils. There was much excitement internationally when some minute and indistinct marks in the hard rocks of South Australia were identified positively as the remains of primitive forms of life at least 600-650 million years old—then the oldest known fossils on earth.

With such a vast tract of old rocks containing few distinguishing marks, the geologist faces serious problems in working out the age relationships of rocks in the field. An accurate idea of these relationships allows him to draw up a history of the rocks in a given region—when they were formed, how they were altered by heat and pressure, when they were uplifted, tilted and fractured, when they were penetrated by volcanic magmas and mineral-containing fluids. Without such precise information, the geologist works only by inspired guesswork, and he is unable to use his knowledge of one area to predict with any accuracy the situation in other, less well-known areas—and accurate predictions are vital in economic geology, the search for minerals.

Unable to determine the absolute ages of Pre-Cambrian rocks, Australian geology was hampered until some very bright geologists in Perth and Canberra began to apply the precise techniques of chemistry and physics. Their quantitative methods were little short of revolutionary in a science as highly generalised and qualitative as geology, and in the mid 1950s and early 1960s Australian geophysicists-cum-geochemists played an important role in making geology both a field study *and* a laboratory science.

Although largely unsung at home, the writings of geological scientists like Professor Ted Ringwood, Dr Bill Compston, Dr John Green, Dr John Richards, Professor John Lovering, Dr Ross Taylor and Associate Professor Richard Stanton became essential reading all over the geological world. Most of these scientists have worked at the Australian National University in Canberra. They developed and refined laboratory techniques for determining the ages of rocks by measuring the long-lasting radioactive decay of elements like uranium, potassium and rubidium. They presented fresh ideas about how igneous rocks are formed within the earth, and how minerals crystallise from volcanic and watery fluids—particularly complex problems to unravel. On even larger scales, their understandings of how the earth and planets were formed have successfully challenged many older theories.

It was no surprise, then, that the American space agency NASA included some Australian geological scientists among the select few to receive precious samples of the rocks brought back from the moon by the Apollo astronauts. Australians working in Canberra, Melbourne and Houston, Texas, analysed the chemical and mineral components of these samples to deduce the ages and likely genesis of lunar rocks.

During the moon mission themselves, several of the leading earth scientists accepted the responsibility for explaining to the general public the scientific significance of the astronauts' observations. I would like to record a word of appreciation for the selfless way in which these expert commentators made themselves available throughout the 24-hour-a-day vigils we kept at the ABC studios for broadcasting the Apollo missions. One of these men was always willing either to be with us in the marathon stretches in the studio or to be on tap by telephone at any hour. At the same time, some were also needed by the NASA mission controllers to be available for calls from the USA. They were heady days (and headachey ones too), and the audience responded with compliments for the Australian scientists.

Even though he is a physicist rather than a geologist, we should not fail to include here our most regular commentator, Dr Brian O'Brien—one of Australia's few space scientists—who is now Director of Environmental Protection in Western Australia. Dr O'Brien built instruments which were flown to the moon's surface for experiments in every one of the six Apollo missions to land there—a rare record in space science.

Professor Ted Ringwood, a bundle of intellectual energy, is probably the world's most adventurous thinker about the complex processes which formed the earth, the moon and the solar system. Previous theorists have been hampered by lack of certain knowledge of what goes on inside the earth at any depth greater than the few thousand metres from which the longest drilling cores can be extracted. Using ultra-high pressure-and-temperature gear at Canberra, Ted Ringwood has managed to subject rocks, and artificial mixtures simulating rock components, to squeezing so massive that their chemical and crystalline characteristics change dramatically, thus reproducing the conditions at depths of thousands of kilometres.

Armed with this information, he has drawn up detailed scenarios of the earth's formation and evolution in a geological sense. His theories about the moon were considered by most as interesting ideas, but too way out. However, the chemical, mineralogical and radioactive information stored in the rocks brought back by the Apollo astronauts has swung opinion in Ringwood's favour, and his theory that the moon was largely formed by the accretion of small solid particles trapped in space near the earth has won wide acceptance. The honours that are his due now flow in—he is a Fellow of the Royal Society and, at 44, the youngest recipient of the Bowie Medal, the highest award of the American Geophysical Union.

One of the most regular criticisms of Australian science has been the comparatively low level of applied research and development. Much of the scientific work underpinning Australian industry has been done overseas, and local scientists function more as adapters and quality controllers than as innovators. There is, of course, a problem of scale. In some industries, a research and development effort is unlikely to pay off without a major financial commitment being maintained over several decades. Only the very biggest firms maintain research laboratories in the million dollar class: BHP, ICI, CRA, ACI, AWA and APM stand out in this regard, but in at least one of these a significant research effort is seriously threatened—when things get tight for commercial firms, only the long-sighted do not cut back their research effort.

Australia has no economically significant groups of small to moderately sized firms engaging in specialised research and development and 'high technology' production—the kind of firms that have flourished in comparably populated countries in Europe. Nor have Australian Government incentive schemes helped establish firms which, in order to enter competitive export markets, may be forced to concentrate on small, cheaply transportable, specialised products such as electronic packages.

Such reliable figures as exist about the industrial R & D (research and development) scene in Australia prove the point: at the end of the 1960s Australian industry was spending about $70 million annually on R & D, but 70 per cent of this was spent by only 6 per cent of the firms devoting any money to R & D; in other words, a few big firms spend big, and a lot of little firms spend little. The Industrial Research and Development Grants scheme, initiated by the Liberal Government and continued by Labor, allocated $14 million over three years to firms for their own R & D projects, but it has been seriously criticised for supporting large firms with existing R & D capabilities at the expense of more flexible and more promising smaller firms.

The largest co-ordinated effort in applied research comes from the Government's own organisations, the most notable being the CSIRO, the Australian Atomic Energy Commission (still languishing for lack of a power reactor after years of anxious waiting), the defence science effort and the Bureau of Mineral Resources. Of these, because of its size and stated purpose, the CSIRO is the most productive (CSIRO stands for the Commonwealth Scientific & *Industrial* Research Organisation); much of its work is directed towards applied objectives in supporting the rural, mining, food and textile industries. Each of these industries has a group of CSIRO laboratories, some of which are heavily dependent on funds provided by the industries themselves; the CSIRO wool laboratories would wither without direct levies from the wool industry. The CSIRO also has some credits in secondary industry.

The multi-million dollar scientific instrument industry based on Dr Alan Walsh's atomic absorption spectrophotometer has been mentioned. Another development in the same money class is the Self-Twist Spinning Machine, conceived and designed in the Geelong laboratories of the Division of Textile Industry. Traditional spinning is a century old, but the new machine is based on a fresh principle: roll two separate threads between rollers, put them in contact with each other, and they 'self-twist' together. Once the bugs had been removed from successive prototype machines, the CSIRO technologists patented a machine which is quieter, more compact, more reliable and some 15 times faster than the old type. Unlike many other Australian innovations, this one was successfully manufactured here by a locally owned firm, Repco Ltd, which is exporting machines at a great rate.

Australia's strength in chemical research has paid off in many fields, but few have quite such potential for national needs in this dry continent as a novel process for purifying water. Patented by the CSIRO under the name Sirotherm, the process has been taken beyond the pilot plant stage by Australia's largest chemical firm, ICI. In principle, the process is simplicity itself—in practice, like any desalination process, it is hard to operate on a competitive, economic scale.

Sirotherm works by passing brackish water (not as salty as sea water), through a special resin which traps the dissolved impurities. The resin, ingeniously developed by Dr Don Weiss of the CSIRO, will yield its impurities to a flush of hot water, and is then ready to draw more excess salts out of more impure water. ICI has begun to plan manufacturing plants for the resin; for economic viability these will have to be located overseas nearer the larger markets.

Two other potential money-spinners from Australian innovations, which also have beneficial side-effects in their reduced environmental impact, are evidence that government-sponsored R & D is not wholly dominant. One comes from a sophisticated and extended programme of research in metallurgy, the other from the fertile mind of a single inventor in the romantic 'backyard workshop'.

The first is the Worcra process for continuous smelting and purification of a variety of ores; this essentially simple, minimum-polluting process is the brainchild of Dr Howard Worner of the British-dominated mining and metals firm, CRA—hence the name. If we do not hear of its widespread introduction over the next 10 years, we shall have an unfortunate example of how a brilliant idea can be killed through lack of adequate support.

The second is the 'orbital engine' of Mr Ralph Sarich, a Perth toolmaker with a flair for finding simple solutions to complex mechanical problems. His compact, economical engine with its few moving parts has great promise; its development to the commercial stage is being backed by the BHP research effort.

THE SLOW POLITICISATION OF AUSTRALIAN SCIENCE

The more radical elements among younger scientists in Australia today have tried to characterise the 'leadership' of science—the Academy of Science, the CSIRO Executive and Chiefs, the senior university professors—as reactionary and politically ineffective. They may sometimes be conservative and reluctant to take strong stands on public issues, but the political criticism cannot, with any justice or knowledge of history, be made to stick. Even though their actions often lacked cohesion and were the result more of private representations to government than of involvement of the scientific community as a whole, the 'leadership' of Australian science managed to win a level of financial support and long-term guarantees for research which was, in retrospect, more than satisfactory.

This is so because research and development were supported by successive Liberal-Country Party Governments in the absence of, indeed in the direct denial of, any overall policy for science in the service of the nation. The 1950s and 1960s saw the consolidation of the CSIRO's position and the funding of several major facilities, notably the astronomical instruments, as evidence of the politician's benign approach to science. The Australian Universities Commission was set up by Sir Robert Menzies and this led to a dramatic expansion in the number and size of universities, all with substantial portions of their finance ($300 million annually) going into research. Three major schemes for making grants to individual researchers or firms were established: the Australian Research Grants Committee, the National Health and Medical Research Council, and the Industrial Research and Development Grants scheme, which collectively allocate $16 million each year.

None of these handouts happened by accident. All were the result of successful lobbying of one sort or another. That this is so little appreciated by younger scientists reflects the complete lack both of scientific writing in the popular press and of the incorporation of Australian scientific history in educational courses, omissions which have resulted in such a low level of knowledge about local science (even within the scientific community) that outsiders are amazed. This perhaps helps to explain why the Liberal-Country Party politicians were so reticent about scientific successes which had been achieved through direct government support—it is reasonable to assume that they just did not notice.

The scene changed at the turn of the last decade. Following as usual in the train of American and British movements, some scientists began to express publicly their concern about the directions science had been taking (note that concern about funding was less noticeable—most of those concerned were reasonably secure under direct or indirect government support). The Social Responsibility in Science movement got under way; this had strong personal and emotional ties to the simultaneous environment-conservation-ecology movement. Both movements scored well in the popular press in the two years leading to the watershed election of December, 1972, when Labor swept into power. Science in the service of man, and not of profits or death, was the catch-cry. The SRS people were, despite their effective publicity, pretty thin among the ranks of scientists, but the environmental angle of the general movement built up a big head of popular steam.

Meanwhile, the 'heavies' of the scientific establishment and a minute handful of people truly expert in science policy matters were pressing the Liberal and Labor Parties alike to define, for the first time in Australia, a co-ordinated and rational policy for science. The Liberals had made the token gesture of adding a 'Science' wing to the existing Department of Education, but their Ministers for Education and Science consistently failed to take science policy seriously, most of them dismissing such a notion as indefinable. However, Labor, in Opposition, formally adopted science into its platform of policies and committed itself to establish a Ministry for Science and Technology. In the event, all we got in December 1972 was a Minister for Science; technology, as before, remained dispersed through other portfolios. This had the unintentioned effect of diminishing the political fallout of the 'anti-science movement', the main thrust of which was really directed against the technological aspects of science.

The new Labor Government also established a Ministry for Environment and Conservation. Both new ministers, Mr Bill Morrison and Dr Moss Cass, appointed some of the more outspoken radicals to their personal staffs. The teeth of the SRS movement were drawn and the environmentalists gave the government an armchair ride for its first 18 months before again voicing concern about the actions and inactions of government and industry.

The Science Minister was 27th out of 27 in the Caucus ballot for Cabinet. Partly because of a resulting low priority in Cabinet, partly because he saw little political advantage in his portfolio ('There are no votes in science,' he had said) and partly because the party platform gave little guidance on administrative and legislative action, it took Mr Morrison over two years to get a long-promised policy advisory body off the ground. The Australian Science and Technology Council (ASTEC) was formed in May 1975 under the chairmanship of Dr J. A. L. Matheson, Vice-Chancellor of Monash University. Those two years of marking time were crucial to the medium-term development of science in Australia. For, while the government made massive commitments to other areas of public funding, such as social security and urban development, science was nudged into a billabong almost without the scientists realising it. The very modest increases in research funds which the government did grant were more than offset by the sharp inflation rate which struck the nation in 1974.

The 'anti-scientists' could be well pleased that, though numerically small, their views appeared to have put the brakes on science, although the deceleration acted indiscriminately across most aspects of research (some politically favoured areas such as analytical work in support of the consumer movement, more food research, and marine science managed to move ahead against the trend). The Government rationalised its position in the introduction to the White Paper launching ASTEC by prefacing its plan of action with talk of 'the growth of public disenchantment with the role of science and technology' and by stating categorically that 'the Australian Government is acutely aware of, and in large measure in sympathy with, public disappointment, disquiet and disillusion associated with many of the products and effects of science and technology'. While it could be said that the scientific evidence for such strong assertions in a formal document about science was so scanty as to be unworthy of a government and to display little understanding of the nature of scientific enquiry (even about opinions), the effect has been to jolt some of the more socially aware scientists into a more open political stance.

Now that their honeymoon period with governments and society at large is over, scientists in Australia are being forced to examine their own affairs and their relationships with political power in a more flexible and realistic way. The second half of the 70s will be crucial years for testing whether Australian scientists will put on a bolder face and join the mainstream of a politicised society.

Opposite: The 64-metre dish of the CSIRO's radio telescope at Parkes, western NSW, was built in 1961 to investigate (and, as it turned out, successfully identify) the sources of radio emissions from deep space. But the Parkes team, in conjunction with Melbourne's Monash University and under the direction of Professor Ron Brown, made a more momentous discovery in 1973. In studying the radio emissions they identified a pattern of absorption bands peculiar to methanimine, a substance believed to be a precursor of the simplest amino acid, glycine; the amino acids are essential components of all protein and therefore of all known forms of living cells. If continuing research reveals the existence of amino acids in deep space, it will greatly strengthen the theory that life on earth originally came from outer space.

Following their momentous discovery of methanimine in space, the Parkes-Monash research team switched its attention to the more complex, and more important, molecules of urea and glycine, two of the 'building blocks of life'.

Top: Professor Ron Brown (centre) and two members of his Monash research team, Dr Peter Godfrey (left) and John Storey, compare their absorption chart for urea with a Parkes computer print-out of a quasar emission; a similar absorption pattern in the print-out would indicate the presence of urea molecules in space. The urea study drew a blank, and glycine is now being investigated.

Right: The control room at Parkes, nerve centre of the hunt for clues to the origin of life and the nature of the universe as a whole.

Opposite: Some 250 kilometres north of Parkes, at Siding Spring Mountain in the Warrumbungle Range, NSW, the huge $16 million Anglo-Australian optical telescope, with its 3.9 metre reflector, peers into space. The new observatory was opened in 1974.

288

The first scientific research undertaken in Australia was in agriculture, and the subsequent success of the nation as a primary producer was greatly aided by the work of the early agricultural scientists. However, there are still many problems to be solved.

Opposite: Locusts have been a problem all over the world ever since man began to cultivate crops. Even today's advanced pesticidal technology has found no effective defence against swarms like this one near Bourke, NSW.

Left: A *Locusta migratoria* feeds in a wheat crop beside a dead comrade, victim of an earlier spraying. On the ground the insects are vulnerable, but the airborne flights continue almost unabated.

Above: A wheat farmer near Moree, NSW, takes stock of the devastation wrought by one small overnight swarm.

Medical research in Australia won national esteem and world attention in the 60s when Sir Macfarlane Burnet and Sir John Eccles were awarded Nobel prizes for their work in immunology and neurophysiology. Newspapers noisily acclaim such 'break-throughs', but for the most part the important, serious research that sometimes leads to such fame is carried out slowly and quietly.

Opposite: Research into the complex mechanics of immunology bring together this specially bred nude mouse and the urbane director of Melbourne's Walter and Eliza Hall Institute, Professor Gus Nossal. Use of these mice is leading to an understanding of rejection in organ transplants, and may lead to further knowledge and perhaps control of cancer.

Left: Sheep are being used at the Howard Florey Institute in investigations of animal adjustments to dietary salt levels, research which is relevant to the pastoral industry and also to the manufacture of baby foods. Here, graduate research assistants Catherine Oddie and Sabariah Schrader compare levels of steroid hormones in sheep's blood.

Below: The director of the Florey Institute, Dr Derek Denton, and his team operating in their fully equipped theatre. The patient is a sheep.

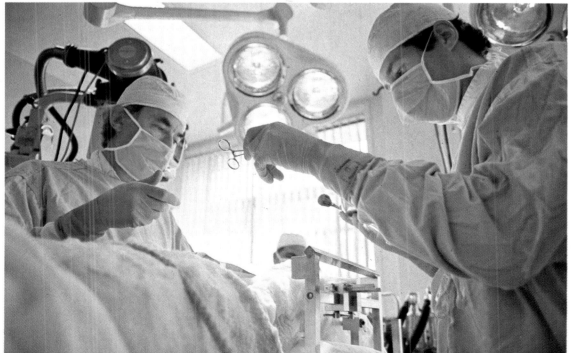

EDUCATION

Dr David Cohen

**'Three million kids into
9,500 schools won't go!'**

The problems of coping with education in Australia before World War II
were relatively simple. The country's slow population growth was paralleled
in school and university enrolments. But the post-war era saw re-enrolment
of discharged military personnel, a greatly increasing population, extension of
compulsory schooling to cover all those aged six to 16 and a big increase in
the number of 17 year olds remaining at school.

In the mid 1950s, less than 10 per cent of the 17 year olds remained at
school. In the mid 1970s, the figure is nearing 40 per cent. In New South
Wales, the most populous State, secondary school enrolments grew by more
than 50 per cent between 1965 and 1972.

Given such a context, how adequate is education in Australia today? This
question may be considered in relation to the organisation of education, financing of education, curricula, teachers and educational research.

Within the six State capital cities lie the key education authorities of Australia.
For historical, economic and geographical reasons, responsibility for providing
free and universal education for school age children was bequeathed to the six
State governments after Federation in 1901. To rationalise the vast personnel
and economic resources required to support education, each State established
a centralised State Education Department, responsible through its Minister
to the State Parliament. Centralised control was intended to ensure a satisfactory education for children attending even geographically remote schools.
'Head Office' was to provide on a state-wide basis uniformly good buildings,
uniformly good teachers, and controlled curricula. Standards could be regularly
checked (indeed, policed) by departmental inspectors visiting all schools in
the State annually, with teacher promotions and salaries dependent upon their
inspectors' reports and assessments. The unfortunate side-effects, including lack
of communication between senior officers and their teachers and students, were
neglected or unrecognised.

As a means of harnessing the seemingly unbridled powers of education
departments—to allocate teachers, land, buildings and their maintenance, furniture, equipment, even curricula and examinations—huge superstructures were

ORGANISATION OF AUSTRALIAN EDUCATION

Opposite: Textbooks and black-
boards are beginning to lose
ground in some schools as small
problem-raising modules, tape recorders, film projectors, television
sets and radios play an increasingly important—and normal—
role in education.

constructed. Bureaucratic processes have evolved to handle the logistics of this huge enterprise. The processes, in turn, have tended to stifle sensitivity for the major purported function of education departments, which is the right of every child to have the best possible educational experience. An educational problem which looms large in Australia in the mid 1970s is: how do you provide three million kids attending 9,500 schools with the best education possible?

State control of the educational systems met the austere expectations of both parents and the majority of teachers at least until after World War II. Planning did not lag too far behind evolving needs in education, and the centralised superstructures were coping adequately.

A slow growth rate tended to conceal inadequacies in educational quality. Over the years, the States inherited a legacy of selectivity, over-centralisation, apathy and shoe-string budgets. Even so, States were reluctant to surrender any of their educational powers to the taxing authority, the Commonwealth. Just three quarters of a century after Federation, the States jealously guarded education as one of the last bastions of State rights.

Accelerated growth after World War II highlighted weaknesses. The huge, unwieldy superstructures often complemented conservative, unimaginative, and even inept decision-making by senior officers. State education departments had been geared to respond only after crises had developed. Responses came too late, with too little. Forward planning was inadequate or non-existent.

Selection board members, seldom education experts, undertook personnel selection roles. Many bright, young and imaginative educators were thus overlooked and they soon fled the unrewarding and inhibitive environment for greener pastures.

The State education departments developed a reputation for rigidity but by the start of the 70s, the situation was brightening. One State Director of Primary Education, addressing a conference of school principals in 1972, confirmed this. 'It is true,' he said, 'that our system is viewed as one of rigidity, one so inflexible that individual schools do not have the opportunity for developing initiative. Many of us have been able to deny this by example. But the fact is that the image is that of a system which is very rigid.' Change was needed. 'Already, I have indicated to inspectors that we should be more concerned with the outcome of education, and less concerned with procedures.' The roles of inspectors are changing in the 70s from supervisory to advisory. Such changing ideas have spread across State boundaries. Within the State educational systems, a number of factors have helped to improve Australia's educational inadequacies. Despite the apparently impersonal nature of the huge bureaucracies, changes of all types can often be traced to the influences of perceptive and sensitive individuals in senior education department administrative posts.

Increasing numbers of top-level Australian educators widened their horizons by looking at thriving educational alternatives overseas. Also, a new breed of administrators has taken up senior positions. Many have extended their educational studies through (formerly unavailable) higher education. For senior educational appointments, higher qualifications have tended to replace the less relevant criterion of senior military service. A corresponding revival of energy and administrative humaneness has seeped back into the State systems. This new breed has a greater depth of understanding of the educational process. Unlike many of their predecessors, they can feel confident and secure while increasingly delegating their authority through the decentralisation of decision-making.

EDUCATIONAL FINANCING

However, by the mid 60s improved decision-making alone was inadequate to meet the educational needs. The available human and physical resources had been allowed to atrophy to unacceptably deficient levels.

Critics and pressure groups claimed that an education crisis existed. Australian education in the mid 60s was regularly described by such words as 'shambles', 'crisis' and 'chaos'. Although shown to be seventh 'richest' of 97 countries surveyed in 1969 by the USA's National Aeronautics and Space Administration, it was an unlucky thirteenth in terms of expenditure per student. Australians were spending $ (US) 123 per student, compared with a typical expenditure of $ (US) 259 per student by developed countries. Yet, expenditure on education had risen astronomically. Total annual Australian expenditure on education was estimated to rise from $74 million in 1950 to $424 million by 1960 and to exceed $1,000 million by 1970. Even so, a survey of needs at that time conservatively estimated that an additional $1,443 million was the minimum needed to overcome the immediate problems of raising educational standards. Reflecting (and exploiting politically) expedient and popular platforms, States begrudged that more than half their treasury budgets were being spent on education and associated activities.

Their dilemma was the fear that acceptance of direct Commonwealth aid to education would further erode State rights. Meanwhile, education increasingly foundered. Ad hoc injections of funds occurred spasmodically to relieve critical areas. For example, a fund was established by industry to assist the development of science laboratories in independent schools. One effect of this was to widen the gap between the 'have' and 'have not' schools. This fund was the precursor of a number of ad hoc Commonwealth legislative acts, seemingly politically motivated rather than the outcome of any rational analysis of educational priorities. In the decade preceding 1973, State educational funds were bolstered by Commonwealth funds for both government and independent secondary schools for the provision of science laboratories and apparatus, and later, of school libraries and books. The quantity and quality of equipment and buildings for libraries and laboratories was spasmodically improved. Often, however, buildings were merely larger and similarly shaped, and failed to reflect the many desirable and frequently proclaimed changes in educational philosophies.

Meanwhile, rich schools became richer. Many of the older established independent schools were handsomely endowed, and also owned large and valuable tracts of prime land, but they were absolved from paying rates and taxes. These 'snob-and-job-appeal' schools (as educationist Henry Schoenheimer described them) progressively increased their fees. By 1972, four such schools had annual fees exceeding $1,000 for day enrolments and $2,250 for boarders.

Yet, many remained independent in name alone. They were often ultra-conservative, meticulously preserving the century-old traditions of their predecessors. Their curricula were generally not innovative. Examinations and narrowly academic objectives, sporting excellence (for those who can excel in football, cricket and rowing), religious observance, character-building, neatness of dress, and military precision in the cadet corps, are the key values in many independent boys schools. And there are corresponding values in many independent girls schools. However, some independent schools could certainly not be identified with such stereotypes. For example, Ascham introduced individualised assignments in the mid 60s in a modified 'Dalton Plan', a unit approach to learning. Frensham has diversified its curriculum offerings, and students may undertake a programme with emphasis upon art and craft. Under Betty Archdale's leadership, Abbotsleigh placed great emphasis upon the development of attitudes and values, as has also Melbourne CEGGS (Morton Hall). The Kings School has introduced 'public service' as an alternative to cadets. Several other examples could readily be cited.

Although often regarded as 'extra-curricula' rather than as *part* of the curriculum for all independent school students, music, art, drama and debating are more readily available than in government schools. Greater stability of staffing, with a far higher proportion of teachers staying for 10 years or more at the same school, and smaller class size, are other positive benefits of independent schooling.

Very recently, several independent schools have moved towards co-education. This liberalisation of policy has occurred, for example, by combining boys' and girls' specialist science classes from neighbouring schools, initially because of economic pressures. Half a dozen schools have become or intend to become co-educational, despite the pressure of 'old boys' or 'old girls' who recall their own school days with strong sentimental feelings and who want their off-spring to carry on the tradition. The pertinent educational and social evidence about co-education has barely been examined.

As the rich schools became richer, deprived schools became poorer. In 1972, a concerned school principal's plea to a State education department requested special consideration for his school 'situated in a depressed area where interest in education is confined to a small minority of parents'. Income from donations and Parents and Citizens Activities was barely sufficient to pay bills, 'let alone supply much-needed equipment, some of which is expensive and beyond the scope of annual departmental requisitions'. Slide projectors or tape recorders would be specially helpful to the children 'who have many disadvant-ages to overcome, and need the best our education system can offer'. Despite favourable endorsement by the district and staff inspectors concerned, the res-ponse from upper echelons was 'Alas, we have no funds!'.

With such an imbalance between rich and poor schools, education was for the first time perceived as a viable issue, as a political platform of Commonwealth importance. The major political parties recognised that education had risen to a vote-catching level. Promises and counter-promises were made. Vote-seeking baits included promises of increased State aid for non-government schools, Australian government subsidies for primary school libraries, and an Australia-wide review of the educational needs of schools.

When the Australian Labor Party was elected in 1972 its leaders declared that 'it's time' for a review of educational priorities in Australia. As a first step, Prime Minister Whitlam announced within one week of his election the forma-tion of an 'Interim Committee for the Australian Schools Commission', chaired initially by the eminent economist and Chairman of the Australian Universities Commission, Professor Peter Karmel.

The outcome of their intensive deliberations was presented, within six months, in a very fine document entitled 'Schools in Australia', and tabled to the Australian Minister for Education, Kim Beazley, in May 1973.

It highlighted deficiencies of human and material resources, major socio-economically based inequalities, inadequacies of teacher education, and the low quality of education including narrowness of curriculum objectives. The report called for the development of the 'needs' concept upon which to base the allocation of government funds. This concept was to include areas of recurrent resources, buildings, libraries, disadvantaged schools and handicapped students, teacher redevelopment (in-service education), and innovation and experimen-tation.

Its most controversial recommendation was the reconsideration of State aid to private schools, also to be based upon need. Determined that all Australian schools should reach minimum acceptable standards by the end of the decade, the Committee recommended the policy of supporting schools financially accord-ing to their needs. The relative estimates of needs were to be based upon data provided by every school in Australia. To avoid criticisms based upon allegedly discriminatory treatment of schools, and to provide a strategy for rapid and objective decision-making, the Committee developed a quantitative 'needs index' based upon school-reported operating expenses, adjusted for State differences. Urgency precluded the use of detailed case studies of schools, or of consideration of individual or qualitative criteria.

Estimated average salaries for full-time teachers and auxiliary staff in rela-tion to school enrolments provided the basis for classifying schools into eight categories, labelled A to H. Schools spending half (or less) of the annual $511 national average per pupil were classified as Category H, and were recommended to receive maximum Australian government subsidy. Schools spending twice the average were classified at Category A, and it was recommended that no further State aid be provided to them.

However, very few schools were rated so as to receive no funds. An appeals committee was constitutd to remedy individual injustices. For example, some

During school terms children from outlying stations live in temporary foster homes provided by a system of children's Bush Hostels. Here, pupils at the Tibooburra Hostel offer their newly cleaned shoes for the daily inspection.

'parent-co-operative' schools had established deliberate smaller-classes policies, and expenditure per pupil was thus inflated despite general economic stresses in these schools. The Karmel Committee's target was to raise expenditure per pupil in Australian schools to 140 per cent of the national average within six years.

The recently changed attitudes towards education are reflected in the increase of federal funding. In 1971-72, $346 million was spent on education; $883 million was spent in 1973-74.

An unresolved set of questions relates to the education of minority groups —the geographically isolated, handicapped children, the migrant child, and Aborigines. For the first time these have at last been identified as problems needing specialised educational provisions. Commonwealth funding has been earmarked to provide secondary school scholarships for all Aborigines, and also to provide substantial funds to isolated rural students. But these problems are not solved merely by raising expenditure per pupil. Fortunately, a number of tertiary institutions are initiating programmes designed to increase the understanding of cultural differences between the longer-term white Australians and the migrant and Aboriginal groups. Correspondence schools and Schools of the Air, using two way radio contact, represent fascinating Australian provisions for the isolated child. Compensation for social isolation remains a challenging problem.

Except in more extreme cases, the child handicapped by learning difficulties has often, in the past, been either undiagnosed or unremedied. Funding for special education, as recommended by the Karmel Report, may hasten the end of neglect for the disadvantaged.

CURRICULA

At least as important as money for education is improvement of the curricula. Historically, centralised educational administration decides curriculum development. State-wide curriculum suggestions were adopted as state-wide prescriptions. These were homogenised offerings of content, meted out in equal doses across the State. This was supported by official textbooks, especially for reading and arithmetic, lesson registers, timetables, schedules, syllabus forms, pupil record cards, all of which supported orderly routines and uniformity. Such homogeneity was heavily reinforced by visits of departmental inspectors.

Under these circumstances, innovation was stifled and variety inhibited. Emphasis upon accuracy and up-to-dateness in keeping records surpassed concern for educational objectives and the student. But this is changing rapidly.

In fact, the 70s may well be the decade of curriculum innovation. Major changes in curriculum are the result of a fresh approach introduced by the new breed of educational administrators in the various States, reinforced by reports from independently established committees in all States which critically examine the directions of Australian education.

Before the 70s, a succession of visiting educational critics deplored the apparent lack of purpose of Australian education. The bureaucracies were efficiently maintaining the machine, but why? Lists of high-sounding educational ideals were mouthed as educational objectives; for example, 'To develop each individual fully to his optimal ability'. But really it was something else which preoccupied the practising teacher when the classroom door closed. The maintenance of a neat and tidy set of classroom records about a quiet, neat, tidy group of children, with neat and tidy books and minds, was the cynic's all-too-accurate description for primary school teachers wishing to make a favourable impression or gain promotion.

For secondary school teachers, it was different. Here, objectives were replaced in practice by the dreaded hurdles of external examinations generally conducted at the end of the fourth and sixth years of secondary school. These examinations have tended to distort what happened in the schools for at least the last two of the previous 10 or 12 years. The trauma of a do-or-die terminal examination lasting two or three hours on each subject was coupled with preparation that included memorising facts to conquer the often re-phrased examination questions from the previous five years.

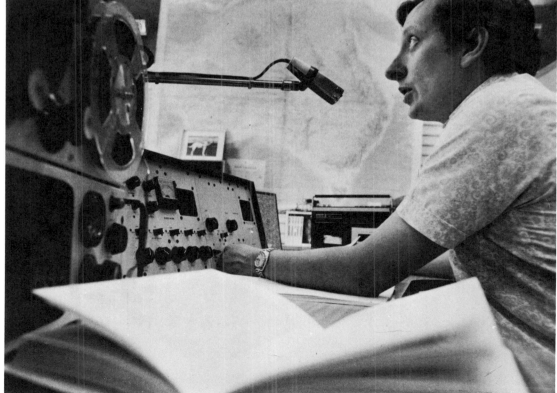

The Alice Springs School of the Air transmits for five hours a day to 35 station homesteads in central Australia, and caters for 70 pupils at levels from pre-school to seventh grade. One of the most distant homesteads is that at Phillip Creek station, 600 km north of the Alice, where 11-year-old Steven Cadzow (*above*) spends from 30 to 90 minutes daily in radio contact with the school. Steven's teachers include Carl Walker (*left*), and their teacher-pupil relationship is five years old.

This academic gamesmanship of teachers outwitting examiners was rivalled by examiners using new techniques to stump the teachers and students. Whatever the strategies used, their effects were to ensure a 'safe' approach to exam preparation, rather than an education concerned with broader objectives. Exams were prepared by a group of anonymous examiners outside schools. The examiners were selected for academic expertise, and were generally unqualified in educational evaluation. The papers were then scored by an anonymous group of markers (enticed by the 'honour' and/or financial incentives offered for each paper). These examinations strangled any autonomy of curriculum which schools purportedly retained. The 'best' teachers in the vicious circle were those whose students performed best. Frequently, this merely identified the school with the best parrots and the teacher with the best crystal ball for predicting questions. Under such circumstances, considered educational ideals could only make a teacher less congruent with 'the system' and less happy in the teaching profession.

Primary school inspectors with new charters and sounder educational objectives are now helping to remould the objectives of primary schools. Likewise, external examination at the end of the fourth year of secondary school has been abandoned. The external matriculation examination at the end of secondary school, traditionally used both for terminal certification and for university selection, has changed. Many States are moving from the short answer, objectively scored retention items of the mid 60s to essay answers which emphasise comparisons, comprehension and interpretation of previously unseen data about current affairs and problems relevant to students. A recent biology exam included questions concerning low-fat diets, prawn yields, another Kon Tiki venture, and Australian racial problems. Such examples show that secondary schools of the 70s are gradually being relieved of traditional exam preparation so that they may concentrate on more long term and significant educational objectives.

The selection of what to teach, and in what sequence, has typically been done in the past by centralised curriculum committees. The committees reinforce the traditional division of the school curriculum into a series of often unco-ordinated subjects such as mathematics, English and social studies. Primary school curricula are usually developed by a select group of teachers and principals (usually nominated by inspectors) under the chairmanship of an inspector (often the initiator of the curriculum revision). Meeting irregularly and infrequently, curriculum committees may take four or more years to produce the document which will receive the director-general's imprint for state-wide adoption. However, the trend in most States since the late 60s has been towards considerably more teacher autonomy. The content and sequence of what is taught today reflects more accurately the interests and abilities of a particular group of learners.

At primary school level, one result of autonomy has been increasing diversity. Despite the apparent confusion in many schools about the architectural and educational aspects of 'open education', there is innovation in this direction, notably in South Australia, Tasmania and Victoria. Larger classrooms have been created by knocking down walls between adjoining rooms. Those who mistakenly believed this was sufficient to create an open classroom have been quickly disillusioned. They have discovered only that doubling the room area has doubled the noise level and other problems without changing basic classroom climate. On the other hand, others have really understood and introduced the more important psychological aspects of openness, through the involvement of students in decision-making about their own learning, what it should include, what materials should be used, where it should take place, and at what rate.

Another aspect of curriculum decision-making is the evaluation of student progress. Traditionally, primary schools have used competitive tests. These show achievement in a possible score out of 10 or by a letter grade A-B-C-D-E. Public examination results of secondary school students have boosted newspaper circulations on the days of publication, as students anxiously pored through the lists of alphabetically arranged or numerically coded sets of results. For other secondary school examination results, a percentage score was given to the student in each subject. The Report Book or Report Sheet, with comments often limited to one sentence, summarised student performances, attitudes, conduct, and attendance. These reports were sent home to parents two or three times a year. They have occasionally been used to provide a basis for initiating discussion between teacher, parent and child, but more often have been fuel for neighbourly discussions about the relative merits of various offspring or of the offending teacher.

Attempts are being made to replace these inadequate and often gravely inaccurate summaries. More progressive schools have introduced regularly scheduled conferences between teachers and parents of each student. Diverse and innovative approaches to reporting are among the fruitful results of curriculum autonomy as it gradually diffuses through Australian schools.

Overall, the current curriculum scene is bright. Fixed content outlines are being replaced by plans which lend themselves to flexibility. Sharply delineated subject areas are being reintegrated to relate more closely to reality and to children's areas of interests. Curricula fully developed and specified within Head Office under the direction of inspectors are being replaced by curricula developed locally in small areas, with community representation, and with the help of field curriculum advisers. Concurrently, simultaneous state-wide implementation is being replaced by regional trials and by gradual and small-scale adoptions. This flexibility permits the adapting of curricula to allow for individual differences in teachers and their students.

Community representation is an extremely significant step and one which should not be underestimated. The history of centralised education in Australia had carried with it, loudly and clearly, the message that the views of the general public about education were unsought and unwanted. In fact, virtually the only time parents were able to enter the schools was in 'Education Week', an annual five day festival to display what didn't happen for most of the year. The opening of schools, and community representation on curriculum and other committees, are a product of the foresight of Ron Reed in Victoria, and of people like David Schapper (former Principal of Maryvale High School), who translated the ideal into action at the local level. The debate on the nature and extent of parental involvement—whether curriculum, financial and organisational aspects should be included—is a healthy and continuing one, since more and more parents are asserting their rights to be heard. The 1970s and 1980s will hopefully see a much closer relationship between educators, parents and local communities.

The trend towards flexibility is also reflected in educational publishing. The outmoded concept of a textbook assumes pre-determined content, identical for all teachers and students alike. In place of the textbook, small self-contained problem-raising units are being developed by the more progressive publishers. Known as modules, they embrace printed and audio-visual items in what is called a multi-media approach. They can be developed to treat each learner as a unique individual, by allowing the student to select the content, sequence and pace of learning.

Improved educational tools are based on a recognition of the need for individual flexibility. The products of the first curriculum project funded by the Australian Government exemplify this. Known as the Australian Science Education Project (ASEP), the junior secondary school science materials produced by its staff have been internationally acclaimed for their success in translating educational ideals into usable classroom form. Project Director Bert Howard's ability to stretch the ASEP budget of $1.25 million over nearly five years was feat enough (the American project known as the Biological Science Curriculum Study [BSCS] used $(US) 4 million over its first four years).

But if one battle for improved educational quality had been waged over autonomy of curriculum, limitations in teacher effectiveness have badly hindered improved quality. Research into teacher effectiveness was confusing and even contradictory in suggesting which characteristics and skills of teachers should be emphasised to improve their effectiveness. Teacher education institutions were the last bastion of conservatism, clutching at a subject approach dominated by history and philosophy of education, teaching methodology, and aspects of educational psychology—with token practice-teaching wedged in between. The Diploma of Education continued in nearly all Australian universities to comprise a diluted one year course, tacked on to a degree in arts, science or commerce. Such courses, devised initially for World War II returned servicemen, were lengthened progressively to two, three and four year courses, as though duration was the key determinant of graduate quality.

What has long been needed, and is still needed as the 70s gallop to their conclusion, is fundamental re-evaluation of the objectives, content, sequence and interrelationship of the components of teacher education. It is incongruous that the traditional teachers college provides a platform for teacher educators who preach about the 'whole child', 'integrated programmes', 'relevance', 'individualised curricula' while their whole environment negates such educational ideals.

One variant of the traditional programme is provided by making practical teaching a more central role in teacher education. For example, for students engaged in a school-based programme being used experimentally in South Australia at the Torrens College of Advanced Education, it is anticipated all other relevant teacher education experiences will arise. The part-time school responsibility of students of the State College of Victoria, in Hawthorn (which prepares some teachers for secondary technical schools), provides a springboard for their college courses. The concurrent BA, Dip.Ed. programme introduced at Macquarie University presents education courses interwoven with cognate courses in arts and sciences, a substantial improvement on the traditional end-on 'Dip.Ed.'

But the 'practise what you preach' model of teacher education remains strangely elusive. Maybe the attainment of such an ideal depends on having the right group of teacher educators working with the right group of prospective teachers. Yet many teacher educators have not kept up with contemporary developments in their fields. They have lacked the 'study leave' provisions of university academics.

Further, the use of matriculation examinations as the major if not sole determinant for selecting prospective teachers is unsuitable. There is more to teaching than the academic gamesmanship required for a pass in matriculation. Promising research in the early 60s by Balson, which attempted to predict likely teaching success from the personality characteristics of applicants, was short-lived. Criteria with seemingly little relevance continue to be used to screen prospective teachers.

Many young people who lacked compassion and love for children were enticed to select teaching careers careers for a different set of reasons, such as the lure of the not only free but also well-subsidised certificate courses at teachers college or degree programmes at university. Such an opportunity made financially feasible an otherwise impossible tertiary qualification. Indeed, it made the penalty of the iniquitous bonding system relatively less forbidding. A survey of prospective teachers enrolled at Monash University in 1967 showed that 74 per cent of science-oriented teachers' scholarship holders, 69 per cent of commerce-oriented teachers' scholarship holders, and 58 per cent of arts-oriented teachers' scholarship holders preferred vocations *other* than teaching, but their scholarships represented economic professional passports.

In New South Wales, the Bell Committee was established in 1971 to investigate teacher education, especially in relation to the wastage among teacher scholarship holders. Their key findings mirrored those from other States. For example, 2,000 of the 14,000 secondary teachers (about 14 per cent) employed at the start of the 1970 school year resigned during that year. More than 33 per cent of the drop-outs expressed dissatisfaction with the education department. Predictably, they complained of inflexibility, authoritarianism, and un-

302

South Australia leads other States in the use of the open classroom system and electronic and other new teaching aids. These children at Ingle Farm primary school, Adelaide, settle in with obvious interest to a tape-recorder session.

sympathetic attitudes to them as individuals. Nearly 33 per cent expressed dissatisfaction with their postings. Probably related to this, 87 per cent of resignations of bonded teachers took place within the first three years of teaching.

Hopefully, the abolition of university fees for all students will now discourage many non-committed students from pledging themselves to teaching via the bond. Certainly, improved selection methods, early detection and release of unsuitable candidates, and penalty-free release of those seeking to opt out of teaching, should be of benefit to all.

The selection and retention of appropriate teachers represents a vital link in the improvement of education. Similarly, within the State systems, the improvement of the teaching force depends on the identification and promotion of prospective leaders. This must be based upon more valid techniques than in the past. The use of unauthoritarian methods, such as judgments by colleagues, has not yet been attempted, but represents a possible alternative. Pre-service and in-service programmes for developing leadership abilities likewise need trial.

In any case, better selection, pre-service education and promotion will still not be enough to maintain an energetic, enlightened, and enthusiastic teaching service.

What else is needed to help teachers cope? A development in the last decade has been a renewed concern for in-service education for teachers. A key finding of the 1973 Karmel Report was that $2.5 million should be made available for the establishment and operation of teacher-initiated education centres for in-service education. Many Australian educators visiting England have spent time at 'Teacher Centres', which, generally governed by a committee containing a majority of practising teachers, conduct courses for the expressed needs of local teachers.

EDUCATION OUTSIDE THE SCHOOLS

Meanwhile, tertiary education has proliferated in availability and diversity. Universities which numbered only six in 1945 have now increased to 17. Since 1950, enrolments have shot up from 30,000 to nearly 150,000. Concurrently, Colleges of Advanced Education (CAE) as additional degree-granting institutions have moved strongly onto the scene. The differences in roles between universities and CAEs are still being clarified. Many colleges are directing their interests to more practical pursuits, including such studies as librarianship, textile sciences, health science, technology and institutional administration.

In the 70s, too, teachers colleges in most States have been granted autonomy. Many are changing their status to CAEs or adopting other multipurpose roles. More importantly, with freedom to advertise for and appoint staff from outside the education departments, there are likely to be notable improvements in the quality and range of teacher education programmes. Many longer-term staff members have been hurriedly induced to return to complete further qualifications after years of intellectual idleness. Others bemoan the fact that their many years of faithful service no longer seem to have any importance, and eagerly await their sixtieth birthday.

In the wider sphere of lifelong education, Australia needs to give urgent thought to developments which have already occurred in many other countries. The need for re-education of adults for new roles, activities and vocations arises from the rapidly changing world in which we live.

At the other end of the educational ladder, except in Tasmania and the ACT, pre-primary education is operated largely by private enterprise, sometimes supported by religious or voluntary organisations. With increasing numbers of working mothers, the availability of childminding centres in industrial areas has also become necessary for socio-economic reasons. Some companies have subsidised on-site centres. Meanwhile, academic debate continues on whether the importance of learning in early childhood would be developed or inhibited by formalising education for the three to six year old. In the longer term, gains in educational achievement from early childhood projects in the

304

USA seemed to dissipate. Nevertheless, irrespective of their educational merits, the provision of childminding facilities as liberators where both parents need or desire to work has become an important part of the emerging social ethos.

The 70s also heralded a renewed commitment to educational research. Two of the most influential Australian educators in the last 40 years have been Dr Ken S. Cunningham and Dr William C. Radford, successive directors of the Australian Council for Educational Research (ACER). Established initially by a grant from the Carnegie Corporation, ACER was subsequently forced into economically rewarding activities to survive. Although both federal and State governments provided token funding, it was inadequate to create a national powerhouse of research. Supplementary income was gained by acting as an agent for overseas curriculum materials, books, etc.

Of course, research performed overseas on educational practices would not breed confidence in the potential usefulness of these research findings in Australia. British research on co-education might illustrate this point. Unlike the one shot short-term research typical of postgraduate theses, research workers at Swansea, Wales, have devoted 25 years to the relative effects of co-education and single sex school education. This research has indicated that, in the British context, co-educational schools are happier and more humane environments for teachers and students. The academic achievement of both girls and boys is better in co-educational schools, markedly so for boys.

But co-education being a social and cultural phenomenon, surely the social and cultural effects on co-educated students represent the most relevant indexes of its effectiveness? Regrettably, such effects are characteristically ignored by educational research because of the difficulties in specifying and measuring them. Additionally, the students studied are not representative of all students, having been drawn largely from grammar schools (ie, high-ability streams). Thus, despite the intensity, thoroughness and dedication of the Swansea research on co-education, the findings lack wide usefulness in Britain and largely ignore vital outcomes. The validity for Australian students is even more remote.

In attempting to mimic the experimental methods of the exact sciences, educational researchers have tried to show that the variation of one closely controlled factor A causes a corresponding change in factor B. The vital questions which differ from the sciences include: for whom, and under what conditions? Unfortunately, in attempting to overcome these pertinent questions, educational researchers have created a reservoir of irrelevant and trivial findings.

It was thus somewhat of a triumph of hope over experience that in 1970 Dr Radford was able to identify five heartening events on the research scene: first, Australian government grants to establish the Australian Advisory Committee on Research and Development in Education (AACRDE); second, grants to provide for research funds related to colleges of advanced education; third, the significant growth of research units in State departments of education and in colleges of advanced education; fourth, the promotion of research into university teaching by the Australian Vice-Chancellors' Committee; finally, the Australian Association for Research in Education was established to promote the extension, dissemination and application of high quality research in education.

Just how effective some of these events have been is open to scrutiny. For example, the funding provided through the AACRDE in 1971 totalled $197,000 across 16 projects, a stark contrast with the research funding of even one American university, often exceeding a million dollars. The first official report of the committee drew attention to the fact that it was convinced 'that there is much research and developmental work in Australian education, quite directly related to existing problems of policy and practice, which should be undertaken, but which cannot proceed because of lack of funds'. Funding to this committee has been increased to $350,000 annually.

The big unanswered question in relation to this research is its influence on practice. Dissemination of research findings in comprehensible and meaningful terms is a prerequisite to effecting change in practices. Then, too, priorities in

305

grants have largely been allocated to academically appealing experiment-oriented projects, at a time when innovative grassroots development projects would have more closely matched the current educational needs. More fundamental changes of educational patterns, including the effects of 'de-schooling', elimination of 'subjects' from curricula, and major variations in traditional school organisational patterns, need exploration.

The recently adopted 'needs' policy for priority funding in education also requires thoughtful and continuing evaluation. In the USA, $10 billion were poured into State and local educational agencies under the 1965 Elementary and Secondary Education Act, in order to improve education for poor children. This American experience has led many to question the wisdom of re-directing money for compensatory educational programmes for disadvantaged children. Educational achievement seems pegged by socio-economic factors. Achievement might be enhanced at least as much by other social policies as by providing additional subsidies to poorer schools. Paradoxically for the educator, the injection of government funds into subsidies for direct increase in incomes, or lowering the taxes of the poor, may have more immediate and direct impacts upon the ultimate improvement of educational achievement.

So, education in Australia is in a state of tremendous change. To the credit of its educational administrators, it has largely conquered the stresses created by massive increases in quantitative demands. Now it is tackling the vital deficiencies in quality that have accrued. Government schools are changing from mere processing agencies of State education departments towards professionally autonomous centres of education whose major concern is the development of its students as individuals. Independent schools likewise are slowly shedding the antiquated traditions of bygone educational eras. Pre-school and tertiary educational facilities are expanding, and their roles are being re-evaluated. Fundamental improvements in Australian education will remain dependent upon people. Central to education, now as always, is the quality of teachers and their concern for individual children.

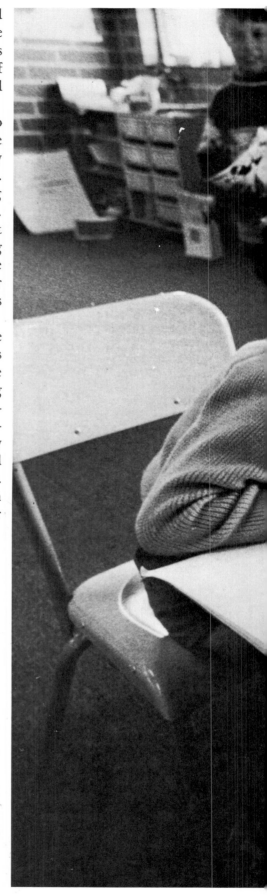

Small and independent working groups, and mutual aid within each group, are central to the new open classroom system at Adelaide's Ingle Farm primary school.

LEISURE

Ian Moffitt

**'A healthy, but not fit,
people . . .'**

The pursuit of leisure is a serious business in Australia. We may not care much about complex Asia, but we've sent some good racing ponies to Malaysia and a batch of great greyhounds to Macao. Those of us who couldn't care less about racing (and there are a lot) dig gardens, paint bedrooms, go to the local flicks, do a hundred-and-one other things. But, en masse, we're leisure lovers: a healthy, but not fit, people with a premature paunch as a symbol of our mindless affluence.

Take the surf. The old Australia was a bronzed lifesaver stamping into the future with a flag unfurling above him and a big yellow A on the front of his green costume. He was a young nation marching nobly out of War and Depression, with Right and Manhood still unquestioned, Patriotism unchallenged, Service and Sacrifice realistic ideals.

We were (we imagined) kings of the creaming-lemonade water, idols of the world, and the lifesaver in peace became the Digger in war, the myth-men melting into each other.

Vic Rushby, my club captain when I was a youth, was my first Australian hero: tall and grey as a Digger monument, straight as steel, iced salt water in his veins. He symbolised that tight-lipped old Australia, a silent storm-man with bare toes planted deep in the wet sand, staring bleak-eyed at the endless wastelands of ocean which rolled into the long, empty North Coast beaches of NSW.

He had a shoe shop in town. Sometimes I saw him kneeling amid the polished leather, rustling white tissue paper in boxes, but I knew that the *real* Vic Rushby stood like a Viking in the surf boat as it plunged into a green trough, the white spray hissing into his steel (or granite?) face. Of course we read about Grace Darling at school, and sang our praises, shrilly, to the Fishermen of England, but Vic and his squad were closer models to emulate—until,

Opposite: Not-quite-sure-about-it on the giant slide at Sydney's Royal Easter Show.

in this decade, the wave of affluence began to undermine the movement. As the President of the Surf Life Saving Association of Australia, Sir Adrian Curlewis, put it: 'The idea of service has become unfashionable'.

The old enemy had been the shark beyond the breakers; the new enemy was the mobile society.

Once kids could only afford to walk or take a tram down to the crumbling surf club pavilions; now they have cars, money, freedom, boards. Eschewing discipline, they turn their backs on institutions and organisations to pursue personal pleasure, and they don't have to give back a thing to the system (including lifesaving). This unique volunteer movement will survive—streamlined training methods and new publicity campaigns have helped—but the media and the stores fill kids' minds today with images more exotic than rescue and resuscitation. They park curtained panel vans along the beach-fronts (mobile boudoirs which rock gently as you pass) and scores of them follow the waves up and down the coast. The old surf club push has become a bit passe, and much of the old idealism has submerged with it.

The agricultural show, especially Sydney's famed RAS Easter spectacular, still survives the past. Every year outside Jimmy Sharman's boxing tent the big drum used to boom like the heart-beat of the 'Easter Show', awakening the primitive in bank-clerks: 'Where are you from, young fella? Tenterfield? Blimey, you're a long way from home, Tenterfield. Well, I'll tell you what we'll do. If you can beat this boy here you get three quid, but if he knocks you out or you squib—what's that? Your mother never had a squib yet? Well, come on up here, Tenterfield . . .'

The tent isn't there any more, but the crowds still stream into the pavilions to see the State's wealth spread before them, and the sideshows are pretty much the same (I once saw an exotic 'French' dancer with MUM tattooed on her arm). Sydney's Easter Show is one of the nation's few old indigenous festivals, and it rekindles childhood memories. 'See death on the French guillotine,' cries a lady in leopard-skin pants, whacking the painted canvas behind her with a sword, 'see the lovely head drop from the lovely shoulders . . .' And: 'The more you clap, the more she takes off . . . lovely girls, daring girls'. Two youths dig into their jeans and saunter, elaborately casual, towards the ticket box. A man glances tentatively at his wife.

Talbot Duckmanton—the business of communicating

Talbot Duckmanton, General Manager of the Australian Broadcasting Commission, is a serious man, smoking a pipe while media storms burst around his head. But sometimes his staff see humour twinkling deep inside him—rather like that pen-picture of Rat peering bright-eyed from his dark burrow in *The Wind in the Willows*. One TV executive saw it when confessing that the staff of This Day Tonight had christened their worm-motif Talbot: 'That's alright,' Duckmanton said solemnly. 'As long as you don't put a pipe in his mouth . . .'

He is a private man, tightly-disciplined, his guard always up—and, interestingly, his work is to channel pleasure (and information) to the masses. He lives in the Sydney suburb of Cheltenham, has a son and three daughters, and, whether admired or not, is a broadcasting professional. 'I'm being facetious,' says the ABC's director of sporting broadcasts, Bernard Kerr, 'but I think it's a pity he went into the executive side—we lost a first-class sporting commentator. You have to control your emotions and give maximum concentration, it's a tre-mendous strain. He was always extremely accurate, and he maintained clarity of diction. He could paint a better picture of a 100 yards race in 10 seconds than anyone I've ever heard . . .'

He drinks sparingly, swims a lot in his home pool, and follows Rugby when not running his public institution, which is a little like walking a tightrope between opposing pressure groups. Born in Melbourne in 1921, he joined the ABC as a cadet announcer in 1939 after leaving Newington College, Sydney, and then went off to the war, becoming an RAAF pilot. Later he covered many ceremonial occasions, the Coronation in 1953, and he played a key role in establishing ABC television. No more calling races; his links now are solid organisations like the Australian Institute of Management, the Australian Administrative Staff College and so on . . .

The philosophy of communications concerns him deeply and he ranges through history for viewpoints—and looks ahead to the home of the future, plugged into a 12-channel cable bearing TV programmes, weather and stock exchange reports; channels on which residents will order the movie they want to see, the page of the library book they want to check. He is all for diversity within a nation, but also fore-sees an Australia with transmitters linked (and perhaps a domestic satellite) so that all Australians can see the same picture at the same time. The prospect does not dismay him, nor does the technological achievement consume him with delight; he quotes G. K. Chesterton to emphasise his confidence in human ability to absorb huge new developments, and force them to fit into a human landscape.

He treads a pretty lonely path, cherishing a special love for radio. 'Radio doesn't deserve to be patronised as a quaint curiosity, because radio didn't merely precede and influence television,' he says. 'It was and still is a cultural medium in its own right, its somewhat restricted resources making unique demands on the imagination, but at the same time bringing with it unique rewards. No television studio can build sets to equal the wonderful constructions of the human mind.'

More than a million Australians flock to the Show every year to pick a box, have a shot, throw a ball, have a free chest X-ray, have a headache powder. The sideshows are nostalgic fun: the spruiker addressing the Maori Prince in mock pidgin, 'How you feeling? You good? Plenty good, eh?', and the Prince telling me later as he carefully studies his fingernails, 'Well, actually, I was a surveyor'.

But the Show is also a recurring sign, as the old touchstones melt everywhere, that the nation's veins have not quite dried up, its heart calcified. The glossy horses and fat cattle wind out of our pastoral past into the petrol-present to create a celebration of unashamed chauvinism; here, beneath the fairy floss and the kewpie dolls, lies the rich dark humus from which we have sprung; increasingly, we no longer take it for granted.

Indiscriminate nostalgia can be a failing. But thousands of Australians are now beginning to discover the past on holiday trips around the country by car and coach. Their appreciation is often imperfect, but it is, at least, a start.

I take a coach tour into the Hunter Valley on a sunny day when even the husbands in the family groups are grudgingly happy. The lush bowl of the valley is stitched with vineyards, a jet unzips the sky above, and we straggle from the coach to inspect a ruined sandstone building: the original homestead of the Wyndham Estate vineyard near Branxton. 'Don't go in there, Kenny,' warns a mother, peering dubiously at the cold fireplaces, the stone strewn floors, the crumbling, empty windows barred against Aborigines and bushrangers. An Alf with a red-brick heart debunks plans to rebuild it, and swigs a can of beer (the rest of us, obediently, sip wine) while his wife murmurs: 'The poor women that lived out here.' Our expectations are much higher these days, and there isn't much of the pioneer spirit left in any of us.

The old and new life styles don't always mix too well either, as I discover at the Hunter Vintage Festival, NSW's new answer to the Barossa Festival. Wine novices wander from tasting-tent to tasting-tent with glasses dangling on string hung round their necks, Don's Party style, and they try valiantly to absorb vineyard lore at wine lectures as pulsating lines of child mini-bike riders roar around outside. If you're not dazed when you go in you are when you come out: one ear registers the mini-bike announcer ('The riders now go into a horseshoe formation . . .') and the other picks up the lecturer ('In November or so the vine starts growing its fruit . . .).

Bruce Petty—cartoonist with a conscience

Bruce Petty always loved drawing: he used to jam the back pages of his State school geography book with Bristol Blenheims and Gloster Gladiators, guns sticking out of every corner. He was living then in his family's yellow weatherboard home on a 12 hectare orchard at Doncaster, Melbourne; they've carved it up now. Bruce lives in a white terrace house in Paddington, Sydney, and he's still drawing.

It is his passion, his obsession, and his job as a cartoonist with The Australian. He gouges deeply into himself, pushing aside drawings as he spurns easy solutions. Sometimes he's still wrestling away at his desk minutes before deadline, scribbled rejects around him as he tries for a telling statement. A long way from the Box Hill High School and his first passion: Australian Rules.

'We used to bowl along to the Church of Christ every Sunday in a 28 Studebaker with yellow celluloid windows flapping,' he told me. 'I had no ambition, really, except sport . . .' His influences then were pretty standard: the local church, Catcher in the Rye, Ulysses, the Goons, a BSA 350, a Standard 12 coupe and girls, and he set out to make his name in Melbourne in 'a Bogart long white waterproof coat, with belt tabs and straps flying about'. He joined a tiny Melbourne firm, and did the lettering for amateur Kodak slides which people sent in, but his spelling was so bad 'they used to lose money over it'.

Well, Topolski and Daumier drawings eventually convinced him that Disney wasn't the ultimate answer, and the beggars in Colombo sparked off his social conscience when he sailed to London in 1953 for a six year stay. He has drawn many times for The New Yorker and Punch, made a national reputation in The Australian, and moved into film as well to project his convoluted insights, and his compassion. Among his most recent projects: two illustrated films for the Indianapolis Museum of Art. He flew to the United States to do those, but usually works with camera and pen in his Paddo studio.

He was planning or doing a few films in 1974—difficult ones, of course. 'I'd like to make some teaching films on hard abstract subjects like law and money and politics and mathematics—not easy things like history and geography,' he said. 'They require merely animation; with my subjects you'd have to wrestle with symbolism and so on . . .' He also wrote the script for a film on cities—with some drawings and a room-size mock-up of a mini-city for the players to stand in—plus the script for a film called Kazzam International, about international affairs. 'It's in theatrical terms —Australia comes in from the bush and applies for an audition for a small part,' he explained. 'It has a role in the war to end all wars, and a walk-on part in the Depression—that sort of thing. And I want to do a film which disentangles a lot of the emotion around Marx, and concentrates without political bias on his attempts to get a better system. Mixing animation and actors . . .'

His joy, in short, is to tinker with the social machine to show how it works—and make us smile at the same time.

There's often a difference too in the life styles of old and new Australians. Some Australian families meet each other once or twice a year in their local Botanic Gardens: elderly sisters dredging snapshots of grandchildren from their handbags before tea in the kiosk, toddlers tossing bread to the ducks amid the mossy-thighed marble nudes. There's a timeless charm in these gatherings (today's toddlers are tomorrow's aging grannies), but New Australians seem to enjoy these family reunions more than Old Australians who mostly don't really *like* children (who reciprocate in later years by shunting the oldies off into institutions and Eventide Homes); the family unit leads a tenuous existence in Australia, where you can't take kids into a posh restaurant, or just about any other place where a shout of childish joy is matched by a glare of anger from older leisure seekers.

Many adults seem immune to the crash and clatter of the poker machines; many are immune to their temptations (in most States they have to be). But for many, the adults-only club is the place to go.

One club is pretty well like another. The compere bounds on stage, flicking the microphone cord as he has seen the top entertainers do a thousand times. 'Good evening, ladies and gentlemen,' he cries. 'Is everybody happy? Getting enough booze down there? No? We'll soon fix that. And now, it gives me very great pleasure to introduce a young lady who is very, very popular at the club. That very sexy sausage with the glorious voice . . .' And out she slithers in powder-blue hotpants and gold calf-length boots.

In another suburb, entertainer John Cootes, ex-priest and ex-Rugby League international, is singing 'Everybody Loves Saturday Night' in a variety of tongues: 'Those of you who have had a classical education will really enjoy this one, I think'.

At the Back o' Bourke, a steakhouse, Gary Tooth sings 'Wallaby Stew' and then swings into a shearing ballad. He's a nuggety, bushy bearded bloke who looks a little like one of the banksia men out of *Bib and Bub*—horticulture is his hobby, orchids his quiet passion—and lives in the NSW Blue Mountains though he hails from Queensland. 'I like the transportation songs best,' he says, 'and I always throw in a lot of Irish stuff.' He is a golden bush singer who could make a packet on the American lecture-song circuit, 'but to sing what I like for a living, this is really beaut'. His roots are deeply planted Down Under.

Glenda Jackson and Bette Davis come to grace our stages. Joan Sutherland returns home, briefly, as a dazzling but all-too-temporary Opera House ornament. *Aida* costs $100,000 to stage and plays to packed houses. Subscription concerts are fully subscribed, home grown ballet and opera vie with one another in the prestige stakes, and Australian drama surges ahead with perhaps more vitality than any other country. Not all that many people out of 13 million actually see these performances; not that many more put aside a Sunday afternoon for the Victorian Arts Centre (though small town museums and folk art centres are popping up like Outback flowers after the rains); and even the Sunbury Rock Festival isn't the drawcard it was, mud or no mud. Mostly it's the 'box' that gets the numbers, and a colour TV set is the current—and expensive—artistic challenge.

We pay for our pleasures, of course. In fact Sydney people, for example, pay among the highest prices in the world for restaurant meals, clothes, household appliances and public transport (such as it is). There is a big shortage of trained staff to help local communities plan and administer leisure facilities, but there is always somewhere to eat. Australians now spend almost $600 million a year on food prepared in commercial kitchens while hoteliers, *restaurateurs*, clubs and the fast food merchants enjoy the boom. In NSW alone people spend about $200 million a year in restaurants, hotels and club dining rooms and another $50 million on take-away food. Nobody starves. But a cardiologist who surveyed Sydney school children says that 12 per cent of Sydney's teenagers now have so high a cholesterol level that their risk of heart disease might be increased threefold.

This pub in the tiny William Creek railway settlement on the southern shores of Lake Eyre, SA, is typical of many smaller outback hotels: it dispenses beer, is the general store, and is the centre for social gatherings and the exchange of information, news and gossip.

The bright lights of the capitals and the bigger towns often blind one to the simple fact that Australia is one of the most beautiful countries on earth. I know scores of unique natural treasures here, and each one is an essay in leisure.

They defy description, these beauties: rain forest and snow country, red desert and mountain streams; Ayers Rock and Katherine Gorge and the Top End where wild buffalo roam and crocodiles still slide into the waterlily lagoons; the apple isle of Tasmania and the bushranger towns and the Indian-Pacific Express, which now spans the continent and is booked out for months ahead (though it lacks the drama of Graham Greene's Stamboul Train, perhaps someone ought to write a light Indian-Pacific TV series starring a fruit-fly inspector); South Australia's Barossa Valley, where the descendants of German settlers grow grapes for Australia's excellent wines; paddle-steamers on the Murray, and the bush race meeting where the punters park light planes, not cars; the opal town of Andamooka, where a fortune lies beneath the red rocks and a .38 pistol lies beneath the miner's pillow. And north Queensland, which thousands of Australians are now discovering . . .

Tropical north Queensland, and the Great Barrier Reef, are sun-ripe: for me (and for many others) a synthesis of memories of Asia and the Pacific in a beautiful new Australian blend. The mainland is exciting enough. Drive through those forgotten little towns up there, in a tropical downpour when they're burning off the cane, and the spectacle is sheer Cecil B. De Mille. A green surf of sugar-cane and bananas rolls to the coast, and out on the pale green sea, scratched with white wave flecks, the Reef's strings of little palm-thatched islands seem to float just above the horizon.

This is a lush but still dangerous Australia, not wallowing in a tropic torpor, its teeth extracted: beware the deadly stonefish spines, the pretty cone shell which can sting you to death, the box jellyfish which is probably more dangerous than the shark. But it is Paradise too for a quarter of a million visitors each year, with planes, helicopters and cruisers now linking these castaway isles to the world's jet routes.

There are, up north, at least 17 resort isles like Dunk and Green and Magnetic and Hayman, Orpheus and Daydream and Paradise Bay and Lindeman. An English Billy Butlin holiday camp schedule fits awkwardly on some, but for the dreamer escape is easy. Green turtles up to 230 kilograms in

Jim Sharman—Brecht, not boxing

Sharman is a magic name in Australia, and it doesn't matter which Sharman you mean: Jimmy, Jimmy or Jim. All three of them—grandfather, father and son—have stamped their images on the national mind, expressing the mood of the nation as it has elevated its pleasures through war and Depression to 70s affluence. Your age dictates which Sharman has impressed you most.

Jim Sharman is Australia's brilliant young stage director and film-maker: his father and grandfather ran the famed Sharman boxing troupe for decades at country and city agricultural shows. His style has certainly soared above theirs; he has swapped the cracked painted fighter backdrops in bush towns for the world's theatrical capitals. But he is in the entertainment business too, and a brief look at his heritage also tells the nation's story—though he is probably tired of the fight stories themselves, which certainly have little place in his serious investigation of theatre.

The elder Jimmy's own grandfather Tom was an Irish bare-knuckle fighter ('Call

that fighting? With chaff-bags on your hands?' he used to snort). Jimmy Sharman I, who died in 1965, was a gravel-voiced fighter-showman who retired in 1911 and took his fight-tent thousands of kilometres around Australia each year. His son Jimmy II carried on, the black and white boxers standing impassively in their silken robes outside the tent as the drum thudded. But Jim Sharman eschewed that role: he attended Randwick High School in Sydney and first attracted attention with magic shows. I asked him once about the boxing tent, and he said: 'Whenever I see those banners I think: "That's the pop culture of Australia".'

He chose a wider stage. 'He has a genius for creating magic in the theatre—a flair for visual effect which I don't think anybody quite equals,' says his agent, Hilary Linstead, in Sydney. Jim himself was in London making a film of The Rocky Horror Show, jetting between London and Sydney in the pursuit of theatrical excellence. And developing a political awareness and learning to project it through theatre—

to use theatre as a political tool with stunning impact. Gentle on the surface; burning with enthusiasms inside.

His work is pleasure, his pleasure work. He has graduated from the reviewers' 'bright young hope' (he doesn't like discussing his age) to brilliant young artistic innovator gathering a team around him 'in a family atmosphere of love and mutual interchange of ideas'. Brecht, not boxing, for him: he took The Threepenny Opera into Sydney Opera House. He had three shows on at once in London in 1973: David Williamson's The Removalists, Superstar, and The Rocky Horror Show stage version, which he also sparked off in Los Angeles and Sydney.

He is a travelling Sharman too, and the road ahead is just opening up. He is lighting it with some brilliant flashes: part of a new world where the main challenge is not how well a man can fight, but how long humanity will survive unless he stops.

weight heave themselves ashore to lay their eggs in the mating season, and underwater observatories are peepholes to a rainbow world of fish and fluted corals.

Dunk Island is an example (it inspired the old book *Confessions of a Beach-comber* by Ted Banfield, who went there for a visit in 1897 and stayed for 25 years). Individual suites nestle beneath umbrellas of palms, and there are 148 species of tropical birds and giant butterflies among the palm groves and in the tropical rain forest. It's easy to understand why some of Australia's 'characters', the true individualists, have fled north from the rat race in the south. The pity of it all is that the Queensland Government has an abysmal attitude towards conservation. Paradise may well become a paradise lost.

Lazing about on coral sands is one form of pleasantly indolent leisure. Another, observedly popular, is the sometimes not-so-gentle-art of sport watching. Despite myths to the contrary, we're more a nation of spectators than particip-ators. One newspaper survey places tennis as the sport which interests the most Australians, followed by swimming, Australian Rules (Australian National Football is the correct name), Rugby (both codes), cricket, soccer, golf, bowls, squash and athletics. The figures and preferences differ sharply from State to State, but swimming, for the fun of it, enjoys the highest level of participation.

Of the competitive sports (only a handful of swimmers take part in races) golf is probably the most popular, though every sport seems to claim a record of some sort for popularity. Golf has well over 400,000 active players and the advantage that you don't have to be fit. In countries like Japan it's a rich man's game, but here almost anyone can play. We have awesome inland deserts ulcerated by drought where red-dust storms engulf tiny outposts, we have a bigger snow area than Switzerland, and we have 20,000 kilometres of golden beaches—but our Japanese visitors revere our golf courses above all, and always find time in a business trip for a few cheap games.

But golf is not leading by much. Skiers in the Snowy Mountains claim that skiing has risen from 17th to fourth in popularity among Australian sports, with at least 300,000 skiing enthusiasts flocking there every winter. Lawn bowls is as popular as it is sedate; almost half the world's bowlers are now Australians. In 1963 we had 150,000 of them; now there are more than 250,000 in more than 2,000 registered clubs. Britain, where Sir Francis Drake put bowls on the map, has only 126,000 bowlers and the United States a mere 6,000.

Organised junior sport has now turned thousands of parents into weekend chauffeurs for their children: football for the boys, netball for the girls. The more aggressive fathers of playing sons sometimes become so involved at games that they spark violence on the sidelines, and it appears that aggression has even permeated netball, with some fathers passing on to their daughters a few rough tactics picked up from watching Rugby League on television.

Delegates at a government sponsored National Seminar on Leisure, held in Canberra, branded Sydney's Rugby League a dirty game and Melbourne's Aus-tralian Rules 'a social disease, not a sport . . . Gladiators turning out for the weekend' (though, like professional boxing, it is obviously here to stay and is superb spectacle as well). The Prime Minister, Mr Whitlam, was adroit in not buying into *that* debate, but he did tell the seminar that planning for leisure will become part of all government and municipal priorities: 'I believe we are on the way to a new concept of schooling in which leisure will be an integral part . . .'.

He did not, of course, mean sitting down at the footy with an Esky full of beer cans; but he did mean that a work-oriented system had thwarted or destroyed the creative capacities of many young Australians so that even their occasional encounters with art, music, literature, craft and sport became intimidating or boring.

Boredom is perhaps a natural concomitant of the 'Lucky Country'. A militant pioneer nation, once radical, is now comfortable and fairly conser-vative, and life for the 'ordinary bloke' is probably more pleasant than in most other countries. In broad terms, the pursuit of leisure in Australia is not especially stimulating intellectually (a Chikko Roll and a cold tube of Resch's on Maroubra Beach are hardly demanding), but neither is it especially harmful. Much leisure time is spent out of doors in what is an essentially healthy climate, and that is all to the good. Blue water mariners abound. They may not all have the steel and whipcord bodies of my old friend Vic Rushby, but they feel good. And a few sets of tennis and 18 holes of golf never did anyone any harm.

But the 19th hole is one of Australia's biggest yet least known problems. Drinking is a popular pastime, and we're good at it (we hate being told that the Belgians drink more than we do). We've learned in recent years to drink and appreciate our own excellent wines, and a few cold beers with a few friends at a weekend out-of-doors barbecue can be the ultimate experience in civilised leisure.

On the other hand, more than 300,000 Australian workers take a 'sickie' every day to recover from hangovers and other effects of alcohol abuse. It's costing industry millions of dollars, and five per cent of the male population and one per cent of the women are on the road to alcoholism.

Australia also breaks world records for road deaths (heedless, aggressive and frequently drunken drivers piloting tomorrow's cars on yesterday's roads), and that is the black underside of leisure which needs massive national attention.

Teenage leisure presents its own problems. The causes are legion, but the generation gap, boredom, the unending quest for 'kicks', and the terrifying prospect of being shunned by one's peers ('Go on, Davo, I dare you . . .') coupled with the comfort of being one of the boys, are often contributing factors. Take Geelong in Victoria, where the co-author of a youth survey, Mr Dennis Challinger, a Melbourne University criminologist, says that one youth in five would resort to stealing 'if he really wanted something and the opportunity came to steal it without being caught'. He adds: 'The survey was designed to assist Geelong in planning facilities for youth, and indicates that for many youths stealing amounts to a leisure time activity'. So glittering is the array of goods spread before youth these days that whipping a few here and there (the bulging supermarkets are happy hunting grounds for teenage shoplifters) is little different, in their minds, from the scrounging their fathers did from the Army.

There's always been teenage violence. The bodgies and the Teddy Boys fought it out with bicycle chains and razors on the wharves of Woolloomooloo back in the feisty 50s. Today, suburban dances sometimes erupt in a brawl, a bloody clash between long-hairs and skinheads. It's not endemic, but it's worrying.

The troubles and the heartbreaks are not peculiarly Australian, but their being symptomatic of a world-wide malaise doesn't make them any the more palatable.

I sit beside a couple of simple old dears in a tea-shop. They are discussing a close friend whose husband has just left her after 40 years of marriage. 'She rang me up,' says one. 'I was expecting her to tell me that God had called her old father home, see. It was the biggest shock of my life. I couldn't believe it—she has to go to work now, of course.' The enticements of modern Australian life had obviously got to the old bloke, but they took it in their stride. 'I don't ever remember better times for young people in the history of Australia—and the older people too,' says her friend. 'They're all catered for . . .'

Perhaps they are. We're eating better, drinking more, exercising less—fired by no national vision, seized with no corporate purpose other than to take it easy while we can. It isn't an admirable life we lead here, but no cruel destiny has overwhelmed us yet. Retribution burns faintly, far ahead, like a bushfire on the dark horizon. And the wind may change.

Opposite: The deadly sea wasp makes Darwin's beaches unsafe for swimming through much of the summer. Natural waterholes are a cool alternative. Here, 18-month-old Stephen Gifford, watched by his parents Sandra and John, celebrates the weekend waterhole pilgrimage to Howard Springs with Dennis Kitching, also from Darwin.

JOHN CARNEMOLLA

Going to the beach is almost a religious ritual for vast numbers of Australians—especially the city dwellers. In Sydney the dedicated beach-goer will drive for 40 kilometres or more, bumper to bumper on a sweltering day, just to 'get away from it all'.

Far left, top: For those who can afford it, Surfers Paradise, 80 kilometres south of Brisbane, is relatively uncrowded and a perfect mecca for jaded southerners intent on escaping the winter cold.

Centre top: The beaches are inhabited primarily by the young— of all ages.

Top: Surf society, Bondi.

Far left: Other fashion fads come and go, but the bikini just gets smaller.

Left: New Year's Day at Bondi Beach, Sydney.

319

Inland Australians head for the water as though by instinct when leisure time comes round—assuming there is any water to head for. If there is, the waves are smaller but the rewards are great.

Opposite: Underpants are swimming trunks for youngsters cooling off in the Tweed River, northern NSW.

Left: Water nymph at Howard Springs, near Darwin.

Below: Anglers enjoy a quiet evening along a backwater of Lake Wendouree near Ballarat, Victoria.

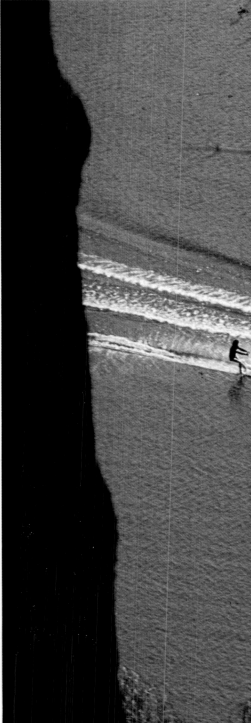

Australians seeking solitude tend to head for the water rather than the bush.

Left: A beachcomber family on a beach fringed by rainforest near Cardwell, northern Queensland.

Below left: A limpid stretch of the Swan River, Perth.

Below: Blue Lake, filling one of three extinct volcanic craters at Mount Gambier, Victoria, is a major attraction for locals and tourists.

Litter, male chauvinism, family togetherness and dressing up are all part of the leisure scene.

Melbourne Cup Day is a moment of national aberration. It is a public holiday in Victoria, and everywhere else in Australia life comes to a standstill as ears and eyes are glued to radios and television screens. At Flemington race course, the site of this equine gala, anything goes—and generally does, as the social set, the would-be social set and the trendies attempt to outdo or outrage one another.

A pop concert at the Melbourne Cricket Ground is a far cry from the old days of Sunday picnics round the bandstand rotunda in the park. This concert attracted a crowd of around 30,000. Dozens of girls were carried from the crush for first aid treatment—heat exhaustion and hysteria were the evils—and the aid area behind the stage looked like a field dressing station, littered with victims. The young lady below was not among them.

Skiing started its climb to popularity in the 1950s when access roads built for and by the Snowy Mountains Hydro-Electric Authority began to open up the snow fields as well. The sport now has more than 300,000 adherents.

Below: Busloads of weekend skiers from Sydney swell the population at Thredbo village. There are long waits for the chairlift.

Bottom: 'If you can walk you can ski' is the motto of one ski school. Skiers aged three or four are not unknown.

Opposite: Ski instructors and members of the Thredbo ski patrol made a night run by the light of hand-held flares. A long exposure captured their trail on film.

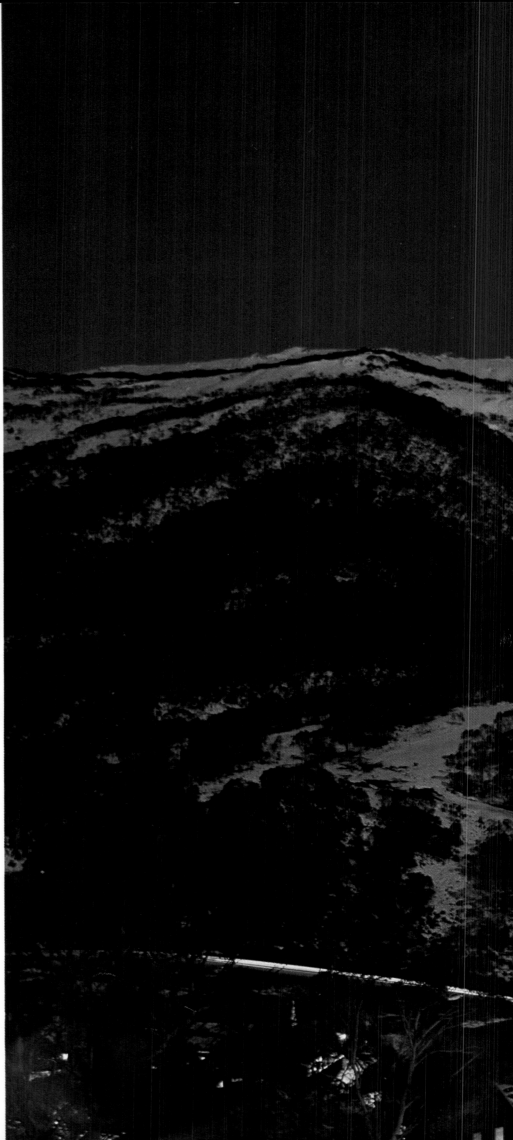

For a young white, growing up in Australia is a relatively painless process. For a young black, the good life is harder to find—and in the urban slums, the poorer reserves, the fringes of country towns like Lismore, Kempsey and Alice Springs, it is sometimes impossible. Nevertheless, interchange and understanding are slowly removing the old barriers, and colour makes no difference at a Melbourne pop concert (*above*) or with playmates in Darwin (*right*).

Above: Not exactly city boys, these three from Alice Springs still enjoy the chance of a head-long gallop across the bed of the out-of-town Todd River. Shayne Johnstone, at all of seven years, gives a no-hands, one-stirrup performance as he challenges 12-year-olds Donald Costello (centre) and David Poots on the grey.

Left: City gimmicks do creep into the bush. Nine-year-old Aron Fishlock, of Mataranka, NT, does a minibike slalom through a forest of termite hills on Elsey station. Elsey was the setting for Mrs Aeneas Gunn's 1908 classic, *We of the Never Never*.

For those whose idea of leisure is an unpeopled landscape, the continent offers almost endless opportunities for solitude.

Top right: A rocky point at a beach near Darwin.

Right: A lone fisherman drags his net past barnacle-encrusted anti-landingcraft defences, mementoes of World War II, at Mindil Beach, Darwin.

Far right: One of many dramatic gorges in the Hamersley Ranges near Wittenoom, WA.

In its attitude towards public expressions of love and affection Australia seems to be moving away from a once prevalent, puritanical wowserism. There is more time in which to enjoy the togetherness and euphoria of being in love.

Opposite: Love in the Botanic Gardens, Melbourne.

Left: Love at Flemington race course, Melbourne.

Below: Love at Woolloomooloo, Sydney.

Nightlife has progressed mightily since the dark ages of the six o'clock swill and deadly Sundays when only the churches were open.

Right: An acrobatic stripper weaves her spell over the audience at the Barrel Theatre, Kings Cross, Sydney.

Below: Members of the Sturt football club enjoy their annual dinner in the banqueting hall of the impressively renovated Old Lion Hotel, Adelaide—a far cry from the 'No meals after 7 pm' mentality that made evenings a misery for visitors and townsfolk alike.

Below centre: Even Hobart, once the 'sleepy hollow' of the State capitals, now draws locals and mainland visitors to its huge Wrest Point hotel and casino.

Below right: Roulette is one of many ways to lose money—or make a lucky kill—at Wrest Point. Two-up, once a national pastime, is regaining popularity in more sophisticated surroundings than an empty garage or a dingy back-street room.

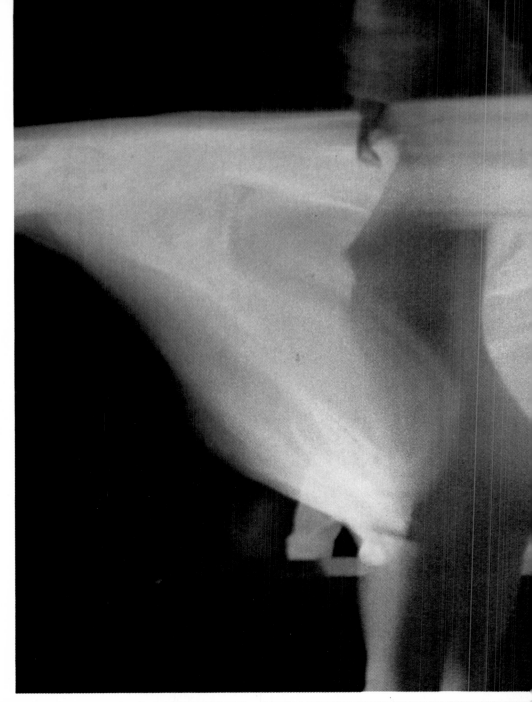

SPORT

Jim Shepherd

'. . . Australia's sports stars have intrigued overseas observers with their obsession to win.'

In recent years there have been many suggestions that Australians are becoming soft and that their traditional sporting dominance is fading. True, there are some weaknesses—but generally, Australian sport is healthy.

Certainly no other country in the world can boast a sporting infatuation which, every day, generates newspaper posters proclaiming the latest sports sensation at the expense of more important world news. And on a per capita basis, no nation can point to so many inner-city sporting venues.

It is fascinating enough that Australia has produced official or acknowledged world champions in athletics, swimming, surfing, billiards and snooker, speedway and motor racing, boxing, golf, tennis, cricket, weight-lifting, softball, high-diving, cycling, barefoot water skiing, kite-flying, pistol shooting, horse riding, yachting and football.

But far more intriguing is the manner in which Australians have achieved so much—that driving force which generates such an intense quest for international competition and such a fierce nationalistic sporting pride among a people regarded as being among the world's most relaxed.

Many theories have been offered for the Australian pre-occupation with sport:

● In the pioneer days, far-flung settlers were forced into pursuing competitive sport as an alternative to the almost complete lack of entertainment and an utter lack of cultural diversions in the Outback.

● The climate permitted the almost year-round pursuit of all the traditional summer sports.

● The comparatively early development of wealthy industries such as wool, beef cattle, wheat and mining generated such an overflow of cash capital that Australians quite naturally drifted into the realms of gambling, sports promotion and the construction of edifices to the mainly commercial glory of sport.

Opposite: A comparatively new event in Sydney's social sporting calendar is the annual run from Martin Place, in the heart of the city, to famed Bondi Beach on the edge of the Pacific Ocean. Top athletes take the race fairly seriously, but hundreds of others—businessmen, housewives, students, children—join in just for the fun of celebrating the outdoor life in a novel way.

341

The Sport of Kings enjoys a large, vocal and free-spending following in Australia. The names of the top thoroughbreds and jockeys are better known than those of most politicians. Here, a tight field moves into the turn at Brisbane's Albion Park race course during a mid-week meeting. (Neil Duncan, *The Australian*)

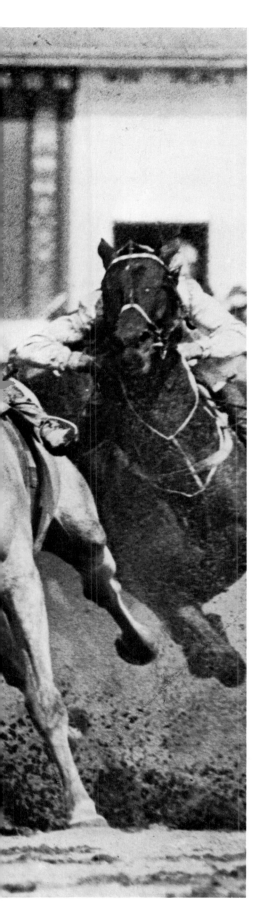

Many historians trace the beginnings of this national pre-occupation back to 1810 and the pioneer days of horse racing at Parramatta, outside of Sydney, and at Hyde Park in Sydney Town proper. However, it is extremely doubtful whether these first races had any long-term effect on the tiny population because the races were organised and competed in solely by the established gentry. The real Australian racing boom began much later with the opening of Randwick Racecourse in 1832 and Flemington in 1840.

It is more likely that the sporting cult began with the spread of bare-knuckle boxing in Sydney around 1814-15 and the emergence by 1856 of semi-professional gamblers who followed the boxing circuit through Redfern, Woolloomooloo and Surry Hills to Parramatta, Windsor, Richmond and Ryde. According to the florid newspaper reports of the day there were dozens of 50 and 75 pound bets on the outcome of the 1827 fight at Parramatta between Young Bailey and John Logan—and one authentic bet of 500 pounds.

A little later the boxing scene in Melbourne was just as hectic (though the financial backing was nowhere near as generous), with recorded fights being held at St Kilda Beach, Carlton, Fitzroy (an area where Altona now stands) and in country districts.

The period from 1850 to 1900 saw intense growth in horse racing, boxing (the sport was legitimised in the 1880s when gloves became compulsory), foot-running, rowing, swimming and cycling—all of them subjects of mercurial betting and, even by today's standards, astonishing attendances. It was certainly in *this* half-century that Australia swung from being a nation of mildly curious observers to being one of fully involved, heavy-gambling enthusiasts who, for a long time, were easy prey for the more unscrupulous entrepreneurs.

Today, Australian sports spectators are far more selective. For instance, they will not pay to watch a top fight if it can be seen for nothing on television. Modern communications have brought them the best of international sport, and they no longer flock to see 'imported' sporting individuals or teams unless they are unquestionably world class.

There is now a hesitant, almost defensive spectator attitude which carries ill-tidings for the fly-by-night speculator, but which provides riches for the entrepreneur who invests in more worthwhile attractions than those offered free at the local Leagues Club or on television.

Despite this defensive attitude, most Australian cities are unique internationally in having vast areas of valuable real estate devoted to sports. Sydney for instance, boasts one racecourse (Randwick) standing on a multi-million dollar *potential* real estate development barely three kilometres in a straight line from the centre of the city . . . and only two kilometres from the city's heart is the multi-billion dollar sporting complex of the Sydney Cricket Ground, Sports Ground and Royal Agricultural Showground.

Melbourne has an entire Olympic Stadium complex about one kilometre from the city centre and, within a five kilometre radius, two major racecourses and no less than 70 major and minor sporting arenas.

Brisbane has its most important racecourse flush against the international airport (a mere 15 minutes' drive from the city centre); a luxurious, ultra-modern indoor sports arena almost exactly at its heart; and the major football, cricket and tennis stadiums within 10 minutes' drive from the City Hall.

Adelaide's major cricket ground is in the middle of the city's most prestigious suburban area, only 20 minutes from the international airport. Perth's most important cricket and trotting arenas are right on the main route from the city to the airport.

If cities can be charged with having a blatant, torrid love affair with sport, Sydney and Melbourne stand accused. Sydney promoters, sporting associations and clubs, suburban councils and the State government have littered the already cluttered Sydney landscape with hundreds and thousands of sporting venues, grounds and fenced-in paddocks masquerading as sports 'stadiums'. Not surprisingly, considering Sydney's penchant for non-planning, precious few are of an acceptable international standard. Despite the proliferation of sites, Sydney community leaders, toying with the idea of applying for the 1988 Olympics, know they would have to build an entirely new Olympic complex.

Incredibly, in view of the size and population of the city, the largest and most famous sporting establishments are positively archaic. The Sydney Cricket Ground, site of the 1938 Empire Games, dates back to the turn of the century and is an architectural nightmare with spires and towers and wrought iron clashing loudly with one fairly modern, concrete-ugly grandstand; despite some attempts at 'modernisation', there is still no cover for more than 25,000 people when the ground is filled to its 68,000 capacity.

But the Sydney Cricket Ground is still the pride of Sydney folk. The greatest cricketers and Rugby footballers and many of the greatest athletes in the world have trod the hallowed turf, and enveloping this ill-balanced mixture of Victoriana and pseudo-modern is an atmosphere one can almost smell . . . the same sort of atmophere that once pervaded another extraordinary Sydney sporting venue, the Sydney Stadium, now demolished to make way for the Eastern Suburbs Railway.

The Stadium, built in 1908, stood for almost 62 years and housed prize-fighters and wrestlers, the world's top entertainers, politicians and trade union leaders, world religious leaders and, once, a symphony orchestra. It was, without a doubt, the world's ugliest indoor sports stadium, indisputably the most uncomfortable, and prone to monumental leaks during rainstorms. But 'The Barn', as Sydney-siders affectionately called the place, produced an almost overpowering elixir of excitement.

While Sydney can claim more sporting arenas per square kilometre than any other Australian city, Melbourne can pride itself on the quality of its sporting venues. As host of the 1956 Olympic Games, Melbourne was obliged to up-date drastically its existing facilities. The improvement plans stimulated by the Games have been pursued into the 1970s . . . a tribute to the more ambitious thinking of Melbourne sporting administrators.

The development at Waverley of Football Park, a ground owned by the Victorian Football League, is a classic example. With the spread of Melbourne's population and the galloping popularity of Australian Rules Football in the city, the VFL decided it was time to make a long-term investment in the future of the game and to end the traditional reliance on the centrally situated Melbourne Cricket Ground as the showcase for the sport. VFL Park is now established and by 1976 will seat 150,000 people, about half under cover, at an estimated cost of $12.5 million.

Melbourne is by far the best-equipped sporting centre in Australia: the Melbourne Cricket Ground, Football Park, Flemington and Caulfield race-courses, the indoor Olympic swimming complex, Olympic Park, the Festival Hall and the magnificent chain of sand-belt golf courses—with Royal Melbourne the pacesetter—all offer sufficient proof of that. And since Melbourne boasts the highest racecourse attendances *and* the annual Melbourne Cup, as well as the largest football, cricket and tennis attendances, it stands unchallenged as the nation's sporting capital.

But despite the Australia-wide obsession with sport, Australia-wide enthusiasm for the *same* sports and the *same* sporting heroes is another matter, perhaps best illustrated by football. In Victoria, Tasmania, South Australia and Western Australia the top code is Australian Rules Football; in NSW and Queensland it is Rugby.

Even the adulation of Australia's world champions suffers from State bias. When Lionel Rose returned in triumph from Tokyo after taking the World Bantamweight Championship from 'Fighting' Harada in 1968, he was disdainfully ignored by journalists at Sydney Airport—and feted in his home town, Melbourne, where a street parade was watched by an exuberant crowd of 250,000. Johnny Famechon received the same treatment when he returned with a world title in 1969, and it is a sad fact that in 1965 when the bulk of the Australian Olympic team (most of the gold medal winners were from Sydney) was

Opposite: Rugby League is the top professional football code in NSW and Queensland. It began in 1907 when a splinter group broke away from Rugby Union, and now enjoys a far greater following than the older game. Here, an Eastern Suburbs man gets his come-uppance from two St George players in a first grade match. (Bill Russell, *The Australian*)

given civic receptions in Melbourne and Sydney, the largest crowds turned out in Sydney. But Melbourne, of course, had after a miserable start presented the 1956 Olympics in a blaze of glory, and Sydney will never live that down.

UNLIMITED ADULATION FOR THE VICTORS

Nevertheless there have been numerous occasions when the entire nation supported an individual, a team—or an animal—with unanimous enthusiasm. Most Davis Cup teams; the 1973-74 World Cup soccer team; legendary boxer Les Darcy; such female stars as Evonne Goolagong, Dawn Fraser, Marjorie Jackson, Betty Cuthbert, Margaret Court, Karen Moras, Lorraine Crapp, Ilsa Konrads and Shane Gould; cyclists like Hubert Opperman, the late Russell Mockridge and Sid Patterson; boxers such as Vic Patrick, Tommy Burns and the late Dave Sands; charismatic cricketers like Keith Miller and Don Bradman; and thoroughbreds like Phar Lap, Peter Pan, Flight, Bernborough, Dalray, Delta, Tulloch and Gunsynd—they have all managed to project whatever magic beam is necessary to mould the rival State factions into one.

Gaining united national support is an intricate business. A multitude of traditions, the economy, even the prevailing climate, have developed vast differences in the behavioural patterns of sporting enthusiasts in Queensland compared with those of Tasmania, or of South Australians compared with their close neighbours the Victorians.

Queenslanders take their sport as it comes, with few frills. The vast majority of post-war Queensland champions have been dour customers, lacking the sophistication of the southerners and the colourful mannerisms that could endear them to the box-office—and the public memory.

Queensland sports watching is a shirt-off, enjoy-the-sun-and-a-few-beers affair. It is a fact of Queensland life that there is more (per capita) rowdiness and public brawling at sporting promotions than in any other State. The almost complete absence of local sport on television may account for the fierce patriotism and sports dedication of Queenslanders, though their sporting tastes are largely the same as those in NSW. Horse racing, trotting, greyhound racing (more recent), boxing, Rugby League, speedway and motor racing, surfing and cricket are the favourites. In season, golf, tennis and swimming are well patronised.

Dawn Fraser—a swimming legend

If you choose to live in the Sydney suburb of Balmain, you will automatically be required to follow some essential ground rules:
Only one Rugby League football team—the Balmain Tigers—is of any real importance.
You must appreciate the historical importance of the area (Balmain is steeped in early Sydney history).
Only one of the district's female sports stars, the legendary Dawn Fraser, can be mentioned in the same breath as any of the great male sports heroes spawned by the waterfront suburb.

No accolade for a sports woman could be higher. In Balmain the pub count is higher than in any other square kilometre of Australia, male dominance of household affairs is almost frightening, and the Balmain Tigers are not simply footballers but demigods in what is still largely a commune of dock workers, wharf labourers and steel workers. Women's Liberation has been ignored in Balmain.

But the Balmainites even named the public baths after Dawn Fraser, a towering tribute when one consideres that Balmain Tigers super stars like Keith Barnes, Joe Jorgenson, Pat Devery and Billy Marsh have yet to accede to even a humble back lane title.

There is ample reason for the unprecedented recognition of Dawn. She is, after all, as any seasoned Balmain pub drinker will tell you, 'one of the boys', a description which is not in any way a reflection on her femininity but rather the ultimate tribute to her sporting prowess and the manner in which she remained, even when universally recognised as the greatest woman sports star of the century, a true-blue Tiger.

Dawn Fraser is now in her middle 30s. She has an unsuccessful marriage behind her, a child a comfortable future as a much sought-after swimming coach in a southern Sydney suburb, and a burning loyalty to Tiger country. Almost two decades of international travel and competition haven't changed that, and it is not difficult to understand the unbreakable link Dawn has with Balmain.

It was in this suburb that she learned her first lessons about life as the youngest of eight children, a sickly child hindered by anaemia and chest complaints. Working long hours in a small Balmain tenement after school she helped her parents with cooking, sewing, and making her own clothes. At 14, Dawn admits, she was on the verge of delinquency and even her swimming career, such as it was in those days, started on the wrong basis.

Dawn first swam competitively with the Balmain League Swimming Club, a professional organisation. When local coach Harry Gallagher recognised her undeveloped talent, an official clearance from the Australian Amateur Swimming Union was necessary before Dawn could pursue a course towards Olympic representation.

It is almost inconceivable, when one remembers the sub-teenage trend of modern swimming, that Dawn Fraser did not seriously devote herself to top level training and competition until she was almost 17—an age which most modern girl champions including the mercurial Shane Gould, believe is the end of the competitive road. A year later, Dawn churned her way into the 1956 Australian Olympic team and into the first stage of her national and, later, international super star phase.

In Melbourne in 1956, she won the Olympic 100 metres freestyle, finished second to Loraine Crapp in the 400 metres, and helped Australia win the relay. Suddenly, Dawn had arrived—a crew-cut, cheeky-faced water urchin who had (all too clearly) far less formal education than

The rodeo is still a major sporting industry and, per capita, Queenslanders are the most enthusiastic fishermen in Australia.

NSW, in comparison, is a mish-mash State with pockets of fierce provincial fervour, bottomless pits of apathy, petty bickering between rival sporting bodies, occasional displays of unexpected sentimentality—and the whole unfathomable mixture is kept on the boil by a battalion of media commentators who are, in many cases, better known than the sporting champions themselves. There never has been and probably never will be any hope of unity—or sanity—while there exist isolated pockets like the Riverina area (an almost fanatical Australian Rules settlement), Illawarra (Rugby League, greyhounds and precious little else), the Far West (horse racing, Rugby League, cricket, trotting and absolutely nothing else allowed) and Newcastle (Rugby League, horse racing, greyhounds, trotting and the speedway, full stop).

The immense television coverage of NSW sport is almost matched by radio coverage of the same events. The Sydney press, pumping out three morning newspapers, two afternoon papers, three 'family' Sunday newspapers, and a profusion of weekly and monthly form guides, speciality newspapers and magazines, adds to the deluge of sporting news . . . a deluge which may have caused the frightening slump in Rugby League and soccer attendances. There have been other casualties. Horse racing patronage is down—partly due at least to the unexpected success of the TAB betting shops; boxing is almost extinct outside of the free bouts staged at Leagues Clubs; attendances at international golf tournaments have slipped drastically; and one lavish international tennis promotion ended as a box-office flop.

NSW sporting administrators agree that the huge media coverage, especially by television, has damaged attendance figures, but they do not put the entire blame on television. Rather, many criticise or blame the peculiar aggression of most of the well-known radio, TV and newspaper commentators who cast a pall of gloom over the sporting scene with their often fiery attacks on every aspect of sport: the administration, the standards, the players.

In Victoria, and particularly in Melbourne, the media are almost overbearingly enthusiastic and are generally unwilling to look too deeply into the

her teammates but who carried off the speechmaking with a confident freshness.

Earlier, Dawn had moved into the headlines, but 1956 was the beginning of a swimming era which even the record-breaking span of Shane Gould never really approached. After Melbourne, Dawn broke world records in all sprint distances with monotonous ease, won two gold and two silver medals at the 1958 Cardiff Commonwealth Games, and set herself for the defence of her Olympic 100 metres freestyle title at Rome in 1960.

Although plagued by a stomach upset, she retained her title, became the first woman in history to win two successive gold medals in the same event—and landed in her first real batch of trouble.

The drama started with Dawn bucking authority and wearing her favourite white tracksuit instead of the official team outfit, and ended with her refusing to swim in the medley relay (she was ill) and slapping the face of teammate Jan Andrew. She was sent to Coventry by her teammates, omitted from Australian teams touring Japan, South Africa and New Zealand, and became the subject of some extraordinary rumours about other matters alleged to have occurred in Rome.

In 1961, still the best sprinter in the world, she crashed the headlines again—by refusing an invitation to join the Australian Republican Party (she claimed it was anti-Royalist), and by spending an hour in the Adelaide City Watchhouse following a minor traffic offence involving a car in which she was a passenger; police later apologised and no charges were laid.

In 1962 Dawn achieved her prime ambition, becoming the first woman to break a minute for 110 yards (59.9 secs), a feat not loosely described as the greatest sporting achievement of the century.

But more was to come.

In 1962, at the Perth Commonwealth Games she won four gold medals and lowered her 110 yards time to 59.5 secs. Nevertheless, it seemed impossible that Dawn, then aged almost 27, could remain on top and achieve the improbable—a third successive gold medal in the Olympic 100 metres freestyle to be contested at Tokyo in 1964.

A few months before the Olympics, Dawn was involved in a tragic accident: the car she was driving crashed on General Holmes Drive near Sydney Airport, killing her mother and leaving Dawn with a chipped vertebra in her neck. Dawn decided, on

recovering, to pursue that third gold.

That she did it—clocking 59.5 secs after a titanic duel with 15 year old American Sharon Stouder—is history. So, too, is another brush with officialdom.

She defied orders and marched in the opening ceremony, and later took part in a light-hearted but foolish escapade in which a flag was souvenired from the Emperor's Palace.

The ASU suspended her for 10 years (the suspension was lifted four years later), but higher powers than the ASU considered her swimming achievements more important and she was awarded the MBE.

Dawn retired from competitive swimming as the greatest woman athlete of her time and (although all her world records have since been broken) is still the greatest swimmer the world has seen.

Out Balmain way, where Dawn still pops in for the occasional 'beer with the boys', nobody wants to know about Shane Gould, who called it quits before she was 17 after only one Olympic Games (Munich, 1972). After all, Dawn went to three Olympics and, like a good Tiger, came home with an incredible four gold medals and that never-to-be-bettered record of three successive wins in the 100 metres freestyle.

more seamy side of sport. The bulk of the population resembles a well-drilled, brainwashed and utterly loyal force. Grand Final day of the Victorian Football League Premiership is maniacal, with overflow crowds of 120,000 or more cramming into the Melbourne Cricket Ground and with city and suburban streets ankle-deep in bunting and streamers. Radio programmes devote days to the Big Football Show, television documentaries pour forth, and otherwise apparently sane people camp for up to a week outside the gates of the Melbourne Cricket Ground—and when the Grand Final is replayed the same night (until 1973 the VFL never allowed a direct telecast anywhere within the State) more than a million viewers, their TV dinners growing gluggy, are glued to the screen.

The same, total involvement is bestowed upon the Melbourne Cup, major motor racing meetings at Sandown Park, boxing matches of worth, international golf tournaments and important tennis matches.

FOOTBALL FEVER: ENDEMIC TO VICTORIA

But it is the football season that drags the last drop of fervour from the Victorian. Small wonder! Nowhere else on earth are some 2.5 million people so consistently bombarded with so much published, filmed and spoken propaganda, blatant publicity, too-obviously concocted half-truths, pictures, posters and parades—and all to do with a single sporting pursuit! And it's not just the media. Every imaginable commodity carries messages about teams, players, the VFL and, in more recent years, the shadow football division, the VFA: canned foods, frozen foods, paper towels, confectionery, soft drinks, hard liquors, T-shirts, underpants and negligees, neckties and cereal boxes, all do their bit of flag-waving. Even babies' napkins come in team colours.

Victorian footballers, past and present, take part in American-style lecture tours (known in Victoria as Sportsmen's Nights). They answer questions from the stages of suburban and country halls, and earn themselves small fortunes. In NSW, where no such hero worship exists, the halls would be close to empty; in Victoria, a handful of known sporting stars can draw a thousand or more fans (at $5-$8 a head) at a whistle-stop country hamlet.

In recent years there has been a slight withdrawal from such community involvement. VFL seasonal spectator aggregates, as percentages of the State's population, have dropped marginally; the actual head count has dropped only slightly. Reasons include economic conditions, the growth of the VFA, greater interest in motor sports, heavier spending on the TAB, tiny gains made by soccer, and a healthy increase in the number of participants in squash, golf, tennis, sailing and surfing.

In Tasmania there are really only three spectator sports: Australian Rules Football (in an unchallengable position as leader), horse racing and, more recently, motor sports. In keeping with the comparatively sleepy nature of the 'Apple Isle', Tasmania is not too involved in sporting hero worship, but there are occasional displays of astonishing loyalty in rural areas. When the tiny town of Scottsdale won the 1973 Tasmanian Premiership by defeating the team from the town of Cooee, the entire Scottsdale population (all 2,800 of them) embarked on a two day celebration that no one will ever forget.

South Australians are reasonably hard to please. Most of the population lives and works around the southern areas of Adelaide and Port Pirie, where they are dutiful spectators of football, horse racing, trotting and some forms of motor sport, notably speedway racing. Adelaide, the focal point of all South Australian sports, resembles Sydney in its slight sporting apathy, its complete lack of Victorian fanaticism, and its general appreciation of any top level sporting competition tempered by utter disdain for mediocre offerings. Baseball and cricket have strong followings, but Adelaide can take or (more often) leave its tennis, golf, swimming, athletics, cycling and boxing.

Following the lead of the VFL, the South Australian National Football League has embarked on an ambitious project at suburban Westlakes, constructing an ultra-modern football and general sports complex to accommodate 80,000.

Opposite: Australian National Football (better known as Aussie Rules, or more simply as 'the footy' in the Rules playing States) is as popular in Victoria, Tasmania, SA and WA as a Roman circus. Club loyalty frequently verges on hysteria, but the game at its best is a brilliant spectacle, with feats of high 'marking' matched by remarkable precision kicking and ball control. Here, Richmond's Kevin Sheedy climbs the back of North Melbourne's Gary Farrant to take a finger-tip mark in the VFL Grand Final, 1974. (Trevor Kolpin, *The Australian*)

Situated next to magnificent waterways, the project could conceivably attract the Commonwealth Games to the city.

Perth, in sporting terms, is a unique city with high attendances at horse racing, trotting, football and cricket and exceptionally high roll-ups for motor sports, topline tennis and hockey. It is the only Australian city apart from Sydney to have hosted the Commonwealth Games. It did so in 1962, turning on a magnificent spectacle at which Australia won 105 medals including a record 38 golds.

Interestingly, Perth has often been singled out for experimental sporting promotions, including a number of semi-international Rugby League games featuring English and French teams. These games against local sides drew respectable crowds—a fine tribute to the broad sporting interest of the average Western Australian who is, after all, raised on Australian Rules Football.

WINNING: A FIERCE AUSTRALIAN GAME

But whatever the State and whatever the sport, Australians have always accepted the fierce competitive spirit and win-at-all-costs philosophy which has been the trademark of the vast majority of modern champions.

From the sculler Stuart McKenzie, who loved to taunt his opponents, to the cyclist Gordon Johnson, whose blockbusting tactics touched·off a major riot in the world championships at Varese, Italy, Australia's sports stars have intrigued overseas observers with their obsession to win.

This was probably first brought home to Australians when London *Daily Mirror* sports writer Peter Wilson described Davis Cup coach Harry Hopman as a 'slave driver' and his teenage wonder boys, Lew Hoad and Ken Rosewall, as 'robots' when they launched themselves in the 1953 Wimbledon championships. Wilson posed a simple question: Was sporting success really worth total involvement at the expense of a normal social life?

Australians, justifiably proud of the international successes of Hoad and Rosewall, ignored the question. Only 20 years later, with the unexpected retirement of Olympic swimming champion Shane Gould, did they begin to appreciate that many adolescent Australians are living a life of sporting drudgery at a time when they are experiencing the pangs of physical and emotional development.

Shane Gould's retirement caused a rift between her coach, Forbes Carlile, and her parents. Carlile astonished many Australians by claiming she 'had let down her country'; her parents protested that Shane had done more than her share in bringing glory to Australian sport and had a right to a life of her own.

This confrontation eventually led the Gould family to move to the NSW country town of Armidale, away from the concentration camp atmosphere of international level Sydney sport.

If nothing else, the incident spotlighted one inescapable fact: behind the vast majority of super champions there have always been the super coaches, the men and women who have at times leapt way ahead of the rest of the world in physical and psychological training techniques—and who produced results. Shane Gould would undoubtedly have become a champion under a Don Talbot, a Frank Guthrie, a Harry Gallagher or any other acknowledged coach, but it is doubtful whether anyone but Carlile could have extracted quite the same measure of brilliance.

Carlile had an unenviable task with Shane Gould, trying to pressure a young girl from a well-to-do Sydney home environment into dedicating herself almost totally to the heartbreaking grind of swimming while her friends naturally drifted into the normal teenage social whirl.

And as Carlile had a problem, so too did Sydney's Harry Gallagher when he first spotted the championship potential in Dawn Fraser, then, on her own admission, 'a bit of a widgie' in the tough suburb of Balmain. Gallagher had to lure Dawn away from the neighbourhood milkbars, wean her off cigarettes and prove to her that 100 per cent application to swimming would hold more ultimate value than remaining a member of a Balmain gang.

Opposite: Swimming coaches have been publicly lambasted for turning star swimmers into sporting automata, but Australian swimmers continue to shatter world records. The water babies start young, competition is fierce, and there's always the chance that today's not-yet-a-teenager will be tomorrow's Jenny Turrall or Stephen Holland. This proud miss flourishes a school championship trophy at Watson's Bay, Sydney. (Rick Stevens, *Sydney Morning Herald*)

And the same challenge faced Percy Cerutty when he finally induced Herb Elliott to settle down seriously to athletics training. Elliott was stubborn, independent and rebellious to the point where he continued smoking against Cerutty's orders when Cerutty was trying to indoctrinate him with the philosophy of his 'Stotan' (Spartan-like) training theories.

All succeeded. All helped, too, to establish what is now an international legend about the 'secrets' of Australian sports training and the 'magical' influences brought to bear on young sportsmen and sportswomen in an endeavour to turn them into machine-like competition winners.

How big a role did this breed of coaches really play?

Sporting history is somewhat confused on this issue. Take tennis coach Harry Hopman. Some factions claim that Hopman was an overrated individual who used nothing more than personality to help Australia to major tennis victories. 'Hopman wasn't worth any 15 points a game to me,' 1957 Davis Cup doubles player Mervyn Rose once said. 'He didn't say a word to me. I was a bit older than the others and I used to like to think for myself . . .'

But Rose, who never had any affinity with Hopman, is countered by Lew Hoad, who liked Hop's discipline. Sedgman, too, admitted Hopman's ability to get players fit, though he often claimed publicly that Hopman couldn't be compared as a tactician with Jack Kramer, Pancho Gonzales or Pancho Segura.

Certainly, excellent and well-respected coaches existed before World War II, but only after the war did coaches really come into their own. Indeed, in the 50s, the country's greatest sporting era, the coaches became nearly as well known as their charges.

Nevertheless, many of the successes of the 70s and a sizeable proportion of those of the 60s were the result of individual perseverance and dedication. Many of the old-guard coaches had by then hung up their training whips. Today, Carlile is probably the last surviving coach from that great period of the 50s.

Since the days when the early settlers held the first race meetings and the bare-knuckle lads broke one another's heads on the eastern States circuit, interest in Australian sport has continually wavered and even, on occasion, followed new lines. Only a handful of sports—horse racing (in particular), Australian Rules Football, cricket and boxing—have remained nationally popular, and on the first

Opposite: Although track and field events attract scant public attention in between Olympic or Commonwealth Games, athletics clubs thrive. Internationally, Australian women are still strong in the sprints, continuing a tradition going back to the early post-war years of Shirley Strickland and Marjorie Jackson; in the gruelling middle and long distance men's events, athletes like these competitors in the NSW 1974 cross country championships are spurred by the feats of such greats as John Landy, Herb Elliott and Ron Clarke. (Mervyn Bishop, *Sydney Morning Herald*)

Jack Brabham—infatuated with mechanical power

The southern Sydney suburb of Hurstville slumbers in neat hectares of red-tiled brick bungalows, each surrounded by the traditional Australian square of neatly-clipped lawn, a haven of concrete garden gnomes, afternoon teas and corner grocers with white aprons.

When one reflects on the Hurstville pre-occupation with community responsibility and the moulding of solid citizens, it comes as no real surprise to remember the area spawned Jack Brabham, three times winner of the World's Racing Driver Championship and without question, the suburb's finest sporting son.

There is still, despite years of exposure to the sophistication of the international sporting scene, a great deal of Hurstville respectability about Brabham.

He remains wealth and fame notwithstanding, a happily married family man with a towering application of ethics to his far-flung chain of business enterprises and without a trace of egotism about the feats which, arguably, made him the most successful Australian sportsman in history.

Brabham's father, Tom, was a Hurstville greengrocer who built up a flourishing business in the 1930s and probably visualised young Jack 'taking over the business' —a powerful parental incentive for hard work in those days. But for reasons young Jack still doesn't understand, the Brabham boy had an early and unquenchable interest in things mechanical.

The Brabhams pandered to this curious childish technical bent, even to the point where Jack was allowed to drive the old family Willys tourer around the spacious backyard when he was barely 10 years of age. There was family disappointment— but no objections—when he asked permission to bypass the fruit and vegetable trade and enter an apprenticeship with Harry Ferguson, a local automotive engineer, who later remembered that . . . 'Jack was a good boy, not brilliant, but a good boy. One thing about him, he never gave me any lip . . .'

Brabham, then as now fiercely patriotic, joined the RAAF when he was 18, served almost three years with the ground crew

and was discharged at 21 even more infatuated with mechanical power and the idea of owning his own Hurstville corner service station and garage.

And it may have happened, had not Brabham met an American named Johnny Schonberg, who proposed an adventurous scheme involving a trip to Darwin to purchase two Army trucks, loading them with automotive spare parts and bringing the booty back for sale in a commodity-starved Sydney market. By an incredible fluke of timing, the pair arrived in Brisbane the same day speedway racing was revived at the Exhibition track and Schonberg, who had raced midget cars in the United States before the war, literally dragged a disinterested Brabham along to the circuit.

In his *Jack Brabham Motor Racing Book*, published in 1960, Brabham admits to being mildly terrified of the midget car action: 'Midget drivers, I thought, must be completely nuts!'. But when Schonberg, his old interest in midget racing reborn, decided to re-enter the sport, Brabham agreed to help him build a racer, a tiny, three of these the whole structure of Australian sport has been based. Boxing has enjoyed some explosive periods of genuine nation-wide interest—the Les Darcy era up to World War I, the Roaring Twenties, the late 30s, and the years immediately after World War II—but it has invariably plummeted to the depths again for no apparent reason.

Cricket's attraction has ebbed and flowed, depending almost entirely on the performances of Australian test teams—a simple formula which can be applied, with few exceptions, to most Australian spectator sports. On the other hand golf's big attractions are imported stars and not the local-boys-made-good, no matter how well Australians may have fared on the US and British circuits.

Track cycling was once an incredibly popular spectator sport in Australia. Crowds 40,000 strong watched racing on the old concrete track that circled the Sydney Cricket Ground during the palmy days of the 1920s and 1930s. Legendary champions like Opperman, Grenda, Spears, Rogers, Guyatt and Lamb pushed the pedals on Sydney's three and Melbourne's two board tracks. Cycling was on the verge of a miserable and humiliating death in the late 60s when the Melbourne Olympic track was demolished and Sydney's few club meetings drew only a handful of spectators, but it was fighting back in the early 70s as a brilliant new breed of young Australian riders burst into international prominence.

PARTICIPATION IS INCREASING AT AN ENCOURAGING RATE

Despite the continual taunts of overseas observers that Australians have become a race of prosperous, blubbery individuals basking in an orgy of self indulgence, it is a fact that more Australians than ever before now take part in some form of sport, be it lawn bowls, football or competitive swimming.

In the late 1940s there were perhaps a thousand or so surfboard riders. Now an estimated 275,000 young board riders try their hand daily in every State. Between 1963 and 1973 the number of squash players increased tenfold to more than 300,000 fairly regular players. There are no definitive figures for the number of social and competitive golfers, but reliable estimates suggest something like 450,000.

The return of the cycling boom saw the sale of 131,000 bicycles in only one year. The extremely successful Little Athletics movement in Victoria caters every weekend for more than 185,000 boy and girl competitors under the age of 12. Sailing has mushroomed, and as many as 400,000 people take to the east

shark-nosed creation which Brabham lovingly grafted together from Army disposals bits and pieces and components taken from an old Amilcar, a Morris Cowley, a Harley-Davidson and a speedway J.A.P. motorcycle engine. When Schonberg's brief infatuation waned, Brabham, with a sizeable investment in the $800 creation, decided to try his hand. He was almost 22. His only association with motor sport was the handful of meetings in which Schonberg had competed.

Among the hard-drinking, chain-smoking speedway driver brigade, Brabham looked exactly what he was: a shy and courteous youngster from a moderately well-to-do suburb with more interest in mechanical engineering than in establishing himself as a Saturday night hero at the Sydney Showground speedway.

But Brabham, much to his own astonishment, was a natural speedway driver with reflexes which steered him clear of crash situations and on to a dozen State and national championships between 1948 and 1951.

But speedway was basically an arena for drivers with heavy right feet. Brabham was eager to explore the mechanical intricacies of legitimate racing at Sydney's old Mt Druitt circuit and perhaps even the road racing headquarters—Mt Panorama at Bathurst.

Equipment was hard to obtain, so Brabham tried his hand in the speedway midget, creating a minor controversy by almost immediately winning the Australian Hill Climb Championship at Rob Roy. He fluked the purchase of a solid little Cooper Mk IV rear-engine racing car, and so impressed the late Reg Shepheard, then Managing Director of the Redex Oil Company, that Shepheard helped him import a brand-new Cooper Bristol racing car in which he became almost unbeatable on local circuits and good enough to lead home many well-known internationals in New Zealand events.

In 1955, Brabham, in formal Hurstville fashion, explained to his wife Betty that he must explore motor racing and either get it out of his system or establish himself

overseas. The Cooper Bristol was sold and Brabham flew to England with modest capital and only a dream: he would give himself eight months to succeed in the heady whirl of English and European racing and then make his decision about the future.

The trip was almost a disaster. He could not purchase a competitive car, was unable to attract the interest of works teams and ended the eight months in the workshop run by the small racing car manufacturer, John Cooper. He made no money, but he built a car on which much of the future of the Cooper factory was to be based—a revolutionary, rear-engined Cooper Bristol sports car which John Cooper allowed him to bring back to Australia.

Brabham duly won the 1955 Australian Grand Prix at Port Wakefield and returned to England in 1956, this time with his wife. John Cooper put him on the payroll, more as a designer and builder than driver, but with the promise of regular competition.

By 1957, Cooper took him away from the drawing boards and put him into the coast waters each weekend. Rock, beach and estuary fishing, most of it strictly for fun, now attracts some 600,000 regular participants.

Similar astonishing figures apply to social cricket, lawn and ten-pin bowling, and non-competitive swimming and surfing. Rugged sports like football have been the losers, with former devotees being lured by the thousands to participate in other enjoyable but less rigorous sporting pursuits.

A little of the old competitive spirit has disappeared from the Australian sporting scene—but certainly not to the extent that sociologists and visiting journalists would have us believe—as the result of a number of factors: an increasingly wide array of recreational diversions, including licensed clubs and off-course betting facilities; the continued growth of the television industry; and the steady rise in car ownership (though cars have had beneficial side-effects in encouraging surfing, fishing, camping and more general exploration of the immense Australian countryside).

There is, of course, no such thing as a 'typical' Australian sportsman. Instead, there is infinite variety. The enthusiastic mid-week lawn bowler or golfer in Melbourne who lives for the weekend's Australian Rules tussle. The tall, tanned Sydney 'surfie' who rises at 4 am to catch the best of the early morning waves and who enjoys a flutter at the Friday night trots. The Queensland deep-sea fishing devotee who wouldn't miss the weekly fight night at Brisbane's Festival Hall. The Perth hockey fanatic whose idea of heaven is Friday night at the rip-roaring Claremont Speedway. The spear fisherman in Adelaide whose Sunday afternoon passion is orienteering in the Adelaide Hills. The sporting shooter from Launceston who follows the local football team with a fervour unmatched by even the most rabid Carlton supporter.

And what does the future hold for Australian sport?

Clearly, nothing less than continued international success in pool and surf swimming, surfboard riding, cricket, golf, tennis and most other ball games; and, certainly, unprecedented successes in the other traditional Australian sports of prizefighting, motorcycle speedway riding, cycling and athletics.

Nothing has really changed in the last half century. Some sports are now more popular than others; world championship successes have been achieved in unexpected areas; some formerly popular sports have almost disappeared but still hover, awaiting the touch of the right promotional genius for their comeback. The public still grumbles about crowding and poor catering at the

Cooper racing team as No. 2 driver to Roy Salvadori. In 1958, Brabham, known to European motor racing fans as the 'Quiet Australian', was No. 1 Cooper driver. In 1959 he became, almost unobtrusively, World Champion. The brilliant Stirling Moss had to play second fiddle to an Australian who had seen his first road race less than eight years previously.

It was the beginning of everything: his own garage in Chessington, a large house near the Cooper factory, a Cessna 180 to fly to Grand Prix engagements. In 1960 he was World Champion again with an incredible five Grand Prix wins in a row. In 1961, he brought a Sydney engineering associate, Ron Tauranac, to England to help him do something no other driver in history had dared—build and race his own Grand Prix racers.

To add the final miracle touch, Brabham began to use Australian-made Repco components. The mighty factories of Ferrari, Porsche, Honda, B.R.M. and the substantial works of Lotus and Cooper were more than a little taken aback by the audacity of the Australian teetotaller. And especially in 1966, when Brabham again won the World Championship, this time driving a Brabham F1 powered by an Australian Repco V8 engine.

It was the first time in motor racing history that a driver had won the World Championship in a car he designed and constructed himself. Ferrari especially was shattered—and then heart-broken when Brabham's No. 2 driver, Dennis Hulme of New Zealand, won the World Championship in 1967 with boss Brabham finishing runner-up. Two all-Australian cars had whipped the best-known Grand Prix works teams!

In 16 years of Grand Prix racing, Brabham lived with tragedy and incredible strain. Champion drivers like Jim Clark, Peter Collins, Jean Behra, Ivor Bueb, Jochen Rindt, Piers Courage, Ricardo Rodriguez, Count von Trips, the Marquis de Portago and dozens more, had been killed. Brabham was the oldest Grand Prix driver in the most lethal sport in the world. It was clearly time to quit.

In 1971, in his normal, quiet manner, Brabham sold his Brabham construction company and other English business enterprises, returned to Australia and invested in a vast complex of commercial pursuits. The Hurstville boy who entered motor sport by building a backyard speedway midget and graduated to designing a Grand Prix car which for at least two years was the best in the world, had made his mark and his fortune. He could do little more.

Australians will continue to win Olympic gold medals, set new world running records and win world boxing championships. Their feats, no matter how brilliant at the time, will remain only passing chapters in international sport. Brabham took on the might and wealth of a dozen companies—many of them, like Ferrari, heavily backed by Government subsidies—and was victorious. There isn't a man in the world capable of emulating his success.

nation's larger sporting arenas, tends to decry a big percentage of individual champions, frequently roots for a team of genuine overseas triers, and always rallies to the cause of a genuine battler.

And will anything really change? Hardly.

The institutions still remain, more firmly entrenched than ever . . . Randwick, the Sydney and Melbourne Cricket Grounds, Flemington, Adelaide Oval, Kooyong and White City. And the old faithfuls are still there, every year . . . the VFL Grand Final, the Melbourne Cup, Sydney and Brisbane Rugby League Grand Finals, the Australian Golf Open, the England-Australia cricket tests, the Sydney-Hobart blue water yachting classic, the Inter-Dominion, Miracle Mile, Austral, the Sheffield and Claxton Shields.

And that unique institution—the Australian sporting public.

Opposite: The march past provides a splendid curtain raiser for a surf lifesaving carnival in NSW. Regular sporting competition keeps members fit for the voluntary beach patrols that rescue about 7,000 people a year at Australian beaches. The history of the Australian Surf Lifesaving movement is studded with heroic rescues and gallant sacrifice. In 1938 about 200 men, women and children were swept out into a treacherous surf at Bondi after a series of sudden sand and wave movements. Surf lifesavers saved all but five in near impossible conditions. Many shark attack victims too have been rescued by surf lifesavers and J. Brinkley of Kirra Beach, Queensland, was fatally mauled while attempting to pull an injured swimmer away from a marauding shark. The movement has lost much of its attraction to young sportsmen with the development of the modern surfboard and the free-wheeling 'image' that goes with it. However, the movement is modernising its techniques and is slowly regaining its ground despite the selfless dedication required of its members.

The traditional Australian-designed surfboat is slowly being replaced as a rescue craft by the high-speed jet boat. However, its popularity in the sporting side of the lifesaving movement remains unchallenged.

Right: With their weight aft and the bows still buried a surfboat crew wrestle with the sweep oar to hold their course and prevent capsize.

Below: Bared backsides minimise chafing in the long tough haul ahead as the Clovelly crew launch their boat at the start of a NSW race.

Below centre: Military-like precision, a vital quality of the rescue and resuscitation drill, is reflected in the determined profiles of a North Cronulla junior team.

Below right: A Victorian crew acknowledges applause during the State's annual Moomba Festival parade.

JOHN CARNEMOLLA

JOHN CARNEMOLLA

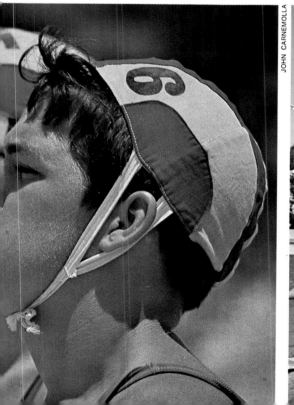

JOHN CARNEMOLLA

Sporting rivalry and spectator bias reaches its peak in the international sporting calendar during the Test cricket matches between Australia and England. In the national sporting arena the Victorian Football League is without equal in the fury of its competition and the partisanship of its Australian Rules followers.

Above right: Australia's wicket-keeper Rodney Marsh appeals for an English wicket at the Sydney Cricket Ground (where spectators on 'The Hill' are noted for their 'ocker' beer drinking and vocal partisanship).

Right: Players set themselves for a high mark—the most skilful and spectacular feature of Australian Rules—in a Carlton-Richmond club game.

Opposite: Vast crowds add a tension to VFL games not experienced by other sports This is particularly so of the Melbourne Cricket Ground, which holds the national attendance record of 121,696, set at the 1970 grand final.

The colourful bedlam of final round football in Melbourne is known as 'football fever'. It infects people of all ages and stratas. Club colours are displayed boldly on anything from the family car to the baby's bedspread early in the season but it's the finals that inspire the most inventiveness and the wildest enthusiasm.

Horseracing, with its attendant gambling, is a truly national sport with a rich heritage of feats and folklore. It is a sport that can halt the nation during the running of the Melbourne Cup or leave a country town deserted for a bush meeting. A relative newcomer to the horse sports is the American-style rodeo—though its spectacular spills and 'Wild West' atmosphere are increasing its popularity.

Above left: An early leader breaks clear of the bunch as the Melbourne Cup field moves into the turn.

Left: In sharp contrast to the lush turf of the Melbourne track, the field spreads wide for the finish in a cloud of dust at a country race meeting at Alice Springs.

Above: Help arrives too late to avoid a bone-jarring spill at a country rodeo meeting.

Climate and fine metropolitan waterways get many thousands of Australians afloat every weekend. Yacht racing is of a high standard and constantly produces winning international boats and crews. Rowing has a much smaller following, but despite fluctuating international fortunes such rowers as Bobby Pearce (Olympic gold medals for singles sculls in 1928 and 1932), and the supremacy of Stuart McKenzie between 1958 and 1962, continue to inspire Australian ambitions.

Above right: Lonely sculler training on the Yarra, Melbourne.

Right: Start of the Sydney-Hobart yacht race, one of the world's ocean racing classics.

Opposite: The Australian-developed 18-foot skiff demonstrates the power in a huge sail area as it effortlessly planes in a light breeze across Sydney Harbour.

366

Above: Ken Rosewall, one of the greatest Australian tennis players of all time, is both the oldest and youngest winner of the Australian Open tournament. He was 18 when he first won in 1953 and he last won it in 1972 at 36. His clashes in the twilight of his career with the brilliant young American player, Jimmy Connors, won him the admiration of tennis followers throughout the world.

Above: A skydiver freefalling above Rockingham, WA.

Left: A series of coloured high-speed electronic flashes demonstrates the action of former broad jump champion, Phil May.

Water skiing is a fast growing sport in Australia and its standard is steadily improving. Australian skiers have already broken the 100 mph barrier for speed skiing and the 75 mph mark for barefoot skiing.

Above: A competitor executes a well-controlled slalom turn at a Victorian championship.

With snowfields comparable to Europe's, resorts are kept busy in the winter months in southern NSW and northern Victoria.

Left: The roof of a chalet provides a launching ramp for some light-hearted ski jump practice.

Below left: Young Australians learn the skills from itinerant European instructors.

FOREIGN RELATIONS

Rohan Rivett

'Complete independence on matters of foreign policy and military policy . . .'

The oldest—and for 150 years easily the most important—Australian relationship overseas was that with Britain. This relationship, largely taken for granted from 1788 until 1941, was jarred by the drama that heralded the beginning of the Pacific war. When the Japanese, within 72 hours, sank both the American fleet at Hawaii and the two major British capital ships off the Malayan coast, Australia found itself in the deadliest peril it had known. There was immediate conflict between Canberra and London about the homeward recall of Australian troops. The celebrated attempt by Winston Churchill to divert A.I.F. veterans from the Middle East to Burma instead of allowing them to come back to an Australia denuded of trained men brought an open breach between Downing Street and the Australian Prime Minister, John Curtin, in Canberra. Curtin appealed unambiguously to the United States for assistance in Australia's hour of need, making it clear that past ties with Britain no longer had any effect on Australia's independent rights to seek friends and support where she wished.

Looking back today, that sharp showdown as 1941 ended and 1942 began can be seen as the beginning of a process now extending over 33 years, whereby, in fits and starts together with long periods of quiescence, Australia has gradually untied itself from London's apron strings. The British at the beginning of the 1960s gave the general trend a sharp acceleration by their decision to throw in their lot with the six European nations that had formed the Common Market under the Treaty of Rome.

Since then, with gathering speed, Australia has sold more and more of her produce and minerals to other countries and has simultaneously bought a smaller proportion of her total imports from Britain with each passing year.

Whereas in 1962-63 Britain was still comfortably the largest market for Australia's exports—taking $401 million worth as compared to $346 million by Japan and $265 million by the USA—nine years later it was taking only a little more than two thirds of what Australia was exporting to the USA and less than one third of Australia's exports to Japan.

Similarly, whereas in 1962-63 the United Kingdom was overwhelmingly the biggest exporter to Australia, selling to Australians goods worth nearly 50 per cent more than those sold by the USA and five times more than those sold by Japan, by 1971-72 Japan was selling nearly two thirds as much as the UK while the USA was selling Australians 15 per cent more.

Yet back in the 1920s and 1930s no-one was surprised that more than two thirds of Australia's total exports went straight to the UK market while an even bigger proportion of Australia's imports came from Britain.

After 142 years as a colony of the British Crown, Australia's status as an independent dominion was officially recognised in 1930 by the Statute of Westminster. However, this was a matter for constitutional lawyers and historians. It did not signify any break or change in the general attitude of affection, respect and reliance which most Australians felt towards Britain. There had been, from

Opposite: Ruined shore defences at Darwin, derelict reminders of Japanese bombing raids during World War II. Sydney, 3,000 km to the south-east as the crow flies, received a few shells fired from submarines, and at least one sub penetrated the harbour defences, but Darwin suffered the brunt of the brief but destructive air attacks.

373

the earliest days of settlement at Port Jackson, an Irish element which had mixed feelings about the British Crown and the strong bonds and sentiments cherished by fellow Australians. But they were a minority and, even during the fierce heat and controversy following the Easter rebellion of 1916, most Australians of Irish origin remained loyal to the British cause.

The homogeneity of the Australian population which had been 98 per cent English, Scottish, Irish or Welsh for 150 years began to break down just before World War II with the admission of refugees, particularly Jews, from Hitler's persecutions.

After the war, following the enthusiastic lead given in 1947 by the Labor Government's Minister for Immigration, the late Mr Arthur Calwell, a great flow of migrants from continental Europe began to change fundamentally the composition of Australia's population. Over the next 27 years nearly two million migrants from countries as far apart as Portugal and Holland on the west to Turkey and Lebanon on the east flowed out to Australia in addition to more than a million migrants from the United Kingdom. Among the continental migrants Italians and Greeks predominated but there were at different times large segments of refugees from the Baltic states and from Hungary.

The overall result of the new, large-scale migration policy followed by all governments from 1947 to 1974 was to reduce the proportion of Australia's population of Anglo-Saxon origin from something well above 98 per cent to just over 80 per cent. The presence of this sizeable minority with no ties of any kind to the British Crown or familiarity with the British parliamentary system or English common law is unquestionably having a considerable impact in the general loosening of the exceptionally strong ties that knit mother country and island continent for the first five generations of white settlement here.

During his prime ministership from 1939 to 1941 and again from 1949 to 1966, Sir Robert Menzies was a great individual force in maintaining the deep traditional friendship with Britain and admiration for British institutions habitual in Australia. In the nine years since his retirement no similar lead has come from Canberra. Nevertheless, even in the mid 70s, it is highly significant that the great majority of the increasing numbers of young Australians going abroad in their late teens and early 20s still go directly or indirectly to London. There are indefinable factors in the British-Australian relationship which can withstand considerable mutual criticism, mockery and occasional public differences.

For the decade ahead it seems certain that the steady erosion of the proportion of Australian trade moving to and from Britain will continue. Even if

Walter Crocker—diplomat extraordinary

Walter Russell Crocker was born on a farm in South Australia in 1902. He was educated at Adelaide University, Balliol College, Oxford, and Stanford University, USA. After serving in the colonial administration of Nigeria he worked for the League of Nations and as Assistant to the Director General of the International Labour Organisation. During the war he was a lieutenant-colonel in the British army and was decorated by the Belgian Government.

He worked at United Nations Headquarters as chief of the Africa Secretariat until 1949 when he was appointed Professor of International Relations at the brand new Australian National University then opened in Canberra. He transferred from the acting vice-chancellorship in 1952 to the Department of External Affairs and was sent as Australia's High Commissioner to India in that year. He then held successively ambassadorships and high commissionships in Indonesia, Canada, India (again) and Nepal, the Netherlands and Belgium, East Africa and finally Italy. He retired from the ambassadorship in Rome in 1970 at the age of 68. He has published a number of books on international problems and in 1971 told the story of his diplomatic career in *Australian Ambassador*, the first major autobiography yet published by an Australian diplomat.

Walter Crocker is slender, tall, straight-spoken, highly perceptive and has an immense background of scholarship and research into the problems of many countries. Only a handful of Australian academics have met with any success in the diplomatic field and among these Crocker has been outstanding.

Unlike some career diplomats in all countries, who tend to tailor their views to those of the minister or ruling faction of the moment, Crocker has been conspicuous for rigid personal independence and intellectual integrity which often led him to express views unpopular with the ministerial team in power in Canberra.

It is some measure of his perceptiveness as an analyst and reporter of the nations where he has represented Australia that, despite this independence, he was continually asked to occupy key posts abroad for the last 18 years of his career. As his writings illustrate Crocker has the assurance and self-reliance which come from an acute intelligence and from 40 years' experience of dealing with politicians and officials of a multitude of races and religions on five continents. Australians have a deserved reputation for denigrating or failing to give full value to fellow Australians with unusual brains and drive. Crocker's record suggests that if the individual is strong enough this prejudice can be overcome triumphantly.

Britain should sever itself from Common Market membership, economists feel it is extremely unlikely that the UK will ever regain anything approaching its once dominant role in the Australian market. Nor can Britain conceivably rival Japan as the main buyer from this country.

In matters of defence the story is parallel. Until the disasters at the beginning of the Pacific war, not one Australian in 20 seriously questioned the belief that Britain was Australia's shield and guardian and that if Britain were involved in any war Australia must be involved also. Since the days of Queen Victoria when Australian contingents went to the Sudan and to South Africa, Australians have fought on land, sea or in the air in every war in which Britain has been involved. Australia's controversial participation in Vietnam in the later 1960s was the first time Australians saw action in a war in which Britain had no part. The Whitlam Government ended that involvement on taking power in December 1972. Australia's actual embroilment was never much more than a token gesture but few Australians can imagine Canberra's decisions about any future action by Australia's armed·forces being seriously influenced by opinions in Whitehall.

Steady evolution—generally slow, occasionally rapid—has marked British-Australian relations since Captain Phillip arrived with the First Fleet in 1788. The Federation of the six States in 1901 and the Curtin appeal to the United States 41 years later can be seen as two decisive points in turning relations from the old absolute reliance on London to the present point of friendship with total independence. Australia is now in the course of becoming more and more involved with her neighbours on the Asian mainland and in the western Pacific and Indian oceans just as Britain, for more than a decade, has been becoming more closely interlocked with the rest of western Europe.

Some Australians believe that within a decade there will be a severance of the traditional, largely formal link with Britain through the Crown. However, anti-monarchist feeling in Australia is so dissipated and muted that a majority seem quite content with the situation where the head of State for Australia (the Queen of Australia) is the English Queen. Events in Washington and in other countries during the 70s have not aroused any Australian enthusiasm for a presidential system. New factors will need to arise before establishment of an Australian republic becomes a serious political issue in the major parties.

THE UNITED STATES: A CLOSE FRIEND BUT . . .

Since the crisis of the Pacific war the most important figure abroad for politically minded Australians has been the President of the United States. Through the first half of the 1940s many, perhaps most, Australians embraced Franklin Delano Roosevelt as Australia's great ally and defender. The ANZUS treaty negotiated in the 1950s seemed to confirm this and the relationship between Canberra and Washington (apart from a brief but painful difference over Suez in 1956) has remained extraordinarily close.

A series of verbal attacks on the policies of the US President in South-east Asia in December 1972 produced considerable rumblings, especially when their full abrasiveness was revealed by publication of the documents at the beginning of 1974. However, most experienced political observers believe that time will erase any doubts then created. In any case, identity of interest in the Pacific, close reliance on the American armament industry and the general tendency of Australians and New Zealanders to get on well with Americans, either in their own countries or in the United States, suggest that the clashes of politicians cannot destroy this strong relationship.

Diplomatic relations began immediately after World War I but were almost entirely concerned with commercial matters until R. G. Casey (now Lord Casey) was sent to Washington in 1940 to open the Legation which was to become very quickly the Australian Embassy. The Pacific war ensured that Washington would become, as it has remained, our most important listening post and most responsible diplomatic point of representation overseas. A series of distinguished Australians, some career diplomats, others politicians, have held the post while other senior envoys over the past two decades have been stationed in New York as Australia's ambassadors to the United Nations.

Whereas until 1942 the closest possible links and interchanges existed between the Australian armed services and those of Britain, the Japanese attack southwards produced a dramatic change which has never since been reversed. Since 1942 both Australia and New Zealand have looked to the USA as their main armourer. While there are alternative sources of certain weapons (the Swedish Bofors gun and the French Mirage plane are instances), most military observers foresee Australia looking to the great factories of the US west coast for those major weapons not produced in Australia during the years immediately ahead.

Many Australians felt, especially during the Vietnam war, that the Australian Government had become as subservient to Washington in matters of diplomatic and military decision, especially in South East Asia, as Australian governments had been to Downing Street right up to World War II. In fact the Dulles policy of communist containment, now largely discredited, was thrust down the throats of successive Australian foreign ministers from Casey to Don Willesee with little more consultation than 19th century British foreign secretaries extended to the various State governments before making their imperial moves across the world.

In part, Australian deference stemmed from the vast contrast in size, population and productivity between the two nations. This gap was emphasised and heightened by the very real sense of obligation felt by Australians throughout the 40s and 50s towards the United States because of the dominant role played by US sailors and airmen in the crucial months of 1942 when Australia seemed virtually defenceless against expected Japanese invasion. The kow-tow approach of Canberra to Washington reached its climax, amid healthy laughter, when the late Harold Holt on the lawns of the White House proclaimed in 1967 that Australia was 'All the way with L.B.J.'.

Today a totally different perspective reigns. The Whitlam Government made abundantly clear to Washington its complete independence in matters of foreign policy and military policy. It is not conceivable that any Labor ministry in Australia in the 70s or 80s could adopt the satellite role towards Washington fully accepted in the later 50s and until 1972 by all ministries in Canberra.

In the sense of size, strength, global significance and influence on others there can never be any thought in our lifetimes of Australia posing as an equal of the United States. But it is the strong conviction of thoughtful Australians that Australia's viewpoint will be best understood and appreciated if the full independence of Australia in matters of military and foreign policy is made clear to Washington at all times. Candour as between friends in private discussion is vastly preferable to public mud-slinging in moments of acute difference.

After 30 years, during which Australia's approach towards the USA was dubbed by critics within Australia as 'Me-tooism', a showdown such as that of December 1972 was probably inevitable and even, in the long term, healthy. In their three decades of global power the Americans have had quite enough sycophants, flatterers and beggars crowding in on Washington. In Australia perceptive Americans can look to find a friend who is not overawed or mendicant. Australia in many ways is following the path of development trodden by the USA more than a century earlier. Physical and geographical parallels abound. Only a very short-sighted Australian, with views unbalanced by ideology, would wish to see anything except a close, mutually helpful and respectful relationship between the English-speaking peoples on opposite sides of the Pacific. The small minority of the extreme Left that has maintained an increasingly anti-American attitude for almost a quarter of a century does not express the view of most Australian trade unionists let alone the entire Australian community.

The 70s brought previously unknown troubles to the American ship of State but the nation proved to have a natural resilience which allowed new leaders and new policies to emerge at a time of national crisis. Australians generally will be looking forward to moving in close step with Americans in many fields in the international sphere long after the governmental differences over Vietnam are forgotten.

The nation closest to the great centres of Australian population is also the nation sharing Australia's viewpoint on the great majority of international issues. As the old British Empire evolved into the British Commonwealth, and now into a Commonwealth of Nations embracing members in six continents, Australia and New Zealand, while each jealous of total independence and full sovereignty, have inevitably come very close in issues affecting the defence and safety of their area. Their strong common approach to the French government over the continuation of atomic testing at Mururoa Atoll is only one instance of a trend that may eventually see the services of Australia and New Zealand training together, sharing identical weapons, making common purchases and generally integrating all aspects of defence in the south-west Pacific.

Over the years Australia has consistently been a bigger exporter to New Zealand than an importer. Partly this is due to industrial development and greater mineral resources; partly it is due to the relative geographic and population sizes of the two countries. Some economists believe that sooner or later Australia and New Zealand must abolish all tariff barriers between the two countries and possibly make a united stance in the sale of major common products such as wool and meat on the markets of the world. The natural and healthy attitude of Wellington at present is to retain every scrap of independence to avoid being swallowed up by New Zealand's much bigger neighbour. There are, happily, no significant points of dispute, jealousy or ill will. Irrespective of the ebb and flow of party politics in both countries, much closer liaison in all fields across the Tasman is assured for the foreseeable future.

Australian relations with Canada have been consistently harmonious but never very close. In the post-war period the two nations have been competitors in attracting migrants from both Britain and continental Europe. Both are major exporters of wheat and there have been lively tussles for the great market places of Asia, notably China. Otherwise, Australian-Canadian relationships have remained singularly unchanging since Australian Federation embraced many aspects of the Canadian Constitution at the beginning of the century. By and large, Australians and Canadians like each other, enjoy meeting and respect each other. But the politics and cultures of each country do not make much impact on the other. New departures in international thinking in the future may change this but at the moment all development of a closer relationship is confined to ministers, parliamentarians and senior public servants meeting at

NEW ZEALAND: NO SIGNIFICANT DISPUTES, JEALOUSY OR ILL WILL

William Robinson—'Mr Mining'

William Sidney Robinson has been dead for a decade but his life and career illustrate better than that of any business man or company executive of 1975 just how much Australian *nous*, imagination and flair can achieve in the international world of business if those talents are harnessed to a unique knowledge of the man's own field. For more than 30 years, W. S. Robinson was 'Mr Mining' of Australia. He not only knew far more about the country's resources of metals and minerals than almost anyone before or since but he had a unique insight into every facet of their extraction, treatment, manufacture and commercial usage both domestically and on the international markets.

Born in Melbourne in 1876 and educated at Scotch College, he was an adviser for the mining industry to a succession of prime ministers from William Morris Hughes in World War I to John Curtin and J. B. Chifley during and after the second conflict.

But his great service was in bringing his own remarkable talents and experience to

the service of the group known in Australian business circles as Collins House. Until he was 30 he was associated with financial journalism, but for half a century thereafter he was deeply involved with almost every development of non-ferrous mining and smelting not only in Australia but in the United Kingdom, Spain, Italy and Burma. Australia's outstanding historian of the mining industry, Geoffrey Blaney, has edited a volume of W. S. Robinson memoirs *If I Remember Rightly*, which spells out the unique place he won in the trust and counsels of international figures ranging from Winston Churchill and the top scientists of Britain to Bernard Baruch and the great multi-millionaires of the mining and metal combines of the USA.

In the 40s a famous American remarked: 'Some men on Wall Street may have heard of Madame Melba, a handful who race horses will recall Phar Lap, but to nearly everyone who matters in mining and finance Australia is represented by W. S. Robinson'.

Yet Robinson avoided publicity like the plague. While his decisions and advice were determining the development, output and eventual sale abroad of millions of tonnes of minerals and metals from Australian mines, factories and workshops, his name and picture seldom appeared in any Australian paper and then, usually, only in some extremely discreet reference on the financial pages.

Yet among people who made the decisions affecting major sections of international commerce between World War I and the 1950s he was pre-eminent. He had a down-to-earth understanding of people and markets, of workers and employers and, above all, of the social, economic and political climate of his own country and of Britain and the United States that was worth tens of millions of pounds to Australia's trade balances. No Australian businessman hitherto has measured up to his stature on the international industrial scene.

various international conferences around the globe, or to such Australian-Canadian links as are established within the professions at similar international gatherings.

South Africa and Rhodesia are today outside the British Commonwealth. Since the Labor victory of December 1972 they have also been very much outside the pale in Canberra because a majority of Australians dislike the apartheid policy followed in Pretoria and, increasingly, in Salisbury. Previously, except when Australian contingents were fighting the Boers at the beginning of the century in South Africa, relations across the Indian Ocean have been harmonious and trade has been mutually profitable.

The whole future of Australian relationships with these two former fellow-members of the British Empire and Commonwealth would seem to hinge largely on the evolution of South Africa and Rhodesia in a continent overwhelmingly controlled elsewhere by black Africans. Those who see eventual disaster and inter-racial warfare in southern Africa will pray that Australia is in no way involved.

With the nations of Europe, Australia's relations have been almost uniformly good and correct in the traditional modes of diplomatic interchange. There have been occasional brushes, the most spectacular being in the 1950s when a Soviet Embassy staff member named Petrov defected in Canberra. The domestic fall-out was enormous, the international impact slight, but for some years thereafter, during the Menzies prime ministership, there was no Russian Embassy in Canberra and no Australian representation in Moscow. In recent years Australia has established a very active and worthwhile listening post for eastern Europe in the Yugoslav capital, Belgrade. The ambassador has been accredited to Bulgaria and Rumania and the post has also been valuable to the migration department recruiting Yugoslavs as citizens for Australia.

Relations with France were habitually harmonious until the 1973 showdown over French nuclear tests at Mururoa Atoll. French defiance of world opinion, especially Pacific, Asian and trade union sentiment, caused the Australian government—with New Zealand always leading the way until very recently—to make the strongest possible protests in Paris and to seek a verdict against France from the World Court.

With the remainder of Europe Australian relations have been smooth and without incident. Migration has been a constant and occasionally controversial subject particularly with governments in Rome, Athens and Valetta which have been major sources of the Mediterranean inflow into Australia.

The Scandinavians, by and large, have resisted Australian blandishments to migrate to a warmer climate but the Dutch have come in great numbers and over a quarter of a century. Thanks to a series of able ambassadors and chief migration officers stationed in The Hague, Dutch-Australian relations could hardly have been better.

Through the 70s and 80s, whatever the evolution or devolution of the Common Market, Australian dealings with Europe—both communist and free enterprise—will certainly concentrate above all on trade.

Some thinking Australians are looking for greater diversification in Australia's market places abroad. They are not happy that such a huge proportion of our vast mineral resources and of our wool clip is now dependent on Japan. It may well be that, by 1980, West Germany, the Soviet Union and possibly France will all take a far larger share of Australia's output of minerals and wool than hitherto.

Through the 60s and into the 70s the general trend has been for migration from western Europe to Australia to dry up or at least to slide slowly down from the peaks reached in the 1950s. Over the last five years Turkey and, to a lesser extent, Spain, emerged as new sources of future Australian populations.

However, the ebb and flow of European economics and of employment and unemployment on the continent makes any fast prediction extremely tentative. What is important for the future is that in millions of minds, from Amsterdam right across to Ankara and from Lisbon to the Vistula, Australia has become established as a reasonable, possible, alternative dwelling place if home conditions suggest a change for either this generation or its children. This has been perhaps the greatest single achievement of Australia in Europe since the death of Hitler.

Today, and for the foreseeable future, any rational government in Canberra will concentrate increasingly on Australian relationships with the countries of Asia and of the Pacific. The swing in this direction since 1945 has probably been the most spectacular change in Australian thinking and emphasis. For generations we were obsessed with Britain and to a lesser extent with continental Europe and the United States. But for the past three decades middle-aged and younger Australians—especially today's students at secondary and tertiary level —are at last being encouraged to think regionally. And the region is enormous. It stretches from the edges of the Middle East where Afghanistan meets Pakistan right across to the easternmost islands of Japan and to the tiny populations scattered over the atolls of the south-eastern Pacific.

In this region live almost 60 per cent of the world's people. Australia and New Zealand in population represent barely two thirds of one per cent of this enormous mass of humanity. Some Australians with ostrich minds tend to shrug hopelessly and say 'Well, what can we, not one in 150, do to meet the gigantic problems of feeding, clothing, housing, and keeping healthy two and a quarter billion human beings?'

Although leaders like Lord Casey and diplomats and other public servants with vision served Australia well in these areas from the 40s onwards, a long-advocated frontal attempt to involve Australia deeply in the struggles of its neighbours had to await the emergence of Mr Whitlam as Prime Minister and Foreign Minister in December 1972. In little more than a year he caused a basic revision in the estimates of Australia formed in the capitals of almost all nations in the region. Whereas, since the Pacific war, Australia had been regarded by many, whatever the ideology of their governments, as a political, economic and military satellite of the United States, the Labor ministry in 1973-74 spelt out, for even the most self-obsessed to read, the signal that it was a truly independent government, not necessarily bound to follow the policies of the White House or the Pentagon. Furthermore it was made clear that Canberra had ideas of its own for the co-operative welfare and development of the area

PEKING RECOGNISED AFTER YEARS OF 'FEIGNING AND HYPOCRISY'

Richard Woolcott—a new breed in diplomacy

Richard Arthur Woolcott is one of the outstanding younger diplomats who entered Australia's foreign service a few years after V-J day.

He began his overseas experience in Moscow in 1952, returning to the Soviet capital as first secretary seven years later. He has held posts in South Africa, Ghana, Singapore and Kuala Lumpur and is probably the most expert handler of relations with the media, both in Canberra and abroad, that the department has yet produced.

Dick Woolcott was a prominent footballer in Victoria and has exceptional verve and enthusiasm for all the tasks that have come his way. Since his return from the high commissionership in Ghana in 1970 he has become an assistant secretary in Canberra with special responsibility in the area of Australia's relationships with her Asian neighbours. As we have seen, these underwent a period of rapid development and considerable change after the Whitlam administration had taken over in December 1972. Dick Woolcott has accompanied the present prime minister and his predecessor, Mr McMahon, on most of their overseas trips and has usually acted as the principal link between the prime minister and the media. He has a good mind for absorption of facts and analysis of them in relation to Australian policy. This has been shown in his speeches and in published reports on the African and South East Asian areas. In 1975 he became Australia's ambassador to Indonesia.

At 46 Dick Woolcott is a whole generation younger than the men who built up the Australian diplomatic service and its reputation abroad during the 40s and 50s. Like his chief in the Department of Foreign Affairs, Mr Alan Renouf, he married a European. Birgit Woolcott is a charming Dane and they have two sons and a daughter.

Dick Woolcott, who comes from a military family, may be taken as representative of the new school of Australian diplomats. They are too young to have had their lives affected, or their political views influenced, by the trauma of the Great Depression. They were at school throughout World War II. For most of them the emergence of the Labor Government in 1972 was a watershed. Many of them had never known one throughout their adolescence or adult lives, or, like Woolcott, had known 20-odd years of ministerial direction from the one party. They tend to be pragmatic, down-to-earth, and to avoid expressions of elitist standards and values such as characterised some of Australia's most distinguished diplomats in previous decades.

The juniors who have followed Woolcott and his contemporaries into Australia's diplomatic service in the past 20 years are inevitably more in his pattern than that of the Sterlings, Crockers, Officers, Cawthornes and other pioneers of Australian representation abroad.

and for the long-needed joint attack by rich and poor nations alike on eviscerating poverty. This is the ogre lurking constantly over much of Asia and over large sectors of the populations on the archipelagoes between Asia and Australia.

The biggest individual change in relationships initiated in December 1972 was the abandonment of the incongruous and rather pathetic pretence that the discredited refugee, Chiang Kai-shek, with the half million of his defeated army, was the ruler of nearly eight hundred million in mainland China. Recognition of Peking and mutual exchange of ambassadors with Canberra ended 23 years of feigning and hypocrisy only excusable in those Australians who are terrified out of their minds by the fear that unless they are utterly subservient they may, as a punishment, be abandoned by Washington.

Throughout the 60s, despite protests from the smallest of the political parties, which had thrived since the mid 50s on anti-Communism, many thousands of Australian farmers had become increasingly dependent on China for putting additional butter on their bread. China, indeed, emerged as the biggest real and potential market for Australian grains, especially wheat. The initiatives of the Australian Ambassador in France, Alan Renouf, who later became head of the Department of Foreign Affairs in Canberra, led to an unexpectedly swift exchange of envoys with mainland China and to a basic change in Australia's understanding with the world's largest nation, the neighbour likely to have the predominant influence in the south Asian and Pacific region for decades to come.

The living standards of the Chinese masses have already been considerably raised from the nadir created by the civil war in the 40s. Probably by 1980 or soon afterwards, China will be turning to Australia as Japan is today for more costly foods such as meat and fruit to supplement what is for most Asians a generally meagre intake of protein and vitamins. On the other hand, much of the output of China's modern industrialisation may gradually make its way onto Australian markets to help pay for China's increasing imports from Australia. The sharply contrasting ideologies of the two nations do not jeopardise this prospect in any way. We have already witnessed spectacular growth in Russo-American commercial interchanges while Britain and Russia continue to post climbing trade figures almost every year.

SEEKING A LASTING REGIONAL PEACE

In the immediate future, as for the past decade, Japan is even more important for the preservation and growth of Australian living standards than China or, indeed, any other nation on the globe. Japanese investment in Australia is still very much smaller than that of the United States or Britain, but this is not the fault of the Japanese. Their great consortia would like a much larger share of the capital cake but Australians, like people in the other countries neighbouring Japan, have become somewhat wary of vaulting Japanese economic ambitions and of the thrust of its big entrepreneurs.

However, the basic facts need no exaggeration. Japan in 1974 had far outdistanced all other customers for most Australian minerals and for wool, and was one of the three largest importers of Australian meat, seafood, fruit and other primary produce. Indeed the replacement of Britain by Japan as a major market for Australian goods and as a supplier of goods to Australia has been perhaps the most dramatic and swift commercial revolution in the 18 decades since white people settled in Australia. It has all happened in a dozen years and there is no sign that the ever-mounting figures of interchange both ways are likely to diminish through the rest of the 70s. In the longer term China, the smaller nations of South-east Asia, and eventually and pre-eminently, India, loom as major absorbers of Australian produce in almost all fields.

In the objective of maintaining peace in the vast area to the north of Australasia almost all governments are as single-minded as Canberra. The explosions at Hiroshima and Nagasaki taught not only the Japanese but all the peoples of the region—and especially their more intelligent rulers—that there is absolutely no future, in fact only annihilation, in any war which involves the major, nuclear powers. Hence, attempts to create a neutral zone in the Indian Ocean and in the Pacific. Hence, also, the very lively concern from Pakistan right across

INDEX

Page numbers in *italic* type refer to captions; numbers in **bold** type refer to Personal Profiles.